Anonymous

The Maryland Society of the Colonial Dames of America, 1899

Anonymous

The Maryland Society of the Colonial Dames of America, 1899

ISBN/EAN: 9783337154387

Printed in Europe, USA, Canada, Australia, Japan

Cover: Foto ©Suzi / pixelio.de

More available books at **www.hansebooks.com**

THE MARYLAND SOCIETY

OF THE

COLONIAL DAMES

OF

AMERICA.

1899.

BALTIMORE:
GUGGENHEIMER, WEIL & CO.
1899.

PREFACE.

THE Maryland Society of the Colonial Dames of America was incorporated December 29th, 1891. It stands, therefore, as regards the date of its formation, second upon the roll of the State societies, and was one of the five that met in convention at Wilmington, Delaware, in May, 1892, to organize the National Federation.

While the requirements for membership have remained substantially the same from the first, some important modifications have been made from time to time, both by the National Conventions and by the several State organizations. Thus, the original Constitution of the Maryland Society recognized the date of the cessation of hostilities, April 11th, 1783, as the close of the colonial period, and accepted services rendered before that date as affording a valid claim to membership. At a meeting of the Maryland society, held March 3d, 1894, it was decided that the Declaration of Independence ought to be taken as the actual conclusion of the colonial period, and the date July 3d, 1776, was established as the limit of eligible service. This modification was proposed, as an amendment to the Constitution, in the National Council of 1894, and, after lying over, under the rules, until the next meeting, was formally adopted by the National Council of 1896.

At the Council which convened in Washington, January, 1893, it was decided that each State society should form its own eligibility list in accordance with the conditions subsisting in the respective States during the colonial period, provided that such lists should be in accordance with the laws of the General Society. Availing themselves of their right, under this provision, the various State societies have deemed it advisable to modify their original eligibility lists in a number of instances, and in this way a certain amount of confusion has necessarily arisen. A further element of confusion consists in the fact that, in the earlier days of the

Society's existence, claims were often presented based on services rendered in States, in which as yet no local society had been formed, and, in passing upon such claims, no other guide was at hand than the somewhat general provisions of the Constitution.

The Maryland Society has always endeavored scrupulously to maintain the standard set up by the National Society and by the local organizations composing it, and, in case of every application for membership, has rigidly adhered to the regulations in force at the time such application was presented. It has, however, been considered unadvisable, in presenting this record of the qualifications of its members, to designate especially those cases which, in consequence of subsequent modifications in the eligibility lists, would not accord with the conditions existing at present. Such a procedure would seem to lend, to regulations more recently adopted, something of the nature of an *ex post facto* operation, and might, it is feared, lead to unfair discrimination. At the same time, the Maryland Society, in thus defining its own position, expressly disclaims all desire to criticise the action of any of its sister societies in this particular, feeling confident that all alike are working in thorough harmony for the general welfare.

The simple and convenient system of arrangement, followed by the Society of Colonial Wars in its Year Books, seems to offer so many advantages that it has been adopted without modification in the present volume. The historical and genealogical work has been done by Dr. Christopher Johnston of the Johns Hopkins University. He has devoted to it much time and labor, and has striven to insure the highest attainable degree of accuracy. In presenting this book, therefore to the members of the Maryland Society of the Colonial Dames of America, the committee to whose charge the preparation of the work has been entrusted, consider that it can be safely accepted as an authority by all students of Maryland history and genealogy.

ELIZA R. BEALL.
MARY TILGHMAN.
HELEN WEST RIDGELY.
Committee

OFFICERS
OF THE
MARYLAND SOCIETY
OF THE
COLONIAL DAMES OF AMERICA.

President,
MRS. FREDERICK von KAPFF.

First Vice-President,
MRS. WILLIAM REED.

Second Vice-President,
MRS. CHARLES MARSHALL.

Recording Secretary,
MRS. EDWARD SHIPPEN.

Corresponding Secretary,
MRS. JOHN THOMSON MASON.

Treasurer,
MRS. HENRY W. ROGERS.

Registrar,
MRS. E. S. BEALL.

Historian,
MISS MARY TILGHMAN.

Managers:
MRS. J. J. JACKSON.
MRS. NICHOLAS G. PENNIMAN.
MRS. JOSEPH KING.
MISS MARY S. HALL.
MRS. JOHN THOMSON MASON.
MRS. J. PEMBROKE THOM.

Advisory Board:
COLONEL CHARLES MARSHALL.
HENRY F. THOMPSON, Esq.
DOUGLAS H. THOMAS, Esq.
DR. CHRISTOPHER JOHNSTON.

Genealogist,
DR. CHRISTOPHER JOHNSTON.

OFFICERS
OF THE
MARYLAND SOCIETY FROM ITS ORGANIZATION,

ELECTED.

President,
1891. MRS. FREDERICK von KAPFF.

First Vice-President,
1891. MRS. WILLIAM REED.

Second Vice-Presidents:
1891. MRS. RICHARD BAYARD.
1894. MRS. EUGENE BLACKFORD.
1896. MRS. CHARLES MARSHALL.

Third Vice-President,
1891. MRS. EUGENE BLACKFORD.

Fourth Vice-President,
1891. MRS. CHARLES RIDGELY, OF HAMPTON.

Recording Secretaries:
1891. MRS. EDWARD SHIPPEN.
1896. MRS. J. J. JACKSON.
1897. MRS. EDWARD SHIPPEN.

Corresponding Secretaries:
1891. MRS. HENRY DIDIER.
1893. MRS. ROBERT ATKINSON.
1893. *MRS. GEORGE R. GOLDSBOROUGH.
1894. MRS. D. GIRAUD WRIGHT.
1898. MRS. JOHN THOMPSON MASON.

Treasurers:
1891. MRS. JOSEPH KING.
1893. MRS. ALEXANDER GORDON.
1894. MRS. HENRY W. ROGERS.

Registrar,
1891. MRS. E. S. BEALL.

Historians:
1891. MISS MARY W. MILNOR.
1893. MISS MARY TILGHMAN.

---

*Pro tempore.

ELECTED.	*Managers:*
1891.	MRS. HORATIO WHITRIDGE.
1891.	MISS MARIAN HOWARD.
1891.	MRS. IREDELL IGLEHART.
1891.	MRS. WINFIELD J. TAYLOR.
1891.	MRS. CHARLES D. FISHER.
1891.	MRS. ROBERT ATKINSON.
1891.	MRS. GEORGE R. GOLDSBOROUGH.
1891.	MRS. OUTERBRIDGE HORSEY.
1891.	MRS. DOUGLAS H. THOMAS.
1891.	MRS. CHARLES MARSHALL.
1891.	MRS. DUNCAN CAMPBELL.
1891.	MISS MARY TILGHMAN.
1891.	MISS AMELIE de PAU FOWLER.
1891.	MRS. ALEXANDER GORDON.
1893.	MRS. EUGENE BLACKFORD.
1893.	MRS. CHARLES RIDGELY, of HAMPTON.
1893.	MRS. D. GIRAUD WRIGHT.
1893.	MRS. HENRY DIDIER.
1893.	MRS. JOSEPH KING.
1893.	MRS. JAMES W. WILSON.
1894.	MRS. RICHARD BAYARD.
1894.	MRS. EDWARD SHIPPEN.
1894.	MRS. WILLIAM B. WILSON.
1894.	MRS. HENRY W. ROGERS.
1894.	MRS. FRANK P. CLARK.
1894.	MRS. NICHOLAS G. PENNIMAN.
1894.	MRS. J. J. JACKSON.
1895.	MISS MARY S. HALL.
1895.	MRS. JOHN THOMSON MASON.
1896.	MISS IDA BRENT.
1896.	MRS. THOMAS CHATARD.
1896.	MRS. AUSTEN JENKINS.
1897.	MRS. JOHN RIDGELY, of HAMPTON.
1898.	MRS. J. PEMBROKE THOM.

Advisory Board:

1896.	COLONEL CHARLES MARSHALL.
1896.	HENRY F. THOMPSON, ESQ.
1896.	DOUGLAS H. THOMAS, ESQ.
1896.	DR. CHRISTOPHER JOHNSTON.

Genealogist,

1893.	DR. CHRISTOPHER JOHNSTON.

INCORPORATORS.

DECEMBER 29, 1891.

MRS. FREDERICK von KAPFF.
MRS. WILLIAM REED.
MRS. RICHARD BAYARD.
MRS. EUGENE BLACKFORD.
MRS. HORATIO WHITRIDGE.
MRS. EDWARD S. BEALL.
MRS. JOSEPH KING.
MRS. HENRY DIDIER.
MRS. ROBERT ATKINSON.

LIST OF MEMBERS.

The degrees of descent, as here given, include the descendant.

Allen, Mrs. Ethan (Eliza Clagett).
    Eighth in descent from Augustine Herman.
    Sixth in descent from James Frisby.
    Sixth in descent from Judge John Brice.
    Sixth in descent from Dr. Charles Carroll.
    Sixth in descent from Zachariah Maccubbin.
    Ninth in descent from Edward Lloyd I.
    Eighth in descent from Colonel Philemon Lloyd.

Armistead, Miss Fannie Carter.
    Sixth in descent from John Armistead.
    Fifth in descent from Colonel John Baylor.
    Seventh in descent from Hon. Lewis Burwell.
    Seventh in descent from Colonel William Fitzhugh.

Armstrong, Miss Mary Hughes.
    Fifth in descent from Colonel John Armstrong.
    Ninth in descent from Brant Arentse Van Schlichtenhorst.
    Eighth in descent from Captain Philip Pieterse Schuyler.
    Eighth in descent from Colonel Peter Schuyler.
    Seventh in descent from Colonel Robert Livingston.
    Seventh in descent from Colonel Henry Beekman I.
    Sixth in descent from Colonel Henry Beekman II.

Assheton, Mrs. William Herbert (Juliet Wilson Wheelwright).
    Sixth in descent from Lieutenant Jeremiah Wheelwright.
    Seventh in descent from Colonel John Wheelwright.
    Eighth in descent from Colonel Samuel Wheelwright.
    Ninth in descent from Rev. John Wheelwright.
    Eighth in descent from Captain James Davis.
    Seventh in descent from Major Charles Frost.
    Seventh in descent from Lieutenant-Colonel William Pepperrell.
    Sixth in descent from Lieutenant Pelatiah Whittemore.
    Ninth in descent from Jeremy Houchin.

LIST OF MEMBERS.

Atkinson, Mrs. Isaac Edmondson (Virginia Duval).
Fourth in descent from Thomas Hawkins.

Atkinson, Mrs. Matthew S.
Fifth in descent from Benjamin Waller.
Fifth in descent from Rev. John Camm.

Atkinson, Mrs. Robert (Laura Robinson).
Fourth in descent from Charles Willson Peale.
Eighth in descent from John Brewer.

Bass, Mrs. John M. (Mary Wharton Berry.)
Seventh in descent from Captain Thomas Clagett.
Seventh in descent from John Dorsey.

Bateman, Mrs. James M. H. (Elizabeth Tench Goldsborough.)
Seventh in descent from Dr. Richard Tilghman.
Sixth in descent from Hon. Richard Tilghman.
Fifth in descent from Hon. Matthew Tilghman.
Fourth in descent from Lieutenant-Colonel Tench Tilghman.
Eighth in descent from Edward Lloyd I.
Seventh in descent from Colonel Philemon Lloyd.
Eighth in descent from Captain James Neale.
Sixth in descent from Nicholas Goldsborough.
Sixth in descent from Tench Francis.

Batré, Mrs. Alfred (Hortense Addison).
Seventh in descent from Colonel John Addison.
Sixth in descent from Colonel Thomas Addison.
Eighth in descent from Richard Smith.
Seventh in descent from Colonel Walter Smith.
Seventh in descent from Colonel Samuel Young.
Sixth in descent from Hon. Daniel Dulany.
Fifth in descent from Walter Dulany.
Sixth in descent from Richard Grafton.

Baughman, Mrs. Mary Jane.
Seventh in descent from Governor Robert Brooke.
Seventh in descent from Captain James Neale.
Eighth in descent from Governor Edward Digges.
Seventh in descent from Governor William Digges.
Eighth in descent from Henry Sewall.

LIST OF MEMBERS.

Bayard, Miss Ellen Howard.
Fourth in descent from Colonel John Eager Howard.
Ninth in descent from John Chew.
Eighth in descent from Samuel Chew.
Sixth in descent from Samuel Chew, M. D.
Fifth in descent from Benjamin Chew.
Sixth in descent from Rev. Thomas Airey.
Twelfth in descent from Captain Edmund Scarburgh.
Eleventh in descent from Colonel Edmund Scarburgh.
Tenth in descent from Major-General John Custis.
Ninth in descent from Colonel John Custis.
Tenth in descent from Sir George Yeardley.
Ninth in descent from Colonel Argall Yeardley.
Eighth in descent from Lieutenant-Colonel John West.
Seventh in descent from John Teackle.
Seventh in descent from Charles Carroll.
Seventh in descent from Colonel John Thompson.
Eighth in descent from Augustine Herman.
Ninth in descent from Colonel Henry Darnall.

Bayard, Mrs. Richard Bassett (Ellen Howard).
Third in descent from Colonel John Eager Howard.
Eighth in descent from John Chew.
Seventh in descent from Samuel Chew.
Fifth in descent from Samuel Chew, M. D.
Fourth in descent from Benjamin Chew.
Fifth in descent from Rev. Thomas Airey.
Eleventh in descent from Captain Edmund Scarburgh.
Tenth in descent from Colonel Edmund Scarburgh.
Ninth in descent from Major-General John Custis.
Eighth in descent from Colonel John Custis.
Ninth in descent from Sir George Yeardley.
Eighth in descent from Colonel Argall Yeardley.
Seventh in descent from Lieutenant-Colonel John West.
Sixth in descent from John Teackle.

Beall, Mrs. Edward Sinclair (Eliza Rebecca Winn).
Seventh in descent from Joseph Winn.
Fourth in descent from Timothy Winn.
Sixth in descent from Daniel Dulany I.
Fifth in descent from Daniel Dulany II.
Eighth in descent from Richard Smith.
Seventh in descent from Colonel Walter Smith.
Eighth in descent from Richard Hall.

Seventh in descent from Captain Thomas Tasker.
Sixth in descent from Hon. Benjamin Tasker.
Seventh in descent from William Bladen.
Sixth in descent from Zachariah Maccubbin.
Sixth in descent from Dr. Charles Carroll.
Ninth in descent from Edward Lloyd I.
Eighth in descent from Colonel Philemon Lloyd.
Ninth in descent from Captain James Neale.
Ninth in descent from Robert Ridgely.
Seventh in descent from Charles Ridgely.
Ninth in descent from Colonel John Dorsey.
Seventh in descent from Captain Richard Hill.

Beall, Miss Louisa Ogle.

Eighth in descent from Colonel Ninian Beall.
Tenth in descent from Acting Governor Robert Brooke.
Ninth in descent from Major Thomas Brooke.
Eighth in descent from Colonel Thomas Brooke.
Seventh in descent from Thomas Brooke, Jr.
Ninth in descent from Richard Smith.
Eighth in descent from Colonel Walter Smith.
Ninth in descent from Richard Hall.
Fifth in descent from Governor Samuel Ogle.
Seventh in descent from Captain Thomas Tasker.
Sixth in descent from Hon. Benjamin Tasker.
Seventh in descent from William Bladen.
Eighth in descent from Dr. Richard Tilghman.
Seventh in descent from Colonel Richard Tilghman.
Sixth in descent from Richard Tilghman III.
Ninth in descent from Edward Lloyd I.
Eighth in descent from Colonel Philemon Lloyd.
Ninth in descent from Captain James Neale.
Ninth in descent from Honorable Henry Sewall.
Eighth in descent from Major Nicholas Sewall.
Seventh in descent from Captain Peregrine Frisby.
Ninth in descent from Colonel William Burgess.
Eighth in descent from Joseph Winn.
Fifth in descent from Timothy Winn.
Seventh in descent from Daniel Dulany I.
Sixth in descent from Daniel Dulany II.
Seventh in descent from Zachariah Maccubbin.
Seventh in descent from Dr. Charles Carroll.
Tenth in descent from Robert Ridgely.
Eighth in descent from Charles Ridgely.
Tenth in descent from Colonel John Dorsey.
Eighth in descent from Captain Richard Hill.

LIST OF MEMBERS.

Beasten, Mrs. Charles (Ella Burns).
Ninth in descent from John Avery.
Eighth in descent from Hercules Sheppeard.
Seventh in descent from Simon Kollock.
Sixth in descent from James Tybout.

Beckwith, Mrs. Franklin H. (Nannie Lawrence Kerfoot.)
Ninth in descent from Acting Governor Robert Brooke.
Eighth in descent from Major Thomas Brooke.
Seventh in descent from Colonel Thomas Brooke.
Eighth in descent from Colonel John Addison I.
Seventh in descent from Colonel Thomas Addison.
Ninth in descent from Richard Smith.
Eighth in descent from Colonel Walter Smith.
Sixth in descent from William Murdock.
Fifth in descent from Colonel Joseph Sim.
Fourth in descent from Roger Nelson.

Belknap, Mrs. Charles (Fanny Wheelwright).
Sixth in descent from Lieutenant Jeremiah Wheelwright.
Seventh in descent from Colonel John Wheelwright.
Eighth in descent from Colonel Samuel Wheelwright.
Ninth in descent from Rev. John Wheelwright.
Eighth in descent from Captain James Davis.
Seventh in descent from Major Charles Frost.
Seventh in descent from Lieutenant-Colonel William Pepperrell.
Sixth in descent from from Lieutenant Pelatiah Whittemore.
Ninth in descent from Jeremy Houchin.

Belt, Mrs. Alfred Mcgill (Ariana Teresa Trail).
Eighth in descent from Major-General John Hammond.

Birckhead, Mrs. James, Jr. (Elizabeth Macaulay).
Third in descent from Lieutenant-Colonel Joseph Thornburgh.

*Black, Mrs. Charles H. (Elizabeth Merryman).
Fourth in descent from John Merryman.
Sixth in descent from Captain Darby Lux.
Fifth in descent from Colonel Darby Lux.
Sixth in descent from Dr. George Buchanan.
Eighth in descent from Honorable James Saunders.

Deceased.

LIST OF MEMBERS.

Blackford, Mrs. Eugene (Rebecca Chapman Gordon).
Seventh in descent from William Biddle I.
Fourth in descent from Colonel Clement Biddle.
Fifth in descent from Honorable Gideon Cornell.
Seventh in descent from Colonel William Fitzhugh.
Eighth in descent from William Freeborn.
Seventh in descent from Gideon Freeborn.
Ninth in descent from Thomas Hazard.
Eighth in descent from George Lawton.
Seventh in descent from Robert Owen.

Blackiston, Mrs. A. Hooton (Elizabeth Price Smith Pearre).
Eighth in descent from Richard Smith.
Seventh in descent from Colonel Walter Smith.
Sixth in descent from Walter Smith, Jr.
Fifth in descent from Dr. Clement Smith.
Eighth in descent from Richard Hall.
Ninth in descent from Hon. Henry Sewall.
Eighth in descent from Major Nicholas Sewall.
Ninth in descent from Colonel William Burgess.
Ninth in descent from Acting Governor Robert Brooke.
Eighth in descent from Major Thomas Brooke.
Seventh in descent from Colonel Thomas Brooke.
Fifth in descent from Colonel Thomas Price.
Seventh in descent from Captain John Worthington.

Blackwell, Mrs. Josiah Low (Helen B. Campbell).
Eighth in descent from William Biddle I.
Seventh in descent from William Biddle II.
Seventh in descent from Nicholas Scull.
Fifth in descent from Captain William Lytle.

Bond, Mrs. Hugh Lennox, Jr. (Jessie Van Rensselaer Beale.)
Sixth in descent from Colonel John Wainwright.
Seventh in descent from Casparus Couyn I.
Sixth in descent from Casparus Couyn II.

Boone, Mrs. Daniel A. (Melanie Carroll.)
Eighth in descent from Colonel Henry Darnall.
Eighth in descent from Charles Carroll.
Tenth in descent from William Mitchell.

LIST OF MEMBERS.

Boyd, Mrs. Allen Richards (Jane Hall Maulsby Ritchie).
Ninth in descent from Colonel Ninian Beall.
Eighth in descent from Colonel William Burgess.
Seventh in descent from Captain Thomas Clagett.
Seventh in descent from James Edmondstone.
Sixth in descent from David Lynn.
Eighth in descent from Thomas Dent.
Ninth in descent from Acting Governor Robert Brooke.
Eighth in descent from Major Thomas Brooke.
Seventh in descent from Colonel Thomas Brooke.
Sixth in descent from Alexander Contee.

Brent, Miss Ida S.
Eighth in descent from Captain George Brent.
Ninth in descent from Honorable Florentius Seymour.
Ninth in descent from Captain James Neale.
Ninth in descent from Honorable Henry Sewall.
Eighth in descent from Colonel Jesse Wharton.
Seventh in descent from Colonel Edward Dorsey.
Fourth in descent from John Lawrence.
Fifth in descent from Jonathan Hager.
Eighth in descent from Joshua Doyne.
Ninth in descent from Cuthbert Fenwick.
Fifth in descent from Colonel Ignatius Fenwick.
Eighth in descent from Michael Taney.
Ninth in descent from Acting Governor Robert Brooke.
Eighth in descent from Roger Brooke.
Ninth in descent from Hon. John Pile.

Brent, Miss Nanine Maria.
Eighth in descent from Captain George Brent.
Ninth in descent from Honorable Henry Sewall.
Eighth in descent from Colonel Jesse Wharton.
Ninth in descent from Governor Florentius Seymour.
Eighth in descent from Joshua Doyne.
Ninth in descent from Captain James Neale.

Brooke, Mrs. John (Esther Willing Brooke).
Fifth in descent from Captain James Hunter.
Fourth in descent from Captain Benjamin Brooke.

Brooks, Mrs. Walter B., Jr. (Fanny Land Bonsal).
Seventh in descent from John Bethel.
Seventh in descent from William Roscoe, Jr.

Brown, Mrs. Arthur George (Mary Elizabeth Alricks).
> Sixth in descent from Peter Alricks.
> Fourth in descent from Honorable John Forbes.

Brown, Miss Ellen Sidney.
> Fifth in descent from Colonel William Buchanan.

Brown, Miss Lizinka Campbell.
> Eighth in descent from William Bladen.
> Seventh in descent from Honorable Benjamin Tasker.
> Fifth in descent from Thomas Polk.
> Sixth in descent from Philemon Hawkins.

Browne, Mrs. Samuel Tracy (Mary Wheelwright).
> Sixth in descent from Lieutenant Jeremiah Wheelwright.
> Seventh in descent from Colonel John Wheelwright.
> Eighth in descent from Colonel Samuel Wheelwright.
> Ninth in descent from Rev. John Wheelwright.
> Eighth in descent from Captain James Davis.
> Seventh in descent from Major Charles Frost.
> Seventh in descent from Lieutenant-Colonel William Pepperrell.
> Sixth in descent from Lieutenant Pelatiah Whittemore.
> Ninth in descent from Jeremy Houchin.

Buchanan, Miss Esther Sidney.
> Fourth in descent from Colonel William Buchanan.
> Fourth in descent from John Smith.
> Fifth in descent from Samuel Smith.
> Fourth in descent from James Calhoun.
> Sixth in descent from Richard Gist.
> Fourth in descent from Dabney Carr.
> Fifth in descent from Colonel Peter Jefferson.
> Sixth in descent from Captain Thomas Jefferson.
> Tenth in descent from Christopher Branch.
> Seventh in descent from Major Peter Field.
> Eighth in descent from Henry Soane.
> Sixth in descent from Colonel Isham Randolph.
> Seventh in descent from William Randolph.
> Eighth in descent from Captain Henry Isham.

Buchanan, Mrs. Roberdeau (Lyla M. Peters).
> Fourth in descent from William Peters.
> Fourth in descent from Dr. Edward Johnson.

LIST OF MEMBERS.

Buell, Mrs. Daniel H. (Ellen Lewis Nye).
Eighth in descent from Colonel John Washington.
Ninth in descent from Colonel Augustine Warner, Sr.
Eighth in descent from Colonel Augustine Warner, Jr.
Ninth in descent from George Reade.
Tenth in descent from Nicholas Martian.
Eighth in descent from Colonel William Ball.
Seventh in descent from John Lewis.
Fifth in descent from Colonel Fielding Lewis.

Burleson, Mrs. Albert Sidney (Adèle Steiner).
Sixth in descent from Colonel Richard Colgate.

Calvert, Mrs. Charles Baltimore (Eleanor Mackubin).
Sixth in descent from Zachariah Maccubbin.
Fifth in descent from Nicholas Maccubbin.
Sixth in descent from Dr. Charles Carroll
Ninth in descent from Captain James Neale.
Ninth in descent from Edward Lloyd I.
Eighth in descent from Colonel Philemon Lloyd.
Sixth in descent from Captain John Worthington.
Seventh in descent from Colonel Nicholas Greenberry.
Seventh in descent from Colonel Henry Ridgely.
Seventh in descent from Colonel William Fitzhugh.
Fifth in descent from Colonel William Fitzhugh (Md.)
Eighth in descent from Colonel Richard Lee I.
Seventh in descent from Colonel Richard Lee II.
Eighth in descent from Henry Corbin.
Sixth in descent from Daniel Dulany I.
Eighth in descent from Richard Smith.
Seventh in descent from Colonel Walter Smith.
Eighth in descent from Colonel George Mason I.
Seventh in descent from Colonel George Mason II.
Eighth in descent from Colonel Gerard Fowke.
Fourth in descent from Colonel Nicholas Worthington.
Ninth in descent from John Brewer.

Camak, Miss M. Annie.
Eighth in descent from John Ogden.

Campbell, Mrs. Duncan (Ella Calvert).
Fifth in descent from Governor Charles Calvert.
Fourth in descent from Honorable Benedict Calvert.
Sixth in descent from Colonel James Martin.

Campbell, Miss Ella Calvert.
    Sixth in descent from Governor Charles Calvert.
    Fifth in descent from Honorable Benedict Calvert.
    Seventh in descent from Colonel James Martin.
    Fifth in descent from Lieutenant-Colonel Micajah Williamson.
    Fifth in descent from Colonel Thomas Goldthwaite.

Canby, Miss Laura.
    Sixth in descent from Thomas Canby.
    Seventh in descent from William Biles (Byles).
    Sixth in descent from Thomas Yardley.
    Seventh in descent from John Woolston I.
    Fifth in descent from John Woolston II.

Carrington, Miss Henrietta Penniman.
    Eighth in descent from Colonel Nicholas Greenberry.
    Eighth in descent from Colonel Henry Ridgely.
    Sixth in descent from Rev. James Macgill.
    Fifth in descent from Colonel Henry Griffith.

Carroll, Mrs. Mary Randolph (Mary Randolph Thomas).
    Fourth in descent from Dr. Philip Thomas.
    Fifth in descent from Honorable John Hanson.
    Sixth in descent from Alexander Contee.
    Seventh in descent from Samuel Hanson.
    Fifth in descent from Colonel Thomas Marshall.
    Eighth in descent from Colonel William Travers.
    Ninth in descent from Governor Isaac Allerton.
    Eighth in descent from Colonel Isaac Allerton.
    Ninth in descent from Elder William Brewster.
    Eighth in descent from William Randolph.
    Seventh in descent from William Colston.

Carroll, Miss Sally Wethered.
    Sixth in descent from Zachariah Maccubbin.
    Sixth in descent from Dr. Charles Carroll.
    Ninth in descent from Edward Lloyd I.
    Eighth in descent from Colonel Philemon Lloyd.
    Ninth in descent from Captain James Neale.
    Ninth in descent from Colonel John Dorsey.
    Ninth in descent from Robert Ridgely.
    Seventh in descent from Charles Ridgely.
    Seventh in descent from Captain Richard Hill.

Sixth in descent from Colonel William Blay.
Seventh in descent from William Pearce.
Fifth in descent from Gabriel Ludlow.

Carter, Miss Mary Coles.
Seventh in descent from Colonel John Carter.
Sixth in descent from Honorable Robert Carter.
Fifth in descent from Honorable John Carter.
Seventh in descent from John Armistead.
Fifth in descent from Robert Carter Nicholas.
Seventh in descent from Colonel Edward Hill.
Eighth in descent from Colonel Miles Cary I.
Seventh in descent from Colonel Miles Cary II.
Sixth in descent from Colonel Wilson Cary.

Cary, Miss Jane Margaret.
Fifth in descent from Colonel Wilson Miles Cary.
Sixth in descent from Colonel Wilson Cary.
Seventh in descent from Colonel Miles Cary II.
Eighth in descent from Colonel Miles Cary I.
Fifth in descent from Archibald Cary.
Eighth in descent from Colonel William Wilson.
Ninth in descent from Captain Thomas Taylor.
Sixth in descent from Honorable John Blair.
Seventh in descent from Archibald Blair.
Fifth in descent from Dabney Carr.
Sixth in descent from Colonel Peter Jefferson.
Seventh in descent from Captain Thomas Jefferson,
Eleventh in descent from Christopher Branch.
Eighth in descent from Major Peter Field.
Ninth in descent from Henry Soane.
Fourth in descent from Colonel Thomas Mann Randolph.
Fifth in descent from Colonel William Randolph of Tuckahoe.
Sixth in descent from Colonel Thomas Randolph.
Seventh in descent from Isham Randolph.
Sixth in descent from Colonel Richard Randolph of Curles.
Seventh in descent from William Randolph.
Eighth in descent from Captain Henry Isham.
Sixth in descent from Honorable Mann Page I.
Seventh in descent from Honorable Matthew Page.
Eighth in descent from Colonel John Page.
Seventh in descent from Honorable Ralph Wormeley II.
Eighth in descent from Honorable Ralph Wormeley I.

LIST OF MEMBERS.

Eighth in descent from Honorable John Armistead.
Seventh in descent from Major John Bolling.
Eighth in descent from Colonel Robert Bolling I.
Ninth in descent from Lieutenant Thomas Rolfe.
Tenth in descent from John Rolfe.
Eighth in descent from Richard Kennon.
Fourth in descent from John Smith.
Fifth in descent from Samuel Smith.

Cary, Mrs. Wilson Miles (Jane Margaret Carr).

Third in descent from Dabney Carr.
Fourth in descent from Colonel Peter Jefferson.
Fifth in descent from Captain Thomas Jefferson.
Ninth in descent from Christopher Branch.
Sixth in descent from Major Peter Field.
Seventh in descent from Henry Soane.
Fifth in descent from Isham Randolph.
Sixth in descent from William Randolph.
Seventh in descent from Captain Henry Isham.
Third in descent from John Smith.
Fourth in descent from Samuel Smith.

Cator, Mrs. James H. (Jeanie Bayly).

Ninth in descent from Captain Richard Bayly.
Tenth in descent from Colonel Edmund Scarburgh.

Chancellor, Mrs. C. W. (Martha Ann Butler).

Fourth in descent from Colonel Thomas Butler.

Chatard, Mrs. Thomas M. (Eleanor Addison Williams.)

Seventh in descent from Captain Stephen Williams.
Fifth in descent from Colonel Joseph Williams.
Ninth in descent from Edward Howell.
Eighth in descent from Major John Howell.
Ninth in descent from Richard Treat.
Eighth in descent from John Deming.
Seventh in descent from John Hawkins.
Seventh in descent from Rev. Stephen Bordley.
Seventh in descent from Michael Miller.
Fifth in descent from James Gittings.
Eighth in descent from Richard Smith.
Eighth in descent from Colonel John Addison.
Eighth in descent from Captain Thomas Tasker.
Eighth in descent from Richard Hall.

Seventh in descent from Charles Ridgely.
Ninth in descent from Colonel John Dorsey.
Fifth in descent from Dr. George Buchanan.

Cheatham, Mrs. Richard (Emma Berry).

Seventh in descent from Captain Thomas Clagett.
Seventh in descent from John Dorsey.

Christopher, Mrs. John G. (Henrietta Shoemaker.)

Sixth in descent from Lieutenant Thomas Shoemaker.
Sixth in descent from Lieutenant Hansyoost Herkimer.
Fifth in descent from Captain Henry Herter.
Sixth in descent from Colonel Richard Colegate.

Clark, Mrs. Frank P. (Mary Maben.)

Sixth in descent from Governor Alexander Spotswood.
Fifth in descent from Bernard Moore.
Seventh in descent from William Aylett I.
Fifth in descent from William Aylett II.
Seventh in descent from Colonel William Dandridge.
Tenth in descent from Governor John West.
Ninth in descent from Colonel John West.
Eighth in descent from Colonel Nathaniel West.
Tenth in descent from Major Joseph Croshaw.

Clarke, Mrs. Henry F. (Belle Taylor.)

Fifth in descent from Colonel James Taylor.
Sixth in descent from Colonel Richard Lee I.
Fifth in descent from Hancock Lee.
Seventh in descent from Isaac Allerton I.
Sixth in descent from Isaac Allerton II.
Eighth in descent from Elder William Brewster.
Seventh in descent from Captain Thomas Willoughby.
Fourth in descent from Captain William Dabney Strother.

Coates, Mrs. Charles Edward (Anna Hunter Roberts).

Sixth in descent from Edward Farmer.

Colvin, Mrs. Alexander B. (Sarah Lightfoot Tarleton.)

Seventh in descent from Honorable Philip Lightfoot.
Fifth in descent from Lieutenant Philip Lightfoot.
Eighth in descent from John Lewis.
Sixth in descent from Colonel Charles Lewis.
Ninth in descent from Colonel Augustine Warner, Jr.

LIST OF MEMBERS.

    Tenth in descent from George Reade.
    Ninth in descent from Henry Corbin.
    Eighth in descent from John Taliaferro.

Comegys, Mrs. Joseph Parsons (Eliza Virginia Thompson).
    Ninth in descent from James Saunders.
    Seventh in descent from Darby Lux.
    Fifth in descent from Daniel Bowly.

Conrad, Mrs. Lawrence Lewis (Sallie Howard Worthington).
    Seventh in descent from Captain John Worthington.
    Fifth in descent from Samuel Worthington.
    Seventh in descent from Thomas Tolley.
    Sixth in descent from Colonel Walter Tolley.
    Eighth in descent from Major-General John Hammond.

Cook, Mrs. George Hamilton (Jane James).
    Seventh in descent from James Claypoole.

Cook, Mrs. Harry C. (Rosalie Dennis.)
    Seventh in descent from Donnack Dennis.
    Fifth in descent from John Dennis.

Coolidge, Mrs. Charles Austin (Sophie Wager Lowry).
    Seventh in descent from Dr. Richard Tilghman.
    Sixth in descent from Colonel Richard Tilghman.
    Fifth in descent from Honorable Matthew Tilghman.
    Eighth in descent from Edward Lloyd I.
    Seventh in descent from Colonel Philemon Lloyd.
    Eighth in descent from Captain James Neale.
    Seventh in descent from Robert Grundy.
    Seventh in descent from Tench Francis.

Cottman, Mrs. Clarence (Susan Noland Powell).
    Eighth in descent from William Powell.
    Fifth in descent from Colonel Levin Powell.
    Seventh in descent from Valentine Peyton.
    Eighth in descent from Burr Harrison.
    Fifth in descent from Colonel Charles Simons.
    Sixth in descent from Major William Douglas.

Cottman, Miss Elizabeth Stewart.
    Eighth in descent from Pieter Alricks.

Sixth in descent from Andrew Boggs.
Fifth in descent from Colonel Miles King.
Ninth in descent from Captain Anthony Armistead.
Tenth in descent from Captain Robert Ellyson.

Cottman, Mrs. J. Hough (Caroline Cary Chubb).

Fourth in descent from Colonel Miles King.
Eighth in descent from Captain Anthony Armistead.
Ninth in descent from Captain Robert Ellyson.

Cox, Mrs. James W., Jr. (Margaret Riggs.)

Seventh in descent from Lieutenant-Colonel Henry Trippe.
Sixth in descent from John Teackle.

Cromwell, Mrs. Kennedy (Sally Bartow Small Franklin).

Sixth in descent from Samuel Rhoads.
Sixth in descent from Thomas Bartow.
Fifth in descent from James Latimer.
Fifth in descent from Captain Jonas Simonds.

Currie, Mrs. C. George (Sarah Crawford Clark).

Eighth in descent from Nathaniel White.
Eighth in descent from Lieutenant William Clark.
Eighth in descent from Captain Roger Clapp.

Cushman, Mrs. Charles D. (Nannie Stewart.)

Fifth in descent from James Dick.

Custis, Miss Clara Douglas.

Ninth in descent from Major-General John Custis.
Tenth in descent from Colonel Edmund Scarburgh.

Custis, Miss Lena Wise.

Ninth in descent from Major-General John Custis.
Tenth in descent from Colonel Edmund Scarburgh.

Custis, Miss Sarah Horsey.

Ninth in descent from Major-General John Custis.
Tenth in descent from Colonel Edmund Scarburgh.

Dammann, Mrs. J. Francis (Aileen B. Cowardin).

Sixth in descent from Colonel John Lewis.

LIST OF MEMBERS.

Dandridge, Miss Anne Spottswood.
Fourth in descent from Alexander Spottswood Dandridge.
Fifth in descent from Nathaniel West Dandridge.
Sixth in descent from William Dandridge.
Sixth in descent from General Adam Stephan.
Sixth in descent from Governor Alexander Spottswood.
Seventh in descent from Colonel Nathaniel West.
Eighth in descent from Colonel John West.
Ninth in descent from Governor John West.
Ninth in descent from Major Joseph Croshaw.
Fifth in descent from Charles Goldsborough I.
Fifth in descent from Honorable Robert Goldsborough.
Seventh in descent from Robert Goldsborough.
Fifth in descent from William Tilghman.
Sixth in descent from Colonel Richard Tilghman.
Sixth in descent from James Lloyd.
Seventh in descent from Colonel Philemon Lloyd.
Eighth in descent from Edward Lloyd I.
Seventh in descent from Robert Grundy.
Ninth in descent from James Neale.
Seventh in descent from Colonel Nicholas Greenberry.
Sixth in descent from Samuel Dickinson.
Eighth in descent from Walter Dickinson.
Seventh in descent from Joseph Ennalls.
Eighth in descent from Bartholomew Ennalls.
Eighth in descent from Dr. John Brooke.
Ninth in descent from Michael Brooke.
Sixth in descent from William Moore.
Seventh in descent from John Moore.

Davies, Miss Jennie Haywood.
Fourth in descent from Captain John Daves.
Sixth in descent from Colonel William Eaton.

*Denman, Mrs. H. B. (Mary Barbara Young.)
Fifth in descent from Colonel Benjamin Young.
Seventh in descent from Colonel Benjamin Rozer.
Eighth in descent from Honorable Thomas Notley.
Eighth in descent from Cuthbert Fenwick.
Eighth in descent from Captain James Neale.
Eighth in descent from Governor Edward Digges.
Seventh in descent from Colonel William Digges.
Eighth in descent from Honorable Henry Sewall.
Eighth in descent from Acting Governor Robert Brooke.
Seventh in descent from Major Thomas Brooke.

*Deceased.

Dorsey, Miss Ella Loraine.

Seventh in descent from Colonel Edward Dorsey.
Seventh in descent from Colonel Nicholas Greenberry.
Seventh in descent from Colonel Henry Ridgely.
Seventh in descent from John Hanson.
Sixth in descent from Samuel Hanson.
Seventh in descent from George Lingan.
Sixth in descent from Captain John Worthington.

Dugan, Mrs. Hammond (Agnes Berry Markoe).

Sixth in descent from Benjamin Chew.
Sixth in descent from Tench Francis.
Fifth in descent from Tristram Thomas.
Fifth in descent from William Perry.
Seventh in descent from Robert Goldsborough.
Sixth in descent from John Goldsborough.
Eighth in descent from Michael Turbutt.
Seventh in descent from Foster Turbutt.
Eighth in descent from John Bozman.

Duke, Mrs. Basil (Henrietta Morgan).

Ninth in descent from Thomas Hazard.
Eighth in descent from Jonathan Hazard.
Ninth in descent from Captain Richard Betts.
Ninth in descent from Lieutenant Ralph Hunt.
Fourth in descent from Lieutenant-Colonel Abraham Hunt.
Fifth in descent from Robert Pearson.

Dunn, Mrs. Herbert O. (Bessie Amanda Webb.)

Sixth in descent from Lieutenant John Knapp.

Duval, Miss Mary Rebecca.

Fifth in descent from John Duval.
Fourth in descent from Marsh Mareen Duval.
Sixth in descent from Rev. Henry Hall.

Earle, Miss Mary Isabel.

Sixth in descent from James Earle.
Fifth in descent from Richard Tilghman Earle.
Eighth in descent from Dr. Richard Tilghman.
Seventh in descent from Colonel Richard Tilghman.
Sixth in descent from Richard Tilghman III.
Fifth in descent from James Tilghman.

LIST OF MEMBERS.

    Ninth in descent from Edward Lloyd I.
    Eighth in descent from Colonel Philemon Lloyd.
    Seventh in descent from James Lloyd.
    Ninth in descent from Captain James Neale.
    Sixth in descent from Samuel Chamberlaine.
    Seventh in descent from Peregrine Frisby.
    Eighth in descent from Thomas Ringgold.
    Sixth in descent from Major William Ringgold.
    Eighth in descent from Simon Wilmer.
    Sixth in descent from Kensey Johns.

Early, Mrs. Alexander R. (Frances Elder Moale.)

    Fifth in descent from John Moale I.
    Fourth in descent from John Moale II.
    Seventh in descent from Major-General John Hammond.
    Seventh in descent from Colonel Nicholas Greenberry.

Emory, Mrs. Campbell D. (Clara Tilton.)

    Eighth in descent from Edward Lloyd I.
    Seventh in descent from Colonel Philemon Lloyd.
    Sixth in descent from Edward Lloyd II.
    Fifth in descent from Edward Lloyd III.
    Fourth in descent from Edward Lloyd IV.
    Eighth in descent from Captain James Neale.
    Seventh in descent from John Rousby I.
    Sixth in descent from John Rousby II.
    Eighth in descent from Henry Morgan.
    Seventh in descent from Colonel William Tayloe.
    Sixth in descent from Colonel John Tayloe I.
    Fifth in descent from Colonel John Tayloe II.
    Eighth in descent from Henry Corbin.
    Sixth in descent from Honorable George Plater.
    Eighth in descent from Richard Woolman.

Fisher, Mrs. Charles D. (Nannie Poultney Dorsey.)

    Fourth in descent from Evan Thomas.
    Seventh in descent from Philip Thomas.
    Seventh in descent from Captain Francis Hutchins.
    Sixth in descent from Colonel John Dorsey.
    Seventh in descent from Colonel Edward Dorsey.
    Eighth in descent from Colonel Henry Ridgely.
    Eighth in descent from Colonel Nicholas Greenberry.

Fisher, Mrs. William A. (Louise Este.)

    Sixth in descent from Lieutenant John Pengilly.
    Fourth in descent from Captain David Este.

LIST OF MEMBERS.

Floyd, Miss Nannie Teackle.

Sixth in descent from Charles Floyd.
Seventh in descent from Colonel William Kendall.
Eighth in descent from Colonel Obedience Robins.
Eighth in descent from Colonel Nathaniel Littleton.
Fifth in descent from Alexander Stockley.
Fourth in descent from Isaac Smith.
Eighth in descent from Lieutenant John Sheppeard.
Ninth in descent from Sir George Yeardley.
Eighth in descent from Colonel Argall Yeardley.
Ninth in descent from Captain Adam Thorowgood.
Seventh in descent from John Teackle.
Fifth in descent from Thomas Teackle.
Tenth in descent from Randall Revell.
Seventh in descent from Lieutenant-Colonel John West.
Ninth in descent from Captain Edmund Scarburgh.
Eighth in descent from Colonel Edmund Scarburgh.
Ninth in descent from Major-General John Custis.
Eighth in descent from Colonel John Custis.

*Fowler, Miss Amélie DePau.

Seventh in descent from John Lyman.
Sixth in descent from John Colt.
Fourth in descent from Peter Colt.
Eighth in descent from William Fowler.

Franklin, Mrs. Fabian (Christine Ladd).

Eighth in descent from William Phelps.
Eighth in descent from Edward Griswold.
Eighth in descent from William Gaylord.
Eighth in descent from Captain Samuel Marshall.
Seventh in descent from Honorable John Gilman.
Eighth in descent from Lieutenant Roger Plaisted.
Seventh in descent from Colonel John Plaisted.

Fisher, Mrs. Ellicott (Mary Tyler).

Seventh in descent from Colonel John Addison.
Sixth in descent from Colonel Thomas Addison.
Fourth in descent from Colonel John Addison.

Fuller, Mrs. Oliver Clyde (Kate Fitzhugh Caswell).

Seventh in descent from Colonel William Fitzhugh.

---

*Great-great-granddaughter of Admiral the Count de Grasse, who commanded the French fleet at Yorktown.

LIST OF MEMBERS.

Fifth in descent from Colonel William Fitzhugh (Md.)
Sixth in descent from Captain Peregrine Frisby.
Seventh in descent from Major Nicholas Sewall.
Eighth in descent from Honorable Henry Sewall
Eighth in descent from Colonel William Burgess.

Gamble, Mrs. Robert Howard (Angelica Robinson).

Seventh in descent from John Brewer.
Fourth in descent from Charles Wilson Peale.

Garrett, Mrs. T. Harrison (Alice Whitridge).

Sixth in descent from Captain John Hall.
Fifth in descent from Colonel John Hall.
Fourth in descent from Colonel Josias Carvil Hall.
Fifth in descent from Honorable William Smith.
Seventh in descent from Richard Gist.
Seventh in descent from William Cattell.
Fifth in descent from Captain Benjamin Cattell.
Eighth in descent from Colonel John Godfrey.
Ninth in descent from James Sanderlain.
Eighth in descent from Honorable Jaspar Yates.
Eighth in descent from Honorable John Cushing I.
Seventh in descent from Honorable John Cushing II.
Sixth in descent from Honorable John Cushing III.
Fifth in descent from Thomas Wallingford.

Gary, Mrs. E. Stanley (Mary Ragan Macgill).

Sixth in descent from Rev. James Macgill.
Seventh in descent from Valentine Peyton.

Gibson, Mrs. Charles H. (Marietta Powell).

Fourth in descent from Levin Powell.
Sixth in descent from Valentine Peyton.

Gibson, Mrs. George T. M. (Eugenia Macgill.)

Sixth in descent from Rev. James Macgill.
Seventh in descent from Valentine Peyton.

Giffen, Mrs. James Fortescue (Louise Elizabeth Wallis).

Sixth in descent from John Teackle.
Fifth in descent from Pollard Edmondson.

Giffen, Miss Lillian.

Seventh in descent from John Teackle.
Sixth in descent from Pollard Edmondson.

Giffen, Miss Louise.
> Seventh in descent from John Teackle.
> Sixth in descent from Pollard Edmondson.

Gill, Mrs. Martin Gillet (Alice Warfield).
> Sixth in descent from Captain John Worthington.
> Seventh in descent from Colonel Nicholas Greenberry.
> Seventh in descent from Colonel Henry Ridgely.
> Seventh in descent from Colonel Edward Dorsey.
> Seventh in descent from Colonel Nicholas Gassaway.

Gill, Mrs. William Harrison (Anna Milby Gray).
> Sixth in descent from Honorable Caleb Cowpland.
> Fifth in descent from Captain Jonathan Cowpland.

Goddard, Mrs. Henry P. (Lida Whitman Acheson.)
> Eighth in descent from Rev. Thomas Hooker.
> Sixth in descent from Honorable John Hooker.
> Seventh in descent from Captain John Stanley.
> Eighth in descent from Captain Thomas Willett.

Goldsborough, Mrs. George Robins (Eleanor Agnes Rogers).
> Third in descent from Colonel Nicholas Rogers.
> Fifth in descent from Dr. George Buchanan.
> Fourth in descent from Lloyd Buchanan.
> Fifth in descent from Philip Jones.
> Eighth in descent from George Saughier.
> Seventh in descent from Captain Thomas Besson.
> Seventh in descent from Honorable Daniel Parke.
> Eighth in descent from Major-General John Custis.

Goldsborough, Mrs. Worthington (Henrietta Maria Wilson Jones.)
> Sixth in descent from Ephraim Wilson.

Goodwin, Miss Elizabeth Taylor.
> Eighth in descent from Robert Ridgely.
> Sixth in descent from Charles Ridgely.

Gordon, Mrs. Alexander (Agnes Armistead).
> Seventh in descent from Colonel William Fitzhugh.
> Seventh in descent from Honorable John Armistead.
> Fifth in descent from Colonel John Baylor.

LIST OF MEMBERS.

Gordon, Miss Margaret.
Eighth in descent from Benjamin Harrison.
Seventh in descent from William Randolph.
Eighth in descent from Colonel John Carter.
Seventh in descent from Honorable Robert Carter.
Sixth in descent from Archibald Cary.
Seventh in descent from Colonel William Fitzhugh.
Sixth in descent from Isham Randolph.
Seventh in descent from Richard Randolph (of Curles).

Gorter, Mrs. Albert L. (Mary Rebecca Thompson.)
Fourth in descent from Commodore Joshua Barney.
Eighth in descent from Robert Ridgely.
Sixth in descent from Charles Ridgely.
Fifth in descent from John Ridgely.
Eighth in descent from Colonel John Dorsey.
Eighth in descent from Richard Smith.
Seventh in descent from Colonel Walter Smith.
Sixth in descent from Walter Smith, Jr.
Eighth in descent from Richard Hall.
Ninth in descent from Acting Governor Robert Brooke.
Eighth in descent from Major Thomas Brooke.
Ninth in descent from Honorable Henry Sewall.
Eighth in descent from Major Nicholas Sewall.
Eighth in descent from Colonel William Burgess.

Gorter, Mrs. Gosse Onno (Mary A. Polk).
Fourth in descent from David Polk.
Seventh in descent from Colonel Hans Hanson.
Sixth in descent from Judge Frederick Hanson.

Green, Mrs. William (Katherine Johnson).
Seventh in descent from Governor Thomas Prince.

Griswold, Miss Ellen Howell.
Sixth in descent from Lieutenant Ebenezer Griswold.
Seventh in descent from Jacob Howell.
Eighth in descent from Francis Collins.
Eighth in descent from Randal Vernon.
Fourth in descent from Major Joseph Howell.

Guest, Mrs. William Woodward (Susan Doll Vail).
Fifth in descent from Sebastian Bauman.

LIST OF MEMBERS.

Hall, Miss Elizabeth Ward.
Eighth in descent from Lieutenant William Stickney.
Eighth in descent from William Ward.
Seventh in descent from Dr. Thomas Pemberton.
Eighth in descent from Honorable John Cutt.
Fifth in descent from Honorable Samuel Blodgett.
Sixth in descent from Colonel Joshua Wingate.
Seventh in descent from Samuel Penhallow.
Eighth in descent from Edward Jackson.
Seventh in descent from William Coleman.
Eighth in descent from Captain Jonathan Wade.
Eighth in descent from Major-General Humphrey Atherton.
Seventh in descent from Lieutenant James Trowbridge.

Hall, Mrs. George W. S. (Mary Bell Moncure).
Fourth in descent from Colonel Thomas Gaskins.
Sixth in descent from Dr. Gustavus Brown.
Eighth in descent from Colonel Gerard Fowke.
Eighth in descent from Colonel William Ball.
Sixth in descent from Colonel Edwin Conway.
Sixth in descent from Colonel Robert Bolling II.

Hall, Miss Mary Stickney.
Eighth in descent from Lieutenant William Stickney.
Eighth in descent from William Ward.
Seventh in descent from Dr. Thomas Pemberton.
Eighth in descent from Honorable John Cutt.
Fifth in descent from Honorable Samuel Blodgett.
Sixth in descent from Colonel Joshua Wingate.
Seventh in descent from Samuel Penhallow.
Eighth in descent from Edward Jackson.
Seventh in descent from William Coleman.
Eighth in descent from Captain Jonathan Wade.
Eighth in descent from Major-General Humphrey Atherton.
Seventh in descent from Lieutenant James Trowbridge.

Hamilton, Mrs. W. T. (Clara Jenness).
Sixth in descent from Captain Richard Jenness.
Fifth in descent from Richard Jenness, Jr.
Fourth in descent from Rev. Samuel McClintock.
Eighth in descent from Captain Henry Dow.
Eighth in descent from Thomas Marston.

LIST OF MEMBERS.

    Ninth in descent from William Eastow.
    Eighth in descent from Captain James Avery.
    Ninth in descent from Honorable John Humfrey.
    Eighth in descent from Lieutenant John Samborne.
    Sixth in descent from Tristram Samborne.
    Fifth in descent from Peter Samborne.
    Sixth in descent from Captain Jonathan Samborne.
    Ninth in descent from Tristram Coffin I.
    Eighth in descent from Tristram Coffin II.
    Ninth in descent from Captain Edmund Greenleaf.
    Eighth in descent from Henry Sherburne.
    Seventh in descent from Captain Samuel Sherburne.
    Ninth in descent from Ambrose Gibbons.

Hamilton, Mrs. Levin Mayer (Sarah Harris).

    Seventh in descent from Samuel Mosely.
    Seventh in descent from Joseph Lynde.
    Eighth in descent from George Denison.
    Eighth in descent from Thomas Stanton.
    Eighth in descent from Hugh Mason.
    Eighth in descent from William Bond.
    Seventh in descent from John Spring.

Harrison, Mrs. Edward Pitts (Carrie Marion Andrews).

    Sixth in descent from Rev. James Macgill.
    Sixth in descent from Colonel Henry Griffith.
    Ninth in descent from Colonel Nicholas Greenberry.
    Eighth in descent from Colonel Edward Dorsey.
    Ninth in descent from Colonel Henry Ridgely.
    Seventh in descent from Henry Ridgely.
    Eighth in descent from Richard Hall.

Haughton, Mrs. Henry Osburne (Sophia Ridgely Alricks).

    Sixth in descent from Pieter Alricks.
    Fourth in descent from Honorable John Forbes.

Hayes, Mrs. John S. (Susan McKim Gordon).

    Seventh in descent from Colonel William Fitzhugh.
    Fifth in descent from Lieutenant Thomas McKim.

Heighe, Mrs. John M. (Sallie Ross).

    Seventh in descent from Governor Thomas Green.

Henry, Mrs. James L. (Kate Kearney).

    Fourth in descent from David Craufurd.

LIST OF MEMBERS.

Heyward, Mrs. Wilson P. (Elizabeth Skinner Wilson).
Fifth in descent from Lieutenant Thomas McKim.
Seventh in descent from Andrew Skinner.
Sixth in descent from Rev. Thomas Airey.

Hill, Mrs. Richard S. (Ida Morgan).
Eighth in descent from Edward Digges.

Hinckley, Mrs. Robert (Eleanora O'Donnell).
Eighth in descent from Sir Edmund Plowden.
Ninth in descent from Thomas Gerard.
Eighth in descent from Captain Robert Slye.
Seventh in descent from Captain Gerard Slye.
Ninth in descent from Governor Giles Brent.

Hodges, Mrs. J. S. B. (Lucy MacDonough Shaler).
Sixth in descent from Ensign Jared Spencer.
Fourth in descent from William Denning.
Ninth in descent from Henry Townsend.
Tenth in descent from Robert Cole.

Hoffman, Mrs. R. Curzon (Eliza Lawrence Dallam).
Tenth in descent from Wolfort Gerrittse van Cowenhoven.
Ninth in descent from Nicasius de Sille.
Eighth in descent from Captain William Lawrence.
Seventh in descent from Captain Henry Johnson.
Eighth in descent from Colonel John Carter.
Eighth in descent from Captain Thomas Todd.

Holladay, Mrs. Samuel W. (Georgianna C. Ord).
Seventh in descent from Garrett Van Swearingen.
Fifth in descent from Thomas Cresap.
Fourth in descent from Daniel Cresap I.
Third in descent from Daniel Cresap II.

Hoogewerff, Mrs. John A. (Edwardine Hiester).
Sixth in descent from Colonel Conrad Weiser.
Fourth in descent from Major-General John Peter Gabriel Muhlenberg.
Fifth in descent from Henry Kendig.

Horsey, Mrs. Outerbridge (Anna Carroll).
Eighth in descent from Colonel Henry Darnall.
Seventh in descent from Charles Carroll.

Hough, Miss Ethel.
Sixth in descent from Richard Hough.
Seventh in descent from John Clowes.
Eighth in descent from Philip Thomas.
Eighth in descent from Captain Francis Hutchins.
Ninth in descent from Richard Snowden.

Howard, Miss Marian Gilmor.
Third in descent from Colonel John Eager Howard.
Eighth in descent from John Chew.
Seventh in descent from Samuel Chew.
Fifth in descent from Samuel Chew, M. D.
Fourth in descent from Benjamin Chew.
Fifth in descent from Rev. Thomas Airey.
Eleventh in descent from Captain Edmund Scarburgh.
Tenth in descent from Colonel Edmund Scarburgh.
Ninth in descent from Major-General John Custis.
Eighth in descent from Colonel John Custis.
Ninth in descent from Sir George Yeardley.
Eighth in descent from Colonel Argall Yeardley.
Seventh in descent from Lieutenant-Colonel John West.
Sixth in descent from John Teackle.

*Howard, Mrs. Charles (Elizabeth Phoebe Key).
Fifth in descent from Philip Key.
Third in descent from Lieutenant John Ross Key.
Eighth in descent from Captain Luke Gardiner.
Seventh in descent from Richard Gardiner.
Seventh in descent from Major William Boarman.
Eighth in descent from Colonel John Jarboe.
Fifth in descent from John Ross.
Eighth in descent from Major John Weire.
Seventh in descent from Edward Lloyd I.
Sixth in descent from Colonel Philemon Lloyd.
Fifth in descent from Edward Lloyd II.
Fourth in descent from Edward Lloyd III.
Third in descent from Edward Lloyd IV.
Seventh in descent from Captain James Neale.
Sixth in descent from John Rousby I.
Fifth in descent from John Rousby II.
Seventh in descent from Henry Morgan.
Sixth in descent from Colonel William Tayloe.
Fifth in descent from Colonel John Tayloe I.

---

* Deceased.

Fourth in descent from Colonel John Tayloe II.
Seventh in descent from Henry Corbin.
Sixth in descent from Attorney-General George Plater
Fifth in descent from Honorable George Plater.
Seventh in descent from Thomas Burford.
Seventh in descent from Colonel John Addison I.
Sixth in descent from Colonel Thomas Addison.
Seventh in descent from Captain Thomas Tasker.

Hunt, Miss Anita Dunbar.

Eighth in descent from Lieutenant Ralph Hunt.
Eighth in descent from Captain Richard Betts.
Ninth in descent from Captain George Brent.
Tenth in descent from Honorable Florentius Seymour.
Tenth in descent from Captain James Neale.
Tenth in descent from Honorable Henry Sewall.
Ninth in descent from Colonel Jesse Wharton.
Ninth in descent from Joshua Doyne.
Eighth in descent from Colonel Edward Dorsey.
Fifth in descent from John Lawrence.
Sixth in descent from Jonathan Hager.
Tenth in descent from Cuthbert Fenwick.
Sixth in descent from Colonel Ignatius Fenwick.
Ninth in descent from Michael Taney.
Tenth in descent from Acting Governor Robert Brooke.
Ninth in descent from Roger Brooke.
Tenth in descent from Honorable John Pile.

Hunt, Mrs. Dunbar (Leila Lawrence Brent.)

Eighth in descent from Captain George Brent.
Ninth in descent from Honorable Florentius Seymour.
Ninth in descent from Captain James Neale.
Ninth in descent from Honorable Henry Sewall.
Eighth in descent from Colonel Jesse Wharton.
Eighth in descent from Joshua Doyne.
Seventh in descent from Colonel Edward Dorsey.
Fourth in descent from John Lawrence.
Fifth in descent from Jonathan Hager.
Ninth in descent from Cuthbert Fenwick.
Fifth in descent from Colonel Ignatius Fenwick.
Eighth in descent from Michael Taney.
Ninth in descent from Acting Governor Robert Brooke.
Eighth in descent from Roger Brooke.
Ninth in descent from Honorable John Pile.

Hunter, Mrs. James W. (Mary Devereux).
    Eighth in descent from Captain James Avery.

Huse, Mrs. Harry P. (Mary Sheward Whitelock).
    Fifth in descent from Isaac Whitelock.
    Eighth in descent from Alexander Beardsley.
    Eighth in descent from William Warner.
    Eighth in descent from Edmund Freeman.
    Ninth in descent from William Bassett of Massachusetts.
    Ninth in descent from Francis Sprague.
    Eighth in descent from Edward Carter.
    Seventh in descent from Robert Carter.
    Eighth in descent from William Cooper.
    Seventh in descent from John Woolston I.
    Fifth in descent from John Woolston II.
    Seventh in descent from Richard Stockton.
    Seventh in descent from William Wood.
    Eighth in descent from Francis Collins.

Iglehart, Mrs. C. Iredell (Anne Calhoun Robinson).
    Seventh in descent from John Brewer.
    Fourth in descent from Charles Willson Peale.
    Sixth in descent from Captain John Hall.
    Fifth in descent from Colonel John Hall.
    Fourth in descent from Colonel Josias Carvil Hall.
    Seventh in descent from Richard Gist.
    Seventh in descent from Honorable William Cattell.
    Fifth in descent from Captain Benjamin Cattell.
    Eighth in descent from Colonel John Godfrey.
    Ninth in descent from James Sanderlain.
    Eighth in descent from Honorable Joseph Yeates.
    Fifth in descent from Honorable William Smith.

Iglehart, Mrs. James D. (Monterey Watson).
    Ninth in descent from Dr. Luke Barber.
    Fifth in descent from Charles Barber.

Jackson, Mrs. John J. (Esther Gill.)
    Eighth in descent from Honorable James Saunders.
    Sixth in descent from Darby Lux.
    Fourth in descent from Daniel Bowly.

Jacobs, Mrs. Jesse Elliott (Margaret Dwight Bell).
    Eighth in descent from Captain Timothy Dwight.
    Sixth in descent from Colonel Timothy Dwight.
    Eighth in descent from Samuel Partridge.

James, Mrs. Norman (Margie Macgill).

Sixth in descent from Rev. James Macgill.
Seventh in descent from Valentine Peyton.

Jenkins, Mrs. E. Austin (Adelaide Lowe).

Eighth in descent from Major John Lowe.
Fifth in descent from Captain Michael Lowe.
Eighth in descent from Captain Henry Hawkins.
Eighth in descent from Samuel Magruder.
Fifth in descent from Joseph Maccubbin.
Fifth in descent from David Polk.
Seventh in descent from Colonel Hans Hanson.
Sixth in descent from Judge Frederick Hanson.

Jenkins, Mrs. Edmund Plowden (Martha Lee Jenkins).

Seventh in descent from Sir Edmund Plowden.
Eighth in descent from Thomas Gerard.
Seventh in descent from Captain Robert Slye.
Sixth in descent from Captain Gerard Slye.
Eighth in descent from Deputy Governor Giles Brent.

Jenkins, Mrs. Harry S. (Katharine Longden Mott).

Ninth in descent from Colonel William Ball.
Fifth in descent from Colonel Burges Ball.

Jenkins, Mrs. Michael (Mary Isabella Jenkins).

Seventh in descent from Sir Edmund Plowden.
Eighth in descent from Thomas Gerard.
Seventh in descent from Captain Robert Slye.
Sixth in descent from Captain Gerard Slye.
Eighth in descent from Deputy Governor Giles Brent.

Jenkins, Mrs. T. Meredith (Sarah Leigh Bonsal).

Seventh in descent from John Bethel.
Seventh in descent from William Roscoe, Jr.

Johns, Mrs. Claude Douglas (Bessy Steiner).

Sixth in descent from Colonel Richard Colgate.

Johnson, Mrs. William Woolsey (Susannah Leverett Batcheller.)

Eighth in descent from Sir John Leverett.

Johnston, Miss Maria Stith.
> Seventh in descent from Major John Stith.
> Fifth in descent from Drury Stith.
> Fourth in descent from Griffin Stith.
> Sixth in descent from Major William Buckner.
> Ninth in descent from Edmund Hobart.
> Eighth in descent from William Bassett (Mass.).

Jones, Mrs. George Alphonzo (Mary Eliza Smith).
> Eighth in descent from Captain James Neale.
> Eighth in descent from Governor William Digges.
> Ninth in descent from Governor Edward Digges.
> Eighth in descent from Henry Sewall.
> Eighth in descent from Cuthbert Fenwick.
> Sixth in descent from Colonel Benjamin Young.
> Eighth in descent from Colonel Benjamin Rozer.
> Ninth in descent from Governor Thomas Notley.
> Sixth in descent from Governor Robert Brooke.
> Tenth in descent from Governor Richard Bennett.

Jones, Mrs. E. Bradley (Nannie Shaw Tiffany).
> Seventh in descent from Colonel Samuel Checkley.

Kerfoot, Mrs. Samuel Humes (Annie Warfield Lawrence).
> Eighth in descent from Honorable Robert Brooke.
> Sixth in descent from Honorable Thomas Brooke.
> Seventh in descent from Honorable John Addison.
> Sixth in descent from Honorable Thomas Addison.
> Eighth in descent from Richard Smith.
> Fifth in descent from William Murdock.
> Fourth in descent from Colonel Joseph Sim.
> Seventh in descent from Colonel Edward Dorsey.

Keyser, Mrs. R. Brent (Ellen McHenry).
> Fourth in descent from Colonel John Eager Howard.
> Fifth in descent from Benjamin Chew.
> Sixth in descent from Samuel Chew.
> Eighth in descent from Colonel Samuel Chew.
> Ninth in descent from John Chew.
> Sixth in descent from Colonel Wilson Miles Cary.
> Seventh in descent from Colonel Wilson Cary.
> Eighth in descent from Colonel Miles Cary I.
> Ninth in descent from Colonel Miles Cary II.
> Sixth in descent from Archibald Cary.

Ninth in descent from Colonel William Wilson.
Tenth in descent from Captain Thomas Taylor.
Seventh in descent from John Blair.
Eighth in descent from Archibald Blair.
Sixth in descent from Dabney Carr.
Seventh in descent from Colonel Peter Jefferson.
Eighth in descent from Captain Thomas Jefferson.
Twelfth in descent from Christopher Branch.
Ninth in descent from Major Peter Field.
Tenth in descent from Henry Soane.
Fifth in descent from Colonel Thomas Mann Randolph.
Sixth in descent from Colonel William Randolph of Tuckahoe.
Seventh in descent from Colonel Thomas Randolph.
Sixth in descent from Colonel Isham Randolph.
Seventh in descent from Colonel Richard Randolph.
Eighth in descent from Colonel William Randolph.
Ninth in descent from Captain Henry Isham.
Seventh in descent from Honorable Mann Page I.
Eighth in descent from Mathew Page.
Ninth in descent from Colonel John Page.
Eighth in descent from Ralph Wormeley II.
Ninth in descent from Ralph Wormeley I.
Ninth in descent from John Armistead.
Eighth in descent from Major John Bolling.
Ninth in descent from Colonel Robert Balling.
Tenth in descent from Lieutenant Thomas Rolfe.
Eleventh in descent from John Rolfe.
Ninth in descent from Richard Kennon.
Fifth in descent from John Smith.
Sixth in descent from Samuel Smith.

Keyser, Mrs. Samuel (Therese Thompson).

Fourth in descent from Daniel Bowly.
Sixth in descent from Darby Lux.
Eighth in descent from Honorable James Saunders.

Keyser, Mrs. William (Mary Hoke Brent).

Eighth in descent from Captain George Brent.
Ninth in descent from Captain James Neale.
Ninth in descent from Honorable Henry Sewall.
Eighth in descent from Colonel Jesse Wharton.
Ninth in descent from Honorable Florentius Seymour.
Fourth in descent from John Lawrence.

LIST OF MEMBERS.

Fifth in descent from Jonathan Hager.
Seventh in descent from Colonel Edward Dorsey.
Eighth in descent from Joshua Doyne.
Ninth in descent from Cuthbert Fenwick.
Fifth in descent from Colonel Ignatius Fenwick.
Eighth in descent from Michael Taney.
Ninth in descent from Acting Governor Robert Brooke
Eighth in descent from Roger Brooke.
Ninth in descent from Honorable John Pile.

Kimball, Mrs. Julius Henry (Emily Nelson Maulsby).

Eighth in descent from Governor Robert Brooke.
Seventh in descent from Thomas Brooke.

King, Mrs. Joseph (Jane Howard).

Third in descent from Colonel John Eager Howard.
Eighth in descent from John Chew.
Seventh in descent from Samuel Chew.
Fifth in descent from Samuel Chew, M. D.
Fourth in descent from Benjamin Chew.
Fifth in descent from Rev. Thomas Airey.
Eleventh in descent from Captain Edmund Scarburgh.
Tenth in descent from Colonel Edmund Scarburgh.
Ninth in descent from Major-General John Custis.
Eighth in descent from Colonel John Custis.
Ninth in descent from Sir George Yeardley.
Eighth in descent from Colonel Argall Yeardley.
Seventh in descent from Lieutenant-Colonel John West
Sixth in descent from John Teackle.

King, Miss Virginia.

Fourth in descent from Colonel Thomas Price.

Latané, Miss Lucy Temple.

Sixth in descent from Honorable William Cocke.
Sixth in descent from Thomas Waring.
Fifth in descent from Francis Waring.
Fifth in descent from Zachary Lewis.

Leakin, Miss Margaret Dobbin.

Seventh in descent from William Hatton.
Ninth in descent from Colonel William Burgess.
Ninth in descent from Honorable Henry Sewall.

LIST OF MEMBERS.

Eighth in descent from Major Nicholas Sewall.
Ninth in descent from Acting Governor Robert Brooke.
Eighth in descent from Major Thomas Brooke.
Sixth in descent from Captain Thomas Middleton.

Lemmon, Mrs. J. Southgate (Fanny Addison Carter Dulany).

Eighth in descent from Richard Smith.
Seventh in descent from Colonel Walter Smith.
Sixth in descent from Daniel Dulany I.
Fifth in descent from Daniel Dulany II.
Eighth in descent from Richard Hall.
Seventh in descent from Thomas Tasker.
Sixth in descent from Honorable Benjamin Tasker.
Seventh in descent from William Bladen.
Eighth in descent from Colonel John Carter.
Seventh in descent from Honorable Robert Carter.

Lewis, Miss Virginia Tayloe.

Seventh in descent from John Lewis.
Fifth in descent from Colonel Fielding Lewis.
Ninth in descent from Colonel Augustine Warner, Sr.
Eighth in descent from Colonel Augustine Warner, Jr.
Sixth in descent from William Bladen.
Fifth in descent from Honorable Benjamin Tasker.
Fourth in descent from Governor Samuel Ogle.
Fifth in descent from Colonel John Tayloe.
Seventh in descent from Henry Corbin.

Ligon, Miss Elizabeth Worthington Dorsey.

Seventh in descent from Colonel John Dorsey.
Seventh in descent from Captain John Worthington.
Seventh in descent from Thomas Tolley.
Sixth in descent from Colonel Walter Tolley.
Seventh in descent from Zachariah Maccubbin.
Eighth in descent from Major-General John Hammond.
Sixth in descent from Colonel John Nash.
Sixth in descent from Captain Abraham Venable.

Littig, Mrs. John Merryman (Mary Clare Ross).

Seventh in descent from Governor Thomas Green.

Livingston, Miss Elizabeth.

Seventh in descent from Robert Livingston.
Sixth in descent from Colonel Philip Livingston.
Fifth in descent from Peter Van Brugh Livingston.

LIST OF MEMBERS.

Lough, Mrs. Ernest St. George (Eloise Lowndes Roman).
Ninth in descent from Captain James Neale.
Ninth in descent from Edward Lloyd I.
Eighth in descent from Colonel Philemon Lloyd.
Seventh in descent from Edward Lloyd II.
Sixth in descent from Edward Lloyd III.
Fifth in descent from Edward Lloyd IV.
Seventh in descent from Honorable George Plater.
Seventh in descent from William Bladen.
Seventh in descent from Thomas Tasker.
Sixth in descent from Honorable Benjamin Tasker.

Lowndes, Mrs. Lloyd (Elizabeth Tasker Lowndes).
Eighth in descent from Captain James Neale.
Eighth in descent from Edward Lloyd I.
Seventh in descent from Colonel Philemon Lloyd.
Sixth in descent from Edward Lloyd II.
Fifth in descent from Edward Lloyd III.
Fourth in descent from Edward Lloyd IV.
Seventh in descent from John Rousby I.
Sixth in descent from John Rousby II.
Eighth in descent from Henry Morgan.
Seventh in descent from Colonel William Tayloe.
Sixth in descent from Colonel John Tayloe I.
Fifth in descent from Colonel John Tayloe II.
Eighth in descent from Henry Corbin.
Seventh in descent from Attorney-General George Plater.
Sixth in descent from Honorable George Plater.
Eighth in descent from Thomas Burford.
Eighth in descent from Colonel John Addison I.
Seventh in descent from Honorable Thomas Addison.
Sixth in descent from William Bladen.
Sixth in descent from Thomas Tasker.
Fifth in descent from Honorable Benjamin Tasker.
Fourth in descent from Christopher Lowndes.
Fifth in descent from Jacob Haldeman.

Luckett, Miss Mary Stacker.
Fifth in descent from William Luckett.
Sixth in descent from Valentine Peyton.
Fifth in descent from Francis Peyton.

Lürman, Mrs. Gustav W. (Elizabeth Cooke Powel).
Fifth in descent from Charles Willing.

Seventh in descent from Edward Shippen.
Tenth in descent from Abraham Isaacsen Ver Planck.
Ninth in descent from Ensign Geleyn Ver Planck.
Seventh in descent from Ensign Philip Ver Planck.
Ninth in descent from Lieutenant William Beekman.
Eighth in descent from Colonel Gerardus Beekman.
Tenth in descent from Honorable Olaff Stevense Van Cortlandt.
Ninth in descent from Honorable Stephanus Van Cortlandt.
Tenth in descent from Captain Philip Pieterse Schuyler.
Tenth in descent from David Provost I.
Ninth in descent from David Provost II.
Seventh in descent from Dr. Richard Tilghman.
Sixth in descent from Colonel Richard Tilghman.
Fifth in descent from Richard Tilghman III.
Eighth in descent from Edward Lloyd I.
Seventh in descent from Colonel Philemon Lloyd.
Eighth in descent from Captain James Neale.
Eighth in descent from Honorable Henry Sewall.
Seventh in descent from Major Nicholas Sewall.
Eighth in descent from Colonel William Burgess.
Sixth in descent from Captain Peregrine Frisby.

Lürman, Mrs. Theodor G. (Nannie Allen Tilghman).

Seventh in descent from Dr. Richard Tilghman.
Sixth in descent from Colonel Richard Tilghman.
Fifth in descent from William Tilghman.
Eighth in descent from Edward Lloyd I.
Seventh in descent from Colonel Philemon Lloyd.
Sixth in descent from James Lloyd.
Eighth in descent from Captain James Neale.
Seventh in descent from Robert Grundy.
Eighth in descent from Garrett van Swearingen.
Eighth in descent from Richard Woolman.

Lyster, Mrs. Henry F. LeH. (Winifred Lee Brent).

Eighth in descent from Deputy Governor Giles Brent.
Fifth in descent from William Brent.
Eighth in descent from Colonel Richard Lee I.
Seventh in descent from Colonel Richard Lee II.
Sixth in descent from Governor Thomas Lee.
Fifth in descent from Thomas Ludwell Lee.
Eighth in descent from Philip Ludwell I.

Seventh in descent from Philip Ludwell II.
Eighth in descent from Colonel John Carter.
Seventh in descent from Honorable Robert Carter.
Sixth in descent from Landon Carter.
Fifth in descent from Robert Wormeley Carter.
Ninth in descent from Benjamin Harrison I.
Eighth in descent from Benjamin Harrison II.
Eighth in descent from Henry Corbin.
Seventh in descent from Honorable Ralph Wormeley II.
Sixth in descent from William Aylett I.
Eighth in descent from Colonel John Armistead.
Eighth in descent from Colonel Henry Darnall.
Fifth in descent from John Wilkins, Jr.
Fifth in descent from George Stevenson.

Macgill, Miss Louisa.

Sixth in descent from Rev. James Macgill.
Seventh in descent from Valentine Peyton.

Mackall, Miss Sally Somervell.

Seventh in descent from Colonel John Mackall.
Sixth in descent from Samuel Beall.
Fifth in descent from James Somervell II.
Eighth in descent from Richard Smith.
Eighth in descent from Colonel Thomas Brooke.

Mackenzie, Mrs. George Norbury (Lucie Tennille Emory).

Seventh in descent from Arthur Emory.
Fifth in descent from Lieutenant Samuel Dyre Betton.

Mackenzie, Miss Mary Gertrude Mackall.

Eighth in descent from Arthur Emory.
Eleventh in descent from Honorable Richard Treat.
Seventh in descent from Colonel Joseph Williams.
Sixth in descent from Lieutenant Samuel Dyre Betton.
Ninth in descent from Captain Stephen Williams.
Ninth in descent from Roger Brooke.
Ninth in descent from James Mackall.
Ninth in descent from Captain Francis Hutchins.
Tenth in descent from Captain James Hance.
Tenth in descent from Governor Robert Brooke.
Tenth in descent from Captain James Neale.
Ninth in descent from Honorable Bartholomew Coppock.
Tenth in descent from Honorable William Parke.

LIST OF MEMBERS.

Ninth in descent from Major John Howell.
Tenth in descent from Honorable John Deming.
Tenth in descent from Honorable Edward Howell.

Mackubin, Miss Florence.

Sixth in descent from Zachariah Maccubbin.
Fifth in descent from Nicholas Maccubbin.
Sixth in descent from Charles Carroll.
Ninth in descent from Edward Lloyd.
Eighth in descent from Colonel Philemon Lloyd.
Ninth in descent from Captain James Neale.
Fifth in descent from Captain Josiah Fay.
Ninth in descent from John Brewer.
Ninth in descent from Colonel Henry Ridgely.

Magruder, Mrs. John Read (Emily Erving Nicholson.)

Fifth in descent from Colonel Joseph Nicholson.
Fourth in descent from Joseph Nicholson, Jr.
Eighth in descent from Edward Lloyd I.
Seventh in descent from Colonel Philemon Lloyd.
Sixth in descent from Edward Lloyd II.
Fifth in descent from Edward Lloyd III.
Fourth in descent from Edward Lloyd IV.
Eighth in descent from Captain James Neale.
Seventh in descent from John Rousby I.
Sixth in descent from John Rousby II.
Seventh in descent from Colonel William Tayloe.
Sixth in descent from Colonel John Tayloe I.
Fifth in descent from Colonel John Tayloe II.
Seventh in descent from Attorney-General George Plater.
Sixth in descent from Honorable George Plater.
Eighth in descent from Henry Morgan.
Eighth in descent from Henry Corbin.

Manly, Mrs. L. Tyson, (Lily Tyson).

Ninth in descent from Acting Governor Robert Brooke.
Ninth in descent from Captain James Neale.
Eighth in descent from Captain Francis Hutchins.
Eighth in descent from Thomas Janney.
Eighth in descent from William Biles.
Seventh in descent from Thomas Yardley.
Fourth in descent from Captain John Joliffe.
Eighth in descent from Valentine Hollingsworth.
Seventh in descent from Henry Hollingsworth.

LIST OF MEMBERS.

Markoe, Mrs. Frank.
>Fourth in descent from Tristram Thomas.
>Fourth in descent from William Perry.
>Fifth in descent from Tench Francis.
>Sixth in descent from Robert Goldsborough.
>Fifth in descent from John Goldsborough.
>Seventh in descent from Michael Turbutt.
>Sixth in descent from Foster Turbutt.
>Seventh in descent from John Bozman.

Marshall, Mrs. Charles (Rebecca Snowden).
>Eighth in descent from Lieutenant Philip Thomas.
>Eighth in descent from Colonel Nicholas Greenberry.
>Fifth in descent from Major Thomas Snowden.
>Fourth in descent from Dr. Charles A. Warfield.
>Fifth in descent from Major Henry Ridgely.
>Eighth in descent from Captain James Neale.
>Eighth in descent from Edward Neale I.
>Seventh in descent from Colonel Philemon Lloyd.
>Sixth in descent from Edward Lloyd II.
>Sixth in descent from Rev. Henry Nicols.

Marshall, Mrs. Edward Athelstan (Sophia Howard).
>Fourth in descent from Colonel John Eager Howard.
>Ninth in descent from John Chew.
>Eighth in descent from Samuel Chew.
>Sixth in descent from Samuel Chew, M. D.
>Fifth in descent from Benjamin Chew.
>Sixth in descent from Rev. Thomas Airey.
>Twelfth in descent from Captain Edmund Scarburgh.
>Eleventh in descent from Colonel Edmund Scarburgh.
>Tenth in descent from Major-General John Custis.
>Ninth in descent from Colonel John Custis.
>Tenth in descent from Sir George Yeardley.
>Ninth in descent from Colonel Argall Yeardley.
>Eighth in descent from Lieutenant-Colonel John West.
>Seventh in descent from John Teackle.

Martin, Mrs. Frank (R. Anna Coates).
>Sixth in descent from Joseph Pennock.
>Seventh in descent from Edward Farmer.

Mason, Mrs. John Thomson (Helen Jackson).
>Ninth in descent from Olaff Stevense van Cortlandt.

Eighth in descent from Matthias Nicoll.
Seventh in descent from Honorable William Nicoll.
Ninth in descent from Kiliaen Van Rensselaer.
Eighth in descent from Colonel Jeremias Van Rensselaer.
Ninth in descent from Captain Edward Richmond.
Ninth in descent from Edward Thurston.
Tenth in descent from Thomas Mumford.
Eighth in descent from Robert Sinclair.
Eighth in descent from Captain Joseph Sylvester.
Ninth in descent from William Cheeseborough.
Eighth in descent from Samuel Cheeseborough.
Ninth in descent from Edward Bangs.

McBlair, Miss Emily.

Seventh in descent from Robert Ridgely.
Fifth in descent from Charles Ridgely.
Seventh in descent from Colonel John Dorsey.

McCandlish, Miss Evelyn Byrd.

Fifth in descent from William Byrd II.
Seventh in descent from Warham Horsmanden.
Fifth in descent from Charles Willing.
Seventh in descent from Edward Shippen.
Seventh in descent from John Lewis.
Eighth in descent from Colonel Augustine Warner, Jr.

McCoy, Mrs. Harry (Elizabeth Pinkney Gray).

Fifth in descent from Colonel Joseph Williams.

McCrackin, Mrs. Alexander (Belle Fitzhugh McPherson).

Fifth in descent from Colonel Robert McPherson.
Eighth in descent from Colonel William Fitzhugh.
Sixth in descent from Colonel William Fitzhugh of Maryland.
Ninth in descent from Honorable Henry Sewall.
Eighth in descent from Major Nicholas Sewall.
Ninth in descent from Colonel William Burgess.

McIlvain, Miss Elizabeth Gunning.

Seventh in descent from William Ashfordley.
Fifth in descent from Thomas Beatty.
Seventh in descent from Andreas Bengston.
Eighth in descent from Governor Jean Paul Jacquett.

LIST OF MEMBERS.

McIntire, Mrs. William Watson (Hortense Monroe Hardesty).
> Sixth in descent from Dr. George Buchanan.
> Fifth in descent from Lloyd Buchanan.
> Sixth in descent from Philip Jones.
> Ninth in descent from George Saughier.
> Eighth in descent from Captain Thomas Besson.
> Fifth in descent from President James Monroe.
> Fourth in descent from Colonel Nicholas Rogers.

McIntosh, Mrs. David Gregg (Virginia Johnson Pegram).
> Fifth in descent from Seth Ward.

McLean, Mrs. Thomas Chalmers (Emily Gordon).
> Eighth in descent from Benjamin Harrison.
> Eighth in descent from Colonel John Carter.
> Seventh in descent from Honorable Robert Carter.
> Sixth in descent from Archibald Cary.
> Seventh in descent from Colonel William Fitzhugh.
> Seventh in descent from William Randolph.
> Sixth in descent from Isham Randolph.
> Seventh in descent from Richard Randolph of Curles.

McSherry, Mrs. H. Clinton (Anna Muhlenberg Hiester).
> Sixth in descent from Colonel Conrad Weiser.
> Fourth in descent from Major-General John Peter Gabriel Muhlenberg.
> Fifth in descent from Henry Kendig.

Mercein, Mrs. Thomas R. (Lucy Schley.)
> Sixth in descent from John Thomas Schley.
> Fifth in descent from David Shriver.
> Seventh in descent from Captain John Worthington.
> Eighth in descent from Colonel Nicholas Greenberry.
> Eighth in descent from Robert Tyler.
> Seventh in descent from Rev. George Murdock.
> Fourth in descent from Colonel Baker Johnson.

Mercer, Mrs. Carroll (Minnie Leigh Tunis).
> Fifth in descent from Samuel Henderson.
> Fifth in descent from Colonel James Martin.

Merritt, Mrs. J. Alfred (Emma Wickes).
> Ninth in descent from Major Joseph Wickes.
> Eighth in descent from Simon Wilmer.

LIST OF MEMBERS.

Eighth in descent from Major James Ringgold.
Ninth in descent from Captain Robert Vaughan.
Eighth in descent from Colonel Hans Hanson.
Eighth in descent from Captain Daniel Pearce.
Eighth in descent from Edward Lloyd I.
Seventh in descent from Colonel Philemon Lloyd.
Sixth in descent from James Lloyd.
Sixth in descent from Rev. Henry Nicols.
Eighth in descent from Captain James Neale.
Sixth in descent from Samuel Chamberlaine.
Ninth in descent from Dr. Richard Tilghman.

Miles, Mrs. Francis T. (Jeanie Wardlaw.)

Fourth in descent from Captain Hugh Wardlaw.

Mills, Mrs. Abraham Gilbert (Mary Chase Steele.)

Fifth in descent from Rev. Thomas Chase.
Fourth in descent from Honorable Samuel Chase.
Fourth in descent from Commodore Joshua Barney.
Fifth in descent from Captain William Steele.

Milnor, Miss Mary Worthington.

Sixth in descent from Joseph Kirkbride.
Ninth in descent from Robert Cole.
Ninth in descent from John Townsend.
Ninth in decsent from Henry Townsend.
Seventh in descent from Captain John Worthington.
Seventh in descent from Thomas Tolley.
Sixth in descent from Colonel Walter Tolley.
Eighth in descent from Major-General John Hammond.
Ninth in descent from Captain James Neale.
Ninth in descent from Job Chandler.
Tenth in descent from Captain Adam Thorowgood.
Ninth in descent from Honorable Henry Sewall.
Eighth in descent from Joshua Doyne.
Sixth in descent from Kensey Johns.
Tenth in descent from John Chew.
Ninth in descent from Samuel Chew.
Fifth in descent from Samuel Worthington.

Minor, Miss Mary Willis.

Fourth in descent from John Minor.
Sixth in descent from Edmund Berkeley I.
Fifth in descent from Edmund Berkeley II.

LIST OF MEMBERS.

    Fourth in descent from Nelson Berkeley.
    Seventh in descent from Honorable Lewis Burwell.
    Eighth in descent from George Reade.
    Ninth in descent from Nicholas Martian.
    Seventh in descent from Colonel John Carter.
    Sixth in descent from Honorable Robert Carter.
    Fifth in descent from Charles Carter.
    Fifth in descent from Landon Carter.
    Eighth in descent from John Armistead.
    Sixth in descent from William Byrd II.
    Seventh in descent from William Byrd I.
    Eighth in descent from Warham Horsemanden.
    Ninth in descent from Thomas Stegge.
    Eighth in descent from Colonel John Page.
    Seventh in descent from Honorable Mathew Page.
    Sixth in descent from Honorable Mann Page I.
    Fifth in descent from Honorable Mann Page II.
    Fourth in descent from Governor John Page.
    Sixth in descent from Nathaniel Burwell.
    Fifth in descent from Robert Carter Burwell.
    Sixth in descent from Honorable John Grymes.
    Eighth in descent from Philip Ludwell I.
    Seventh in descent from Philip Ludwell II.
    Ninth in descent from Benjamin Harrison I.
    Eighth in descent from Benjamin Harrison II.
    Eighth in descent from Ralph Wormley I.
    Seventh in descent from Ralph Wormley II.

Mitchell, Miss Elizabeth Farnandis.
    Seventh in descent from Samuel Hanson.
    Sixth in descent from Walter Hanson.
    Seventh in descent from Colonel Edward Dorsey.

Moore, Mrs. Benjamin P. (Florence Sparks.)
    Fifth in descent from Richard Derby.

Moore, Mrs. Henry (Maria McBlair).
    Seventh in descent from Robert Ridgely.
    Fifth in descent from Charles Ridgely.
    Seventh in descent from Honorable John Dorsey.

Morris, Mrs. Charles Manigault (Clementine Hanson McAllister).
    Fourth in descent from Colonel Richard McAllister.
    Fifth in descent from Captain Matthew Dill.

LIST OF MEMBERS.

Morris, Miss Elizabeth M.

Seventh in descent from Honorable Lewis Morris I.
Sixth in descent from Honorable Lewis Morris II.
Fifth in descent from Honorable Lewis Morris III.
Eighth in descent from Colonel James Graham.
Eighth in descent from Major Abraham Staats.
Eighth in descent from Lieutenant William Beekman.
Sixth in descent from Gabriel Manigault.
Eighth in descent from Colonel Thomas Broughton.
Seventh in descent from Honorable Ralph Izard.
Sixth in descent from Peter De Lancy.
Ninth in descent from Philip Pieterse Schuyler.
Tenth in descent from Brant Arentse van Schlichtenhorst.
Eighth in descent from Sir Nathaniel Johnson.
Ninth in descent from Honorable Olaff Stevense van Cortlandt.
Eighth in descent from Honorable Stephanus van Cortlandt.
Seventh in descent from Honorable Cadwallader Colden.
Fifth in descent from Colonel Richard McAllister.
Sixth in descent from Captain Matthew Dill.

Mudge, Mrs. Edmund Tileston (Caroline Florence Keyes).

Fourth in descent from Governor John Brooks.

Mullan, Mrs. John (Rebecca Williamson).

Eighth in descent from Garrett Van Swearingen.
Ninth in descent from William Mitchell.

*Mullikin, Mrs. Richard Oden (Mary Blaine Hays).

Fourth in descent from Ephraim Blaine.
Eighth in descent from Joannes de Haes.

Mullikin, Miss Sophie Margaret.

Ninth in descent from Joannes de Haes.
Fifth in descent from Ephraim Blaine.

Murdoch, Miss Sallie Howard.

Eighth in descent from Colonel Samuel Young.

Murray, Mrs. Francis Key (Anna Morris).

Seventh in descent from Anthony Morris.
Fifth in descent from Charles Willing.

*Deceased.

Seventh in descent from Edward Shippen.
Fourth in descent from Honorable Benedict Calvert.
Fifth in descent from Governor Charles Calvert.

Nicholas, Miss Cary Ann.

Fourth in descent from Robert Carter Nicholas.
Seventh in descent from Colonel John Carter.
Sixth in descent from Honorable Robert Carter.
Seventh in descent from Colonel Miles Cary I.
Sixth in descent from Colonel Wilson Cary.
Seventh in descent from John Armistead.
Eighth in descent from Captain Thomas Taylor.
Seventh in descent from Colonel William Wilson.

Nicholas, Miss Elizabeth Cary.

Fourth in descent from Robert Carter Nicholas.
Seventh in descent from Colonel John Carter.
Sixth in descent from Honorable Robert Carter.
Seventh in descent from Colonel Miles Cary I.
Sixth in descent from Colonel Miles Cary II.
Fifth in descent from Colonel Wilson Cary.
Seventh in descent from Colonel John Armistead.
Eighth in descent from Captain Thomas Taylor.
Seventh in descent from Colonel William Wilson.
Fourth in descent from Edward Ambler.

Nicholas, Mrs. Wilson Cary (Augusta Neville).

Fourth in descent from John Moale I.
Third in descent from John Moale II.
Sixth in descent from Major-General John Hammond.
Sixth in descent from Colonel Nicholas Greenberry.

Nicholson, Mrs. Charles G. (Emilie Jane Goldsborough.)

Sixth in descent from Robert Goldsborough.
Fifth in descent from Charles Goldsborough.
Fourth in descent from Honorable Robert Goldsborough.
Seventh in descent from Colonel Nicholas Greenberry.
Seventh in descent from Bartholomew Ennalls.
Sixth in descent from Joseph Ennalls.
Seventh in descent from Colonel Henry Ridgely.
Sixth in descent from Captain John Worthington.
Fifth in descent from Thomas Worthington.
Fourth in descent from Major Nicholas Worthington.

LIST OF MEMBERS.

Norris, Mrs. Owen (Margaret Tilghman Owen).
Seventh in descent from Dr. Richard Tilghman.
Sixth in descent from Colonel Richard Tilghman.
Fifth in descent from William Tilghman.
Eighth in descent from Edward Lloyd I.
Seventh in descent from Colonel Philemon Lloyd.
Sixth in descent from James Lloyd.
Eighth in descent from Captain James Neale.
Seventh in descent from Robert Grundy.
Eighth in descent from Richard Woolman.
Eighth in descent from Garrett van Swearingen.

Ober, Mrs. Robert (Rosa Woolfolk).
Fifth in descent from Secretary Thomas Nelson.
Fourth in descent from Major John Nelson.
Eighth in descent from Colonel John Page.
Seventh in descent from Honorable Matthew Page.
Sixth in descent from Honorable Mann Page.
Seventh in descent from William Byrd I.
Sixth in descent from William Byrd II.
Fifth in descent from William Byrd III.
Eighth in descent from Colonel John Carter.
Seventh in descent from Honorable Robert Carter.

O'Donnell, Mrs. Columbus (Caroline Jenkins).
Seventh in descent from Sir Edmund Plowden.
Eighth in descent from Thomas Gerard.
Seventh in descent from Captain Robert Slye.
Sixth in descent from Captain Gerard Slye.
Eighth in descent from Deputy Governor Giles Brent.

O'Ferrall, Mrs. Frank F. (Annie B. Wetherill).
Eighth in descent from Christopher Wetherill.
Eighth in descent from Lieutenant Richard Stockton.
Sixth in descent from Captain Jacob Morgan.

Orrick, Mrs. Henry Abert (Martha Burroughs Levering.
Sixth in descent from Solomon Wright.
Fifth in descent from Solomon Wright, Jr.
Seventh in descent from William Coursey.

Paca, Miss Juliana Tilghman.
Eighth in descent from Aquila Paca.
Fifth in descent from Honorable William Paca.

Eighth in descent from Dr. Richard Tilghman.
Seventh in descent from Colonel Richard Tilghman.
Sixth in descent from Honorable Matthew Tilghman.
Tenth in descent from John Chew.
Ninth in descent from Edward Lloyd.
Eighth in descent from Colonel Philemon Lloyd.
Ninth in descent from Captain James Neale.

Page, Mrs. William C. (Rosalie Bell Williams.)

Sixth in descent from Carter Braxton.
Eighth in descent from Honorable Robert Carter.
Ninth in descent from Colonel John Carter.
Ninth in descent from Christopher Robinson.
Ninth in descent from Colonel Moore Fauntleroy.
Fifth in descent from Colonel Thomas Marshall.
Eighth in descent from William Randolph.
Ninth in descent from John Armistead.
Seventh in descent from William Colston.
Eighth in descent from Major William Gooch.
Eighth in descent from Colonel William Travers.
Eighth in descent from Colonel Isaac Allerton.
Ninth in descent from Governor Isaac Allerton.
Tenth in descent from Elder William Brewster.
Eighth in descent from Colonel Christopher Wormley.
Ninth in descent from Captain Thomas Willoughby.
Seventh in descent from Rev. John Camm.

Parran, Mrs. James Bourne (Jeannette Briscoe Thomas).

Fifth in descent from Major William Thomas.
Eighth in descent from Colonel John Jarboe.
Seventh in descent from Major William Boarman.
Ninth in descent from Acting Governor Robert Brooke.
Eighth in descent from Colonel Baker Brooke.
Ninth in descent from Governor Leonard Calvert.
Eighth in descent from Richard Marsham.
Eighth in descent from Captain Luke Gardiner.
Seventh in descent from Colonel John Courts.
Sixth in descent from John Courts.
Eighth in descent from Captain Robert Henley.
Eighth in descent from Colonel Philip Briscoe.
Seventh in descent from Captain John Briscoe.
Fifth in descent from Samuel Briscoe.
Eighth in descent from Colonel Humphrey Warren.
Ninth in descent from Governor William Stone.
Eighth in descent from John Stone.

LIST OF MEMBERS.

Seventh in descent from Captain Thomas Stone.
Eighth in descent from Richard Boughton.
Sixth in descent from Judge Walter Hanson.
Seventh in descent from Samuel Hanson.
Eighth in descent from John Hanson.

Parsons, Mrs. Joel Burton (Amelia Griffith Andrews).

Sixth in descent from Rev. James Macgill.
Sixth in descent from Colonel Henry Griffith.
Ninth in descent from Colonel Nicholas Greenberry.
Eighth in descent from Colonel Edward Dorsey.
Ninth in descent from Colonel Henry Ridgely.
Seventh in descent from Henry Ridgely.
Eighth in descent from Richard Hall.

Payson, Mrs. Herbert (Sally Carroll Brown).

Seventh in descent from Charles Carroll.
Eighth in descent from Colonel Henry Darnall.

Pearre, Miss Mary Smith Worthington.

Eighth in descent from Richard Smith.
Seventh in descent from Colonel Walter Smith.
Sixth in descent from Walter Smith, Jr.
Fifth in descent from Dr. Clement Smith.
Eighth in descent from Richard Hall.
Ninth in descent from Honorable Henry Sewall.
Eighth in descent from Major Nicholas Sewall.
Ninth in descent from Colonel William Burgess.
Ninth in descent from Acting Governor Robert Brooke.
Eighth in descent from Major Thomas Brooke.
Seventh in descent from Colonel Thomas Brooke.
Fifth in descent from Colonel Thomas Price.
Seventh in descent from Captain John Worthington.

Penniman, Mrs. George Dobbin (Harriet Wilson Dushane).

Ninth in descent from Acting Governor Robert Brooke.
Eighth in descent from Roger Brooke.
Ninth in descent from Captain James Neale.
Ninth in descent from Richard Smith.
Eighth in descent from Richard Smith, Jr.
Seventh in descent from John Broome.
Sixth in descent from Captain John Broome.
Seventh in descent from Thomas Howe.
Sixth in descent from James Somervell.

LIST OF MEMBERS.

Fifth in descent from Colonel Alexander Somervell.
Fifth in descent from James Duke.

Penniman, Mrs. Nicholas G. (Rebecca Dobbin.)

Seventh in descent from Colonel John Dorsey.
Seventh in descent from Richard Hill.

Penniman, Miss Rebecca.

Eighth in descent from Colonel Nicholas Greenberry.
Fifth in descent from Colonel Henry Griffith.
Eighth in descent from Colonel Henry Ridgely.
Sixth in descent from Henry Ridgely.
Sixth in descent from Rev. James Macgill.
Eighth in descent from Colonel John Dorsey.
Ninth in descent from Captain Richard Hill.

Pennington, Miss Elizabeth Lloyd.

Ninth in descent from Edward Lloyd I.
Eighth in descent from Colonel Philemon Lloyd.
Seventh in descent from Edward Lloyd II.
Sixth in descent from Edward Lloyd III.
Fifth in descent from Edward Lloyd IV.
Eighth in descent from John Rousby I.
Seventh in descent from John Rousby II.
Ninth in descent from Henry Morgan.
Eighth in descent from Colonel William Tayloe.
Seventh in descent from Colonel John Tayloe I.
Sixth in descent from Colonel John Tayloe II.
Ninth in descent from Henry Corbin.
Eighth in descent from Attorney-General George Plater.
Seventh in descent from Honorable George Plater.
Ninth in descent from Colonel John Addison I.
Eighth in descent from Honorable Thomas Addison.
Ninth in descent from Captain Thomas Tasker.
Ninth in descent from Captain James Neale.
Seventh in descent from Colonel John Winder.
Fifth in descent from William Winder.
Fourth in descent from Governor Levin Winder.
Eighth in descent from Honorable Henry Sewall.
Seventh in descent from Major Nicholas Sewall.
Eighth in descent from Colonel William Burgess.

Phenix, Miss Florence.

Eighth in descent from Richard Smith.
Seventh in descent from Colonel Walter Smith.

LIST OF MEMBERS.

Sixth in descent from Walter Smith, Jr.
Fifth in descent from Dr. Clement Smith.
Ninth in descent from Acting Governor Robert Brooke.
Eighth in descent from Major Thomas Brooke.
Seventh in descent from Colonel Thomas Brooke.
Fifth in descent from Colonel Thomas Price.

*Philpot, Miss Mary Dennison.

Fourth in descent from Brian Philpot.
Third in descent from Ensign Brian Philpot.
Eighth in descent from John Chew.
Seventh in descent from Samuel Chew.
Fifth in descent from Dr. George Buchanan.
Fourth in descent from General Andrew Buchanan.
Seventh in descent from Colonel Walter Smith.
Eighth in descent from Richard Hall.
Ninth in descent from Acting Governor Robert Brooke.
Eighth in descent from Major Thomas Brooke.
Eighth in descent from Honorable Henry Sewall.
Seventh in descent from Colonel Nicholas Sewall.
Eighth in descent from Colonel William Burgess.

Pitts, Mrs. Sullivan (Ellen Lloyd Goldsborough).

Seventh in descent from Robert Goldsborough.
Sixth in descent from Charles Goldsborough.
Fifth in descent from Honorable Robert Goldsborough.
Sixth in descent from Colonel Richard Tilghman.
Seventh in descent from Colonel Nicholas Greenberry.
Seventh in descent from John Moore.
Sixth in descent from William Moore.
Eighth in descent from Walter Dickinson.
Sixth in descent from Samuel Dickinson.
Eighth in descent from Bartholomew Ennalls.
Seventh in descent from Colonel Henry Ennalls.
Seventh in descent from Joseph Ennalls.
Eighth in descent from Captain James Neale.
Eighth in descent from Henry Morgan.
Eighth in descent from Edward Lloyd I.
Seventh in descent from Colonel Philemon Lloyd.
Sixth in descent from Edward Lloyd II.
Fifth in descent from Edward Lloyd III.
Fourth in descent from Edward Lloyd IV.
Sixth in descent from James Lloyd.

*Deceased.

LIST OF MEMBERS.

Seventh in descent from Robert Grundy.
Sixth in descent from Dr. William Murray (Cambridge).
Fifth in descent from Dr. William Murray (Chestertown).
Sixth in descent from Rev. Daniel Maynadier I.
Fifth in descent from Rev. Daniel Maynadier II.
Seventh in descent from John Rousby I.
Sixth in descent from John Rousby II.
Seventh in descent from Colonel William Tayloe.
Sixth in descent from Colonel John Tayloe I.
Fifth in descent from Colonel John Tayloe II.
Seventh in descent from Attorney-General George Plater.
Sixth in descent from Honorable George Plater.
Eighth in descent from Henry Corbin.

Poe, Mrs. Neilson, Jr. (Alice Henrietta Minis.)

Seventh in descent from Robert Livingston.
Sixth in descent from Colonel Philip Livingston.
Fifth in descent from Robert Livingston II.
Sixth in descent from John Swift I.
Fifth in descent from John Swift II.
Sixth in descent from Colonel Jacob Kollock.
Seventh in descent from Hercules Sheppeard.
Eighth in descent from Captain John Avery.

Polk, Miss Anna Maria.

Fifth in descent from David Polk.
Seventh in descent from Colonel Hans Hanson.
Sixth in descent from Judge Frederick Hanson.

Polk, Mrs. William Stewart (Louisa Ellen Minor Anderson).

Fourth in descent from Garland Anderson.
Fourth in descent from Garrett Minor.

Poultney, Mrs. Arthur E. (Emily Chapman Blackford.)

Eighth in descent from William Biddle I.
Fifth in descent from Colonel Clement Biddle.
Sixth in descent from Honorable Gideon Cornell.
Ninth in descent from William Freeborn.
Eighth in descent from Gideon Freeborn.
Tenth in descent from Thomas Hazard.
Ninth in descent from George Lawton.
Eighth in descent from Robert Owen.
Eighth in descent from Colonel William Fitzhugh.
Fifth in descent from John Minor.

LIST OF MEMBERS.

    Eighth in descent from Colonel John Carter.
    Seventh in descent from Honorable Robert Carter.
    Seventh in descent from William Byrd II.
    Ninth in descent from Warham Horsmanden.
    Tenth in descent from Captain Thomas Stegge.

Poultney, Mrs. Eugene (Leila Livingston Minis).
    Seventh in descent from Robert Livingston.
    Sixth in descent from Colonel Philip Livingston.
    Fifth in descent from Robert Livingston II.
    Sixth in descent from John Swift I.
    Fifth in descent from John Swift II.
    Sixth in descent from Colonel Jacob Kollock.
    Seventh in descent from Hercules Sheppeard.
    Eighth in descent from Captain John Avery.

Powell, Miss Sarah Harrison.
    Eighth in descent from William Powell.
    Fifth in descent from Colonel Levin Powell.
    Seventh in descent from Valentine Peyton.
    Eighth in descent from Burr Harrison.
    Fifth in descent from Colonel Charles Simons.
    Sixth in descent from Major William Douglass.

Powell, Mrs. William S. (Elizabeth Bowen Smith).
    Ninth in descent from Elder William Brewster.
    Eighth in descent from John Alden.
    Eighth in descent from Constant Southworth.
    Ninth in descent from Rev. Thomas Thacher.
    Tenth in descent from Rev. Ralf Partridge.
    Eighth in descent from Lieutenant Francis Peabody.
    Eighth in descent from Captain George Denison.

Presstman, Mrs. Benjamin (Matilda Winthrop Hooper).
    Fifth in descent from General Henry Hooper.
    Eighth in descent from Bartholomew Ennalls.
    Sixth in descent from Rev. Thomas Airey.
    Eighth in descent from Hugh Roberts.
    Ninth in descent from Captain James Neale.
    Ninth in descent from Edward Lloyd I.
    Eighth in descent from Colonel Philemon Lloyd.
    Eighth in descent from Dr. Richard Tilghman.
    Seventh in descent from Colonel Richard Tilghman.
    Seventh in descent from Thomas Robins.

LIST OF MEMBERS.

Sixth in descent from George Robins.
Seventh in descent from Rev. Henry Nicols.

Preston, Mrs. J. Alexander (Achsah Ridgely Carroll).

Sixth in descent from Zachariah Maccubbin.
Sixth in descent from Dr. Charles Carroll.
Ninth in descent from Edward Lloyd I.
Eighth in descent from Colonel Philemon Lloyd.
Ninth in descent from Captain James Neale.
Ninth in descent from Colonel John Dorsey.
Ninth in descent from Robert Ridgely.
Seventh in descent from Charles Ridgely.
Seventh in descent from Captain Richard Hill.
Sixth in descent from Colonel William Blay.
Seventh in descent from William Pearce.

Price, Mrs. Sterling W. (Mary Sterling.)

Ninth in descent from Captain Thomas Todd.

Proudfit, Miss Mary Couper.

Sixth in descent from James Logan.

Ramsay, Mrs. Henry Ashton (Julia White Cooke).

Seventh in descent from Colonel Henry Whiting.
Seventh in descent from Colonel Peter Beverly.

Ramsay, Miss Martha Parker.

Fifth in descent from David Ramsay.
Seventh in descent from Philip Key.
Seventh in descent from Dr. Gustavus Brown.
Eighth in descent from Colonel Henry Whiting.
Eighth in descent from Peter Beverly.

Randall, Mrs. Alexander Barton (Jane Randolph Harrison).

Fifth in descent from Honorable Nathaniel Harrison.
Sixth in descent from Benjamin Harrison II.
Seventh in descent from Benjamin Harrison I.
Fifth in descent from Honorable Cole Diggs.
Sixth in descent from Honorable Dudley Diggs.
Seventh in descent from Honorable Edward Diggs.
Eighth in descent from Sir Dudley Diggs.
Seventh in descent from Colonel William Cole.
Fourth in descent from William Byrd III

Fifth in descent from William Byrd II.
Sixth in descent from William Byrd I.
Eighth in descent from Captain Thomas Stegge.
Seventh in descent from Warham Horsmanden.
Ninth in descent from Sir Warham St. Leger.
Fifth in descent from Charles Willing.
Seventh in descent from Honorable Edward Shippen.
Fifth in descent from Colonel Thomas Mann Randolph.
Sixth in descent from Colonel William Randolph of Tuckahoe.
Seventh in descent from Colonel Thomas Randolph.
Eighth in descent from William Randolph.
Ninth in descent from Captain Henry Isham.
Seventh in descent from Honorable Mann Page I.
Eighth in descent from Honorable Mathew Page.
Ninth in descent from Colonel John Page.
Eighth in descent from Ralph Wormley II.
Ninth in descent from Ralph Wormley I.
Sixth in descent from Archibald Cary.
Ninth in descent from Colonel Miles Cary I.
Tenth in descent from Captain Thomas Taylor.
Seventh in descent from Colonel Richard Randolph of Curles.
Eighth in descent from Major John Bolling.
Ninth in descent from Colonel Robert Bolling I.
Tenth in descent from Lieutenant Thomas Rolfe.
Eleventh in descent from John Rolfe.
Ninth in descent from Richard Kennon.
Fifth in descent from President Thomas Jefferson.
Sixth in descent from Colonel Peter Jefferson.
Seventh in descent from Captain Thomas Jefferson.
Eleventh in descent from Christopher Branch.
Eighth in descent from Major Peter Field.
Ninth in descent from Henry Soane.
Seventh in descent from Isham Randolph.
Seventh in descent from Colonel Francis Eppes IV.
Eighth in descent from Colonel Francis Eppes III.
Ninth in descent from Colonel Francis Eppes II.
Tenth in descent from Colonel Francis Eppes I.
Fifth in descent from Robert Carter Nicholas.
Sixth in descent from Dr. George Nicholas.
Seventh in descent from Honorable Robert Carter.
Eighth in descent from Colonel John Carter.
Eighth in descent from Honorable John Armistead.
Sixth in descent from Colonel Wilson Cary.

LIST OF MEMBERS.

Seventh in descent from Colonel Miles Cary II.
Eighth in descent from Colonel William Wilson.
Eighth in descent from John Smith.
Sixth in descent from Samuel Smith.

Redwood, Mrs. Frank T. (Mary Buchanan Coale.)

Fifth in descent from Thomas McKean.
Sixth in descent from Dr. George Buchanan.
Fifth in descent from General Andrew Buchanan.
Sixth in descent from Joseph Borden.
Fifth in descent from Thomas Hopkinson.
Sixth in descent from Colonel William Hammond.
Ninth in descent from Richard Smith.
Eighth in descent from Colonel Walter Smith.
Seventh in descent from Walter Smith, Jr.
Ninth in descent from Richard Hall.
Tenth in descent from Acting Governor Robert Brooke.
Ninth in descent from Major Thomas Brooke.
Fifth in descent from Richard Brooke.
Ninth in descent from Captain James Neale.
Tenth in descent from Honorable Henry Sewall.
Ninth in descent from Major Nicholas Sewall.
Tenth in descent from Colonel William Burgess.

Reed, Mrs. William (Emily McKim).

Seventh in descent from William Ashfordley.
Fifth in descent from Thomas Beatty.
Seventh in descent from Andreas Bengston.
Eighth in descent from Governor Jean Paul Jacquett.

Reynolds, Mrs. William (Nora Meade Lightfoot).

Sixth in descent from Honorable Philip Lightfoot.
Fourth in descent from Lieutenant Philip Lightfoot.
Seventh in descent from John Lewis.
Fifth in descent from Colonel Charles Lewis.
Eighth in descent from Colonel Augustine Warner, Jr.
Ninth in descent from George Reade.
Eighth in descent from Henry Corbin.
Seventh in descent from John Taliaferro.

Ridgely, Mrs. Charles (Margaretta Sophia Howard).

Third in descent from Colonel John Eager Howard.
Seventh in descent from Robert Ridgely.
Sixth in descent from Colonel John Dorsey.
Seventh in descent from Samuel Chew.
Sixth in descent from Captain Richard Hill.

Ridgey, Mrs. John (Helen West Stewart).

> Tenth in descent from Elder William Brewster.
> Tenth in descent from John Alden.
> Tenth in descent from Captain Miles Standish.
> Tenth in descent from William Collier.
> Fifth in descent from Captain John Morton.
> Sixth in descent from Brian Philpot.
> Ninth in descent from Samuel Chew.

*Ringgold, Mrs. James T. (Isabelle Elizabeth Egerton.)

> Seventh in descent from Captain John Hall.
> Fifth in descent from Aquilla Carvil Hall.
> Sixth in descent from Colonel Thomas White.

Ritchie, Mrs. John (Betty Harrison Maulsby).

> Eighth in descent from Acting Governor Robert Brooke.
> Seventh in descent from Major Thomas Brooke.
> Sixth in descent from Colonel Thomas Brooke.
> Fifth in descent from Alexander Contee.

Robbins, Mrs. Henry S. (Frances Fuller Johnston.)

> Eighth in descent from Major John Stith.
> Sixth in descent from Drury Stith.
> Fifth in descent from Griffin Stith.
> Seventh in descent from Major William Buckner.
> Tenth in descent from Edmund Hobart.
> Ninth in descent from William Bassett (Mass.)

Roberts, Mrs. John B. (Mary M. Ellicott.)

> Seventh in descent from Philip Thomas.
> Seventh in descent from Captain Francis Hutchins.
> Fourth in descent from Evan Thomas.

Robinson, Miss Louisa Hall.

> Eighth in descent from John Brewer.
> Fourth in descent from Charles Willson Peale.
> Sixth in descent from Captain John Hall.
> Fifth in descent from Colonel John Hall.
> Fourth in descent from Colonel Josias Carvil Hall.
> Seventh in descent from Richard Gist.
> Seventh in descent from Hon. William Cattell.
> Fifth in descent from Captain Benjamin Cattell.

*Deceased.

Eighth in descent from Colonel John Godfreey.
Ninth in descent from James Sanderlain.
Eighth in descent from Honorable Jasper Yeates.
Fifth in descent from Honorable William Smith.

Rogers, Mrs. Charles Lyon (Ann Rebecca Grogan).

Eighth in descent from Garrett van Swearingen.

Rogers, Mrs. Henry W. (Fanny Johnson Dennis.)

Seventh in descent from Donnack Dennis.
Fifth in descent from John Dennis.
Eighth in descent from Colonel Nathaniel Littleton.
Seventh in descent from Colonel Southey Littleton.
Ninth in descent from Randall Revell.
Eighth in descent from Honorable James Saunders.
Sixth in descent from Darby Lux.
Sixth in descent from Thomas Jennings.
Fifth in descent from Robert McPherson.
Fifth in descent from Governor Thomas Johnson.

Roman, Miss Louisa Lowndes.

Ninth in descent from Captain James Neale.
Ninth in descent from Edward Lloyd I.
Eighth in descent from Colonel Philemon Lloyd.
Seventh in descent from Edward Lloyd II.
Sixth in descent from Edward Lloyd III.
Fifth in descent from Edward Lloyd IV.
Seventh in descent from Honorable George Plater.
Seventh in descent from William Bladen.
Seventh in descent from Thomas Tasker.
Sixth in descent from Honorable Benjamin Tasker.

Rowland, Miss Elizabeth Mason.

Eighth in descent from Colonel George Mason I.
Seventh in descent from Colonel George Mason II.
Sixth in descent from Colonel George Mason III.
Fifth in descent from Thomson Mason.
Sixth in descent from Major Abraham Barnes.
Seventh in descent from Stevens Thomson.
Eighth in descent from Colonel Gerard Fowke.
Ninth in descent from Captain Adam Thorowgood.
Seventh in descent from Captain Anthony Armistead.
Sixth in descent from Captain Robert Armistead.

Rowley, Mrs. C. W. (Margaret Hughes Armstrong.)
   Fifth in descent from Colonel John Armstrong.
   Ninth in descent from Brant Arentse Van Schlichtenhorst.
   Eighth in descent from Captain Philip Pieterse Schuyler.
   Eighth in descent from Colonel Peter Schuyler.
   Seventh in descent from Robert Livingston.
   Seventh in descent from Colonel Henry Beekman I.
   Sixth in descent from Colonel Henry Beekman II.

Screven, Mrs. George P. (Ellen Buchanan.)
   Fifth in descent from Dr. George Buchanan.
   Fourth in descent from General Andrew Buchanan.
   Fourth in descent from Thomas McKean.
   Fifth in descent from Joseph Borden.
   Eighth in descent from Richard Smith.
   Seventh in descent from Colonel Walter Smith.
   Sixth in descent from Walter Smith, Jr.
   Eighth in descent from Richard Hall.
   Ninth in descent from Honorable Henry Sewall.
   Eighth in descent from Major Nicholas Sewall.
   Ninth in descent from Colonel William Burgess.
   Eighth in descent from Edward Lloyd I.
   Seventh in descent from Colonel Philemon Lloyd.
   Sixth in descent from Edward Lloyd II.
   Fifth in descent from Edward Lloyd III.
   Fourth in descent from Edward Lloyd IV.
   Eighth in descent from Captain James Neale.
   Sixth in descent from Rev. Daniel Maynadier I.
   Fifth in descent from Rev. Daniel Maynadier II.
   Seventh in descent from Colonel William Tayloe.
   Sixth in descent from Colonel John Tayloe I.
   Fifth in descent from Colonel John Tayloe II.
   Eighth in descent from Henry Corbin.
   Sixth in descent from Honorable George Plater.
   Seventh in descent from John Rousby I.
   Sixth in descent from John Rousby II.
   Eighth in descent from Col. John Addison I.
   Seventh in descent from Col. Thomas Addison.
   Eighth in descent from Capt. Thomas Tasker.
   Eighth in descent from Henry Morgan.

Semmes, Mrs. John E. (Frances Carnan Hayward).
   Sixth in descent from John Risteau.
   Fourth in descent from John Robert Holliday.

Eighth in descent from Colonel John Addison I.
Seventh in descent from Colonel Thomas Addison.
Eighth in descent from Captain Thomas Tasker.
Eighth in descent from Henry Morgan.
Tenth in descent from Captain Thomas Todd.

Semple, Mrs. Percy (Meta Powell Hollyday).

Fifth in descent from James Hollyday.
Fifth in descent from Levin Powell.
Fifth in descent from Humphrey Brooke.
Eighth in descent from Dr. Richard Tilghman.
Seventh in descent from Colonel Richard Tilghman.
Ninth in descent from Edward Lloyd I.
Eighth in descent from Colonel Philemon Lloyd.
Ninth in descent from Captain James Neale.
Fifth in descent from George Robbins.

Shawhan, Mrs. Charles S. (Narcisse Tayloe Maupin.)

Seventh in descent from Colonel John Tayloe I.
Sixth in descent from Colonel John Tayloe II.
Eighth in descent from Henry Corbin.
Sixth in descent from Honorable George Plater.
Seventh in descent from Governor Samuel Ogle.
Seventh in descent from Honorable Benjamin Tasker.
Eighth in descent from William Bladen.

Sibley, Mrs. Clarence (Nannie Thomas Markoe).

Sixth in descent from Benjamin Chew.
Sixth in descent from Tench Francis.
Fifth in descent from Tristram Thomas.
Fifth in descent from William Perry.
Sixth in descent from John Goldsborough.
Seventh in descent from Robert Goldsborough.
Eighth in descent from Michael Turbutt.
Seventh in descent from Foster Turbutt.
Eighth in descent from John Bozman.

Shippen, Mrs. Edward (Rebecca Lloyd Nicholson).

Fifth in descent from Colonel Joseph Nicholson.
Fourth in descent from Joseph Nicholson, Jr.
Eighth in descent from Colonel William Burgess.
Seventh in descent from Captain Edward Burgess.
Sixth in descent from Captain James Smith.
Eighth in descent from Thomas Hynson.

Seventh in descent from Colonel John Hynson.
Eighth in descent from Edward Lloyd I.
Seventh in descent from Colonel Philemon Lloyd.
Sixth in descent from Edward Lloyd II.
Fifth in descent from Edward Lloyd III.
Fourth in descent from Edward Lloyd IV.
Seventh in descent from John Rousby I.
Sixth in descent from John Rousby II.
Eighth in descent from Henry Morgan.
Seventh in descent from Colonel William Tayloe.
Sixth in descent from Colonel John Tayloe I.
Fifth in descent from Colonel John Tayloe II.
Eighth in descent from Henry Corbin.
Seventh in descent from Attorney-General George Plater.
Sixth in descent from Honorable George Plater.
Eighth in descent from Colonel John Addison I.
Seventh in descent from Honorable Thomas Addison.
Eighth in descent from Captain Thomas Tasker.
Eighth in descent from Captain James Neale.
Eighth in descent from Lieutenant-Colonel John West.
Tenth in descent from Captain Edmund Scarburgh.
Ninth in descent from Colonel Edmund Scarburgh.
Tenth in descent from Sir George Yeardley.
Ninth in descent from Colonel Argall Yeardley.
Tenth in descent from Captain Adam Thorowgood.
Ninth in descent from Governor Richard Bennett.

Simpson, Mrs. Edward (Camilla Ridgely).
Eighth in descent from Robert Ridgely.
Sixth in descent from Charles Ridgely.
Fifth in descent from John Ridgely.
Fifth in descent from James Sterett.
Fourth in descent from Captain John Sterett.
Eighth in descent from Colonel John Dorsey.
Eighth in descent from Francis Hutchins.
Seventh in descent from Colonel John Mackall.
Sixth in descent from James John Mackall.
Sixth in descent from William Bowie.
Fifth in descent from Governor Robert Bowie.
Sixth in descent from Allen Bowie.
Fifth in descent from Captain Fielder Bowie.
Seventh in descent from Valentine Hollingsworth.
Sixth in descent from Henry Hollingsworth.
Sixth in descent from William Ghiselin.
Fifth in descent from Reverdy Ghiselin.

LIST OF MEMBERS.

Sioussat, Mrs. Albert Willis (Annie Middleton Leakin).
> Seventh in descent from William Hatton.
> Ninth in descent from Colonel William Burgess.
> Ninth in descent from Honorable Henry Sewall.
> Eighth in descent from Major Nicholas Sewall.
> Ninth in descent from Acting Governor Robert Brooke.
> Eighth in descent from Major Thomas Brooke.
> Sixth in descent from Captain Thomas Middleton.

Slingluff, Mrs. Fielder C. (Mary Johnston.)
> Fifth in descent from Honorable Robert Morris.
> Eighth in descent from Major-General John Hammond.
> Sixth in descent from John Moale I.
> Eighth in descent from Colonel Nicholas Greenberry.

Sloan, Mrs. Robert Neale (Louise Gittings Littig).
> Fifth in descent from James Gittings.
> Sixth in descent from Dr. George Buchanan.
> Fifth in descent from Captain John Sterett.
> Sixth in descent from John Ridgely.

Smith, Mrs. Benjamin Franklin (Mary Dorsey Evans).
> Eighth in descent from Colonel John Dorsey.

*Smith, Mrs. Chandler Price (Henrietta Gaither).
> Eighth in descent from Colonel William Burgess.
> Eighth in descent from Colonel Edward Dorsey.
> Ninth in descent from Colonel Henry Ridgely.
> Seventh in descent from Henry Ridgely.
> Ninth in descent from Colonel Nicholas Greenberry.
> Seventh in descent from Colonel John Dorsey.
> Seventh in descent from Captain John Worthington.
> Sixth in descent from Colonel Walter Tolley.
> Seventh in descent from Thomas Tolley.
> Eighth in descent from Robert Ridgely.
> Sixth in descent from Charles Ridgely.

Smith, Miss Clementine.
> Seventh in descent from Richard Smith.
> Sixth in descent from Colonel Walter Smith.
> Fifth in descent from Walter Smith, Jr.
> Fourth in descent from Dr. Clement Smith.

*Deceased.

Eighth in descent from Acting Governor Robert Brooke.
Seventh in descent from Major Thomas Brooke.
Sixth in descent from Colonel Thomas Brooke.
Fourth in descent from Colonel Thomas Price.

Smith, Mrs. Frederick Henry (Elizabeth Gairdner).
Fifth in descent from Barnaby McKinnie.

Smith, Miss Josephine Hopkinson.
Sixth in descent from Thomas Hopkinson.

Smith, Mrs. Robert C. (Mary Elizabeth Rhoads Smith.)
Sixth in descent from Daniel Smith.
Fifth in descent from Robert Smith.
Fourth in descent from Daniel Smith, Jr.
Seventh in descent from William Cooper.
Sixth in descent from Joseph Cooper.
Eighth in descent from Mahlon Stacy.
Seventh in descent from Honorable John Smith of Pennsylvania.
Fifth in descent from Thomas Raper.
Seventh in descent from Joseph Kirkbride.
Sixth in descent from Mahlon Kirkbride.
Sixth in descent from John Bacon.
Seventh in descent from John Blunston.
Fourth in descent from Colonel Edward Thomas.
Seventh in descent from Robert Lucas.

Smith, Miss Sallie Cox.
Seventh in descent from Richard Smith.
Sixth in descent from Colonel Walter Smith.
Fifth in descent from Walter Smith, Jr.
Fourth in descent from Dr. Clement Smith.
Eighth in descent from Acting Governor Robert Brooke.
Seventh in descent from Major Thomas Brooke.
Sixth in descent from Colonel Thomas Brooke.
Fourth in descent from Colonel Thomas Price.

Smith, Mrs. Thomas Marsh (Helen Randolph Parry).
Sixth in descent from Nathaniel Fitz Randolph.
Third in descent from Lieutenant Edward Fitz Randolph.
Sixth in descent from Richard Hartshorne.
Sixth in descent from Thomas Watson.
Sixth in descent from Thomas Canby.

LIST OF MEMBERS.

Smith, Miss Virginia Hope Bryant.
    Sixth in descent from Anthony Walke.
    Fifth in descent from Anthony Walke, Jr.
    Eighth in descent from Colonel Anthony Lawson.
    Ninth in descent from Colonel Richard Lee.
    Eighth in descent from Honorable John Armistead.
    Eighth in descent from Colonel Edward Moseley.
    Sixth in descent from Edward Hack Moseley.
    Ninth in descent from Colonel William Kendall.
    Tenth in descent from Captain John Gookin.
    Eighth in descent from Honorable Lewis Burwell.
    Tenth in descent from Captain Adam Thorowgood.

Smith, Mrs. Virginia McBlair.
    Eighth in descent from Robert Ridgely.
    Sixth in descent from Charles Ridgely.
    Eighth in descent from Colonel John Dorsey.

Snead, Mrs. Charles W. (Susan Upshur Snead.)
    Seventh in descent from Donnack Dennis.
    Fifth in descent from John Dennis.

Spencer, Mrs. Jervis (Julia Williamson).
    Eighth in descent from Garrett Van Swearingen.
    Eighth in descent from William Mitchell.

Steele, Miss Rosa.
    Ninth in descent from Acting Governor Robert Brooke.
    Eighth in descent from Major Thomas Brooke.
    Seventh in descent from Colonel Thomas Brooke.
    Fifth in descent from Colonel Joseph Sim.
    Eighth in descent from Colonel John Addison.
    Seventh in descent from Colonel Thomas Addison.
    Ninth in descent from Richard Smith.
    Eighth in descent from Colonel Walter Smith.
    Fourth in descent from General Roger Nelson.

Steuart, Miss Henrietta.
    Fifth in descent from Dr. George Steuart.
    Eighth in descent from Governor Edward Digges.
    Seventh in descent from Colonel William Digges.
    Eighth in descent from Bartholomew Ennalls.
    Seventh in descent from Colonel Henry Ennalls.
    Eighth in descent from Honorable Henry Sewall.

Steuart, Miss Mary Elizabeth.
> Fifth in descent from Dr. George Steuart.
> Eighth in descent from Governor Edward Digges.
> Seventh in descent from Colonel William Digges.
> Eighth in descent from Honorable Henry Sewall.
> Seventh in descent from Colonel Henry Ennalls.
> Eighth in descent from Bartholomew Ennalls.

Stewart, Mrs. David (Alice Gerry).
> Seventh in descent from Captain Richard Jenness.
> Sixth in descent from Richard Jenness, Jr.
> Fifth in descent from Rev. Samuel McClintock.
> Ninth in descent from Captain Henry Dow.
> Ninth in descent from Thomas Marston.
> Tenth in descent from William Eastow.
> Ninth in descent from Captain James Avery.
> Tenth in descent from Honorable John Humfrey.
> Ninth in descent from Lieutenant John Samborne.
> Seventh in descent from Tristram Samborne.
> Sixth in descent from Peter Samborne.
> Seventh in descent from Captain Jonathan Samborne.
> Tenth in descent from Tristram Coffin I.
> Ninth in descent from Tristram Coffin II.
> Tenth in descent from Captain Edmund Greenleaf.
> Ninth in descent from Henry Sherburne.
> Eighth in descent from Captain Samuel Sherburne.
> Tenth in descent from Ambrose Gibbons.

Stiles, Mrs. Edmund (Monterey Watson Randall).
> Tenth in descent from Dr. Luke Barber.
> Sixth in descent from Charles Barber.

Stockbridge, Mrs. Henry, Jr. (Helen Maria Smith.)
> Eighth in descent from Lieutenant Samuel Smith.
> Ninth in descent from Governor John Webster.
> Eighth in descent from Major Aaron Cook.

Stokes, Miss Eliza Hughes.
> Sixth in descent from Samuel Chamberlaine.
> Eighth in descent from Robert Tyler.
> Seventh in descent from Thomas Robins.
> Sixth in descent from George Robins.
> Ninth in descent from Edward Lloyd I.
> Eighth in descent from Colonel Philemon Lloyd.

LIST OF MEMBERS.

Ninth in descent from Captain James Neale.
Eighth in descent from Dr. Richard Tilghman.
Seventh in descent from Colonel Richard Tilghman.
Sixth in descent from Rev. George Murdock.

Story, Mrs. B. T. (Jeannie Washington Campbell.)

Ninth in descent from Colonel Gerard Fowke.
Tenth in descent from Captain Richard Townshend.
Sixth in descent from Colonel Henry Ashton.

Strother, Mrs. Nelson (Emily Viele).

Fifth in descent from Captain Zebulon Butler.
Fifth in descent from Comfort Sands.

Sullivan, Mrs. Felix R. (Elizabeth Tayloe Buchanan).

Fifth in descent from Dr. George Buchanan.
Fourth in descent from General Andrew Buchanan.
Fourth in descent from Thomas McKean.
Fifth in descent from Joseph Borden.
Eighth in descent from Richard Smith.
Seventh in descent from Colonel Walter Smith.
Sixth in descent from Walter Smith, Jr.
Eighth in descent from Richard Hall.
Ninth in descent from Honorable Henry Sewall.
Eighth in descent from Major Nicholas Sewall.
Ninth in descent from Colonel William Burgess.
Eighth in descent from Edward Lloyd I.
Seventh in descent from Colonel Philemon Lloyd.
Sixth in descent from Edward Lloyd II.
Fifth in descent from Edward Lloyd III.
Fourth in descent from Edward Lloyd IV.
Eighth in descent from Captain James Neale.
Sixth in descent from Rev. Daniel Maynadier I.
Fifth in descent from Rev. Daniel Maynadier II.
Seventh in descent from Colonel William Tayloe.
Sixth in descent from Colonel John Tayloe I.
Fifth in descent from Colonel John Tayloe II.
Eighth in descent from Henry Corbin.
Sixth in descent from Honorable George Plater.
Seventh in descent from John Rousby I.
Sixth in descent from John Rousby II.
Eighth in descent from Colonel John Addison I.
Seventh in descent from Colonel Thomas Addison.
Eighth in descent from Captain Thomas Tasker.
Eighth in descent from Henry Morgan.

Tait, Mrs. John R. (Anna D. M. Tiernan.)
    Ninth in descent from John Rolfe.
    Eighth in descent from Garrett Van Swearingen.

Tarleton, Mrs. Robert (Sallie Bernard Lightfoot).
    Sixth in descent from Honorable Philip Lightfoot.
    Fourth in descent from Lieutenant Philip Lightfoot.
    Seventh in descent from John Lewis.
    Fifth in descent from Colonel Charles Lewis.
    Eighth in descent from Colonel Augustine Warner, Jr.
    Ninth in descent from George Reade.
    Eighth in descent from Henry Corbin.
    Seventh in descent from John Taliaferro.

Taylor, Mrs. B. Jones (Mary Frances Wigfall).
    Fifth in descent from Theodore Trezevant.
    Fifth in descent from Rev. Levi Durand.
    Eighth in descent from Arthur Fenner.
    Seventh in descent from Thomas Fenner.
    Ninth in descent from William Harris.
    Tenth in descent from William Arnold.
    Ninth in descent from Richard Waterman.
    Sixth in descent from Louis Timothy.
    Ninth in descent from William Carpenter.
    Tenth in descent from Edward Smith.
    Eighth in descent from Benjamin Smith.
    Seventh in descent from Simon Smith.
    Ninth in descent from Chad Brown.
    Ninth in descent from Richard Borden.
    Eighth in descent from Thomas Borden.
    Ninth in descent from Stephen Arnold.

Taylor, Mrs. Winfield J. (Decima Shubrick Heyward.)
    Sixth in descent from Captain Thomas Heyward.
    Fourth in descent from Judge Thomas Heyward.
    Fifth in descent from Honorable Thomas Shubrick.
    Fourth in descent from Colonel Thomas Shubrick.
    Sixth in descent from Isaac Motte.
    Seventh in descent from Honorable William Cattell.
    Fifth in descent from Captain Benjamin Cattell.
    Eighth in descent from Colonel John Godfrey.
    Eighth in descent from Honorable Jasper Yeates.
    Ninth in descent from James Sanderlain.

LIST OF MEMBERS.

Thom, Mrs. J. Pembroke (Catherine Grosh Reynolds).

Ninth in descent from Captain Richard Betts.
Ninth in descent from Lieutenant Ralph Hunt.
Fourth in descent from Lieutenant-Colonel Abraham Hunt.
Fifth in descent from Robert Pearson.
Ninth in descent from Thomas Hazard.

Thomas, Mrs. Douglas H. (Alice Lee Whitridge.)

Seventh in descent from Honorable John Cushing I.
Sixth in descent from Honorable John Cushing II.
Fifth in descent from Honorable John Cushing III.

*Thomsen, Mrs. John J. (Emmalena Lilly.)

Eighth in descent from Captain Miles Standish.

Thompson, Miss Charlotte de Macklot.

Ninth in descent from Honorable James Saunders.
Fifth in descent from Daniel Bowly.
Seventh in descent from Darby Lux.

Thompson, Miss Elizabeth Young.

Fourth in descent from Commodore Joshua Barney.
Eighth in descent from Robert Ridgely.
Sixth in descent from Charles Ridgely.
Fifth in descent from John Ridgely.
Eighth in descent from Colonel John Dorsey.
Eighth in descent from Richard Smith.
Seventh in descent from Colonel Walter Smith.
Sixth in descent from Walter Smith, Jr.
Eighth in descent from Richard Hall.
Ninth in descent from Acting Governor Robert Brooke.
Eighth in descent from Major Thomas Brooke.
Ninth in descent from Honorable Henry Sewall.
Eighth in descent from Major Nicholas Sewall.
Eighth in descent from Colonel William Burgess.

Tiffany, Mrs. L. McLane (Evelyn May Bayly).

Eighth in descent from Benjamin Harrison I.
Ninth in descent from Governor Edward Digges.
Ninth in descent from Colonel William Cole.
Eighth in descent from Colonel William Fitzhugh.
Seventh in descent from Colonel Henry Fitzhugh.

---

*Deceased.

Ninth in descent from Edmund Bowman.
Tenth in descent from Colonel Edmund Scarburgh.
Fifth in descent from Captain Sebastian Cropper.
Fourth in descent from General John Cropper.
Sixth in descent from Captain Richard Bayly.

Tilghman, Miss Mary.

Seventh in descent from Dr. Richard Tilghman.
Sixth in descent from Colonel Richard Tilghman.
Fifth in descent from William Tilghman.
Eighth in descent from Edward Lloyd I.
Seventh in descent from Colonel Philemon Lloyd.
Sixth in descent from James Lloyd.
Eighth in descent from Captain James Neale.
Seventh in descent from Robert Grundy.
Eighth in descent from Garrett Van Swearingen.
Eighth in descent from Richard Woolman.

Tilton, Miss Elizabeth.

Eighth in desent from Edward Lloyd I.
Seventh in descent from Colonel Philemon Lloyd.
Sixth in descent from Edward Lloyd II.
Fifth in descent from Edward Lloyd III.
Fourth in descent from Edward Lloyd IV.
Eighth in descent from Captain James Neale.
Seventh in descent from John Rousby I.
Sixth in descent from John Rousby II.
Eighth in descent from Henry Morgan.
Seventh in descent from Colonel William Tayloe.
Sixth in descent from Colonel John Tayloe I.
Fifth in descent from Colonel John Tayloe II.
Eighth in descent from Henry Corbin.
Sixth in descent from Honorable George Plater.
Eighth in descent from Richard Woolman.

Tompkins, Mrs. John Almy (Anna Albertine Shriver).

Fourth in descent from David Shriver.

Trimble, Mrs. David C. (Sallie Scott Lloyd.)

Eighth in descent from Edward Lloyd I.
Seventh in descent from Colonel Philemon Lloyd.
Sixth in descent from Edward Lloyd II.
Fifth in descent from Edward Lloyd III.
Fourth in descent from Edward Lloyd IV.

LIST OF MEMBERS.

Eighth in descent from Captain James Neale.
Sixth in descent from Rev. Daniel Maynadier I.
Fifth in descent from Rev. Daniel Maynadier II.
Seventh in descent from Colonel William Tayloe.
Sixth in descent from Colonel John Tayloe I.
Fifth in descent from Colonel John Tayloe II.
Eighth in descent from Henry Corbin.
Sixth in descent from Honorable George Plater.
Seventh in descent from John Rousby I.
Sixth in descent from John Rousby II.

Turnbull, Mrs. Alexander Nisbet (Olivia Cushing Whitridge).

Sixth in descent from Captain John Hall.
Fifth in descent from Colonel John Hall.
Fourth in descent from Colonel Josias Carvil Hall.
Fifth in descent from Honorable William Smith.
Seventh in descent from Richard Gist.
Seventh in descent from Honorable William Cattell.
Fifth in descent from Captain Benjamin Cattell.
Eighth in descent from Colonel John Godfrey.
Ninth in descent from James Sanderlain.
Eighth in descent from Honorable Jasper Yeates.
Eighth in descent from Honorable John Cushing I.
Seventh in descent from Honorable John Cushing II.
Sixth in descent from Honorable John Cushing III.
Fifth in descent from Thomas Wallingford.

Turnbull, Mrs. John O. (Sophia Gough Carroll.)

Sixth in descent from Zachariah Maccubbin.
Sixth in descent from Dr. Charles Carroll.
Ninth in descent from Edward Lloyd I.
Eighth in descent from Colonel Philemon Lloyd.
Tenth in descent from Captain James Neale.
Ninth in descent from Colonel John Dorsey.
Ninth in descent from Robert Ridgely.
Seventh in descent from Charles Ridgely.
Seventh in descent from Captain Richard Hill.
Sixth in descent from Colonel William Blay.
Seventh in descent from William Pearce.

Tyson, Mrs. John Snowden (Mary Roberts).

Sixth in descent from Edward Farmer.

Van Antwerp, Mrs. Thomas C. (Margaret Percival Wright.)

Eighth in descent from Richard Hall.

von Kapff, Mrs. Frederick (Anne Donnell Smith).
    Fourth in descent from John Smith.
    Fourth in descent from Honorable William Smith.
    Ninth in descent from Sir George Yeardley.
    Eighth in descent from Colonel Argall Yeardley.
    Seventh in descent from Lieutenant-Colonel John West.
    Eighth in descent from Colonel Edmund Scarburgh.
    Ninth in descent from Major-General John Custis.
    Eighth in descent from Colonel John Custis.
    Sixth in descent from John Teackle.

von Kapff, Mrs. Frederick, Jr. (Annie Sharp Brown.)
    Sixth in descent from Lieutenant Thomas McKim.

Waller, Mrs. Robert Alexander (Lena Watson).
    Eighth in descent from Captain Thomas Todd.

Ward, Mrs. Frank X. (Ellen Topham Evans).
    Fifth in descent from Governor Thomas Johnson.

Washburn, Mrs. Charles W. (Kate Styles Spence.)
    Sixth in descent from Zachariah Maccubbin.
    Sixth in descent from Dr. Charles Carroll.
    Ninth in descent from Edward Lloyd I.
    Eighth in descent from Colonel Philemon Lloyd.
    Ninth in descent from Captain James Neale.
    Ninth in descent from Colonel John Dorsey.
    Ninth in descent from Robert Ridgely.
    Seventh in descent from Charles Ridgely.
    Tenth in descent from Captain Richard Hill.
    Ninth in descent from Elder John Whipple.
    Eighth in descent from Captain John Whipple.
    Seventh in descent from Matthew Whipple.
    Eighth in descent from Samuel Appleton.
    Fifth in descent from Robert Traill.

Wetmore, Mrs. Russell (Amy D'Arcy Wilson).
    Fifth in descent from Lieutenant Thomas McKim.

White, Mrs. Miles, Jr., (Virginia Purviance Bonsal.)
    Seventh in descent from John Bethel.
    Seventh in descent from William Roscoe, Jr.

LIST OF MEMBERS.

Whitelock, Mrs. George (Louise Clarkson).
Seventh in descent from Matthew Clarkson.
Seventh in descent from Colonel Abraham de Peyster.

Whitney, Mrs. George E.
Seventh in descent from Garrett Van Swearingen.

Whiting, Mrs. C. Clarence (Minna Armistead).
Seventh in descent from Colonel William Fitzhugh.
Seventh in descent from Honorable John Armistead.
Fifth in descent from Colonel John Baylor.

Whitridge, Mrs. Horatio L. (Elizabeth Buchanan Hall.)
Fifth in descent from Captain John Hall.
Fourth in descent from Colonel John Hall.
Third in descent from Colonel Josias Carvil Hall.
Fourth in descent from Honorable William Smith.
Sixth in descent from Richard Gist.
Sixth in descent from Honorable William Cattell.
Fourth in descent from Captain Benjamin Cattell.
Seventh in descent from Colonel John Godfrey.
Eighth in descent from James Sanderlain.
Seventh in descent from Honorable Jasper Yeates.

Whitridge, Mrs. William H. (Elizabeth Graham.)
Seventh in descent from John Teackle.
Twelfth in descent from Captain Edmund Scarburgh.
Eleventh in descent from Colonel Edmund Scarburgh.
Ninth in descent from Randall Revell.
Tenth in descent from Major-General John Custis.
Ninth in descent from Colonel John Custis.
Ninth in descent from Lieutenant-Colonel John West.

Williams, Mrs. Charles Phelps (Juliet Marie Riley).
Sixth in descent from Colonel Benjamin Young.
Eighth in descent from Colonel Benjamin Rozer.
Ninth in descent from Honorable Thomas Notley.
Ninth in descent from Governor Edward Digges.
Eighth in descent from Colonel William Digges.
Ninth in descent from Honorable Henry Sewall.
Ninth in descent from Acting Governor Robert Brooke.
Eighth in descent from Major Thomas Brooke.
Ninth in descent from Captain James Neale.
Tenth in descent from Governor Richard Bennett.

Williams, Miss Elizabeth Chew.
> Tenth in descent from John Chew.
> Ninth in descent from Honorable Samuel Chew.
> Ninth in the descent from Captain Thomas Clagett.
> Eighth in descent from Colonel John Dorsey.
> Ninth in descent from Attorney-General Richard Smith.
> Eighth in descent from Colonel Walter Smith.
> Seventh in descent from Walter Smith.
> Ninth in descent from Richard Hall.
> Tenth in descent from Acting-Governor Robert Brooke.
> Ninth in descent from Major Thomas Brooke.
> Tenth in descent from Honorable Henry Sewall.
> Ninth in descent from Major Nicholas Sewall.
> Tenth in descent from Colonel William Burgess.

Williams, Mrs. John Witherspoon (Augusta Rebecca Howell).
> Fifth in descent from Honorable John Stockton.

Williams, Miss Rebecca Dalrymple.
> Sixth in descent from Captain Stephen Williams.
> Fourth in descent from Colonel Joseph Williams.
> Eighth in descent from Edward Howell.
> Seventh in descent from Major John Howell.
> Eighth in descent from Richard Treat.
> Seventh in descent from John Deming.

Williams, Miss Sue Campbell.
> Sixth in descent from Colonel Joseph Williams.
> Ninth in descent from William Parke.
> Fifth in descent from Lieutenant-Colonel Micajah Williamson.
> Fifth in descent from General Elijah Clarke.

Wilson, Miss Ella Chapman.
> Ninth in descent from Honorable James Saunders.
> Seventh in descent from Honorable Darby Lux.
> Fifth in descent from Daniel Bowly.
> Sixth in descent from Lieutenant Thomas McKim.
> Eighth in descent from Captain Edmund Craske.
> Seventh in descent from Captain John Craske.
> Sixth in descent from Captain John James.

Wilson, Miss Emma.
> Ninth in descent from Honorable James Saunders.

Seventh in descent from Darby Lux.
Fifth in descent from Daniel Bowly.
Sixth in descent from Lieutenant Thomas McKim.
Eighth in descent from Captain Edmund Craske.
Seventh in descent from Captain John Craske.
Sixth in descent from Captain John James.

Wilson, Mrs. James W. (Ellinor Donnell von Kapff.)
Fifth in descent from John Smith.
Fifth in descent from Honorable William Smith.
Tenth in descent from Sir George Yeardley.
Ninth in descent from Colonel Argall Yeardley.
Eighth in descent from Lieutenant-Colonel John West.
Ninth in descent from Colonel Edmund Scarburgh.
Tenth in descent from Major-General John Custis.
Ninth in descent from Colonel John Custis.
Seventh in descent from John Teackle.

Wilson, Miss Mary Bowly.
Eighth in descent from Hon. James Saunders.
Sixth in descent from Darby Lux.
Fourth in descent from Daniel Bowly.
Fifth in descent from Lieutenant Thomas McKim.

Wilson, Mrs. William B. (Jane Marshall Wilson.)
Seventh in descent from Captain Edmund Craske.
Sixth in descent from Captain John Craske.
Fifth in descent from Captain John James.

Winchester, Mrs. H. Carroll (Fannie Albert Hosmer).
Ninth in descent from Thomas Hosmer.
Eighth in descent from Stephen Hosmer.
Seventh in descent from Captain Thomas Hosmer.
Fifth in descent from Honorable Titus Hosmer.
Fifth in descent from Major-General Samuel Holden Parsons.

Winn, Miss Mary.
Seventh in descent from Joseph Winn.
Fourth in descent from Timothy Winn.
Sixth in descent from Daniel Dulany I.
Fifth in descent from Daniel Dulany II.
Eighth in descent from Richard Smith.
Seventh in descent from Colonel Walter Smith.

Eighth in descent from Richard Hall.
Seventh in descent from Captain Thomas Tasker.
Sixth in descent from Honorable Benjamin Tasker.
Seventh in descent from William Bladen.
Sixth in descent from Zachariah Maccubbin.
Sixth in descent from Dr. Charles Carroll.
Ninth in descent from Edward Lloyd I.
Eighth in descent from Colonel Philemon Lloyd.
Ninth in descent from Captain James Neale.
Ninth in descent from Robert Ridgely.
Seventh in descent from Charles Ridgely.
Ninth in descent from Colonel John Dorsey.
Seventh in descent from Captain Richard Hill.

Wood, Mrs. Joseph C. (Florence Bell.)
Eighth in descent from Captain Timothy Dwight.
Sixth in descent from Colonel Timothy Dwight.
Eighth in descent from Samuel Partridge.

Woodruff, Mrs. George C. (Lucy E. Crawford.)
Eighth in descent from William Bassett.
Tenth in descent from Benjamin Harrison I.
Ninth in descent from Benjamin Harrison II.
Eighth in descent from Benjamin Harrison III.
Seventh in descent from Benjamin Harrison IV.
Sixth in descent from Benjamin Harrison V.
Fifth in descent from Captain Moses Este.
Seventh in descent from Lieutenant John Pengilly.
Ninth in descent from John Armistead.

Woods, Mrs. Daniel C. (Maria Louisa Crane.)
Fifth in descent from Honorable John Adams.
Ninth in descent from John Alden.
Ninth in descent from Lieutenant-Colonel Edmund Quincy.
Seventh in descent from Colonel John Quincy.
Ninth in descent from Honorable Richard Treat.
Eighth in descent from Governor Robert Treat.
Ninth in descent from Samuel Bass.
Tenth in descent from Rev. Thomas Shepard.
Ninth in descent from Rev. Thomas Shepard, Jr.
Tenth in descent from William Tyng.
Ninth in descent from Captain James Neale.
Ninth in descent from Governor Richard Bennett.

Eighth in descent from Richard Hall.
Fifth in descent from Benjamin Hall.
Ninth in descent from Acting Governor Robert Brooke.
Eighth in descent from Major Thomas Brooke.
Seventh in descent from Colonel Henry Lowe.
Sixth in descent from William Murdock.
Eighth in descent from Colonel John Addison I.
Seventh in descent from Colonel Thomas Addison.
Ninth in descent from Richard Smith.
Eighth in descent from Colonel Walter Smith.

Wright, Mrs. D. Giraud (Louise Sophie Wigfall).

Fifth in descent from Theodore Trezevant.
Fifth in descent from Rev. Levi Durand.
Eighth in descent from Arthur Fenner.
Seventh in descent from Thomas Fenner.
Ninth in descent from William Harris.
Tenth in descent from William Arnold.
Ninth in descent from Richard Waterman.
Sixth in descent from Louis Timothy.
Ninth in descent from William Carpenter.
Tenth in descent from Edward Smith.
Eighth in descent from Benjamin Smith.
Seventh in descent from Simon Smith.
Ninth in descent from Chad Brown.
Ninth in descent from Richard Borden.
Eighth in descent from Thomas Borden.
Ninth in descent from Stephen Arnold.

Zunts, Miss Sue Howard.

Seventh in descent from Edmund Howard.
Eighth in descent from Colonel William Stevens.
Eighth in descent from Colonel Thomas Holliday.

INDEX OF ANCESTORS AND DESCENDANTS.

ADAMS, HON. JOHN, 1735-1826. Signer of the Declaration of Independence. President of the United States.
Woods, Mrs. Daniel C.

ADDISON, COLONEL JOHN, I., ——1705. Captain, 1692. Colonel, 1695. Member of Council of Maryland, 1691-1705.
Kerfoot, Mrs. Samuel Humes.
Fisher, Mrs. Ellicott.
Steele, Miss Rosa.
Batré, Mrs. Alfred.
Chatard, Mrs. Thomas M.
Shippen, Mrs. Edward.
Beckwith, Mrs. Franklin H.
Pennington, Miss Elizabeth Lloyd.
Woods, Mrs. Daniel C.
Lowndes, Mrs. Lloyd.
Sullivan, Mrs. Felix R.
Screven, Mrs. George P.
Howard, Mrs. Charles.

ADDISON, COLONEL JOHN, II. Lieutenant - Colonel, 3d Battalion Maryland Flying Camp, 1776.
Fisher, Mrs. Ellicott.

ADDISON, COLONEL THOMAS, 1679 - 1727. Member of Council of Maryland, 1721-1727.
Fisher, Mrs. Ellicott.
Kerfoot, Mrs. Samuel Humes.
Steele, Miss Rosa.
Batré, Mrs. Alfred.
Shippen, Mrs. Edward.
Beckwith, Mrs. Franklin H.

Pennington, Miss Elizabeth Lloyd.
Woods, Mrs. Daniel C.
Lowndes, Mrs. Lloyd.
Sullivan, Mrs. Felix R.
Screven, Mrs. George P.
Howard, Mrs. Charles.

AIREY, REVEREND THOMAS, 1701-1765. Rector of Great Choptank Parish, Dorchester County, 1728-1765.
Bayard, Miss Ellen Howard.
Howard, Miss Marian Gilmor.
Bayard, Mrs. Richard Bassett.
King, Mrs. Joseph.
Marshall, Mrs. Edward Athelstan.
Heyward, Mrs. Wilson P.
Presstman, Mrs. Benjamin.

ALDEN, JOHN, 1599-1687. Last surviving signer of Mayflower Compact. Member of Captain Miles Standish's Duxbury Company, 1643. Assistant, 1633-41, '50-86. Deputy, 1641-49. Deputy - Governor, 1666. Member of the Council of War, 1646, '53-60, '67, '71, '75-76, Plymouth Colony.
Woods, Mrs. Daniel C.
Ridgely, Mrs. John.
Powell, Mrs. William S.

ALLERTON, GOVERNOR ISAAC, ——1659. Deputy-Governor of Plymouth Colony, 1621-1624.

INDEX OF ANCESTORS AND DESCENDANTS.

Carroll, Mrs. Mary Randolph.
Clarke, Mrs. Henry F.
Page, Mrs. William C.

ALLERTON, COLONEL ISAAC, 1630-1702. Major, under Colonel John Washington, of Virginia Forces, in expedition against the Indians, 1675. Lieutenant-Colonel, 1680. Member of the Virginia House of Burgesses, 1676. Member of Council, 1683.
Carroll, Mrs. Mary Randolph.
Clarke, Mrs. Henry F.
Page, Mrs. William C.

ALRICKS, PIETER. Appointed, 1673, Commandant on the South River or Delaware. Deputy-Governor of the Colonies on the Delaware, 1673-74. Member of the First Assembly of the Province of Pennsylvania, 1682-83; one of the Provincial Councillors, 1685-1689.
Haughton, Mrs. Henry Osburne.
Brown, Mrs. Arthur George.
Cottman, Miss Elizabeth Stewart.

AMBLER, EDWARD, 1733-1767. Collector of the Port of York. Member of the Virginia House of Burgesses.
Nicholas, Miss Elizabeth Cary.

ANDERSON, GARLAND. Member of Committee of Safety, Hanover Co., Va., 1775. Delegate to Convention held at Richmond, 1775.
Polk, Mrs. William Stewart.

APPLETON, SAMUEL, 1625-1692. Ipswich, Mass. Deputy to the General Court, Colony of Massachusetts Bay, six terms, between 1668-80. Captain, 1675. Major and Commander-in-Chief of Massachusetts troops, 1675. In command at Springfield, Hatfield, and at the Great Swamp Fight. Assistant, 1681-86, '89-92.
Washburn, Mrs. Charles W.

ARMISTEAD, CAPTAIN ANTHONY. Member of the Virginia House of Burgesses, 1693-'96. Captain of Horse, Elizabeth City Co., 1699.
Cottman, Miss Elizabeth Stewart.
Cottman, Mrs. J. Hough.
Rowland, Miss Elizabeth Mason.

ARMISTEAD, HONORABLE JOHN. Lieutenant-Colonel of Horse, Gloucester Co., Va., 1680; Burgess, 1685; Member of the Council of Virginia, 1687-98.
Page, Mrs. William C.
Armistead, Miss Fannie Carter.
Reynolds, Mrs. William.
Gordon, Mrs. Alexander.
Woodruff, Mrs. George C.
Minor, Miss Mary Willis.
Carter, Miss Mary Coles.
Nicholas, Miss Cary Ann.
Nicholas, Miss Elizabeth Cary.
Smith, Miss Virginia Hope Bryant.
Keyser, Mrs. R. Brent.
Randall, Mrs. Alexander Barton.
Cary, Miss Jane Margaret.
Whiting, Mrs. Clarence.
Lyster, Mrs. Henry F. LeH.

ARMISTEAD, CAPTAIN ROBERT, ——1742. Member of the Virginia House of Burgesses, 1714.
Rowland, Miss Elizabeth Mason.

ARMSTRONG, COLONEL JOHN, 1718-1795. Surveyor of

84

Cumberland Co., Penna. Served in Braddock's campaign. Commanded expedition against Indians at Kittanning, September 8, 1756. Served at Forts Loudoun and Pitt, 1764. Member of Congress, 1778-80, 1787-88.
Armstrong, Miss Mary Hughes.
Rowley, Mrs. C. W.

ARNOLD, STEPHEN, 1622-1699. Rhode Island. Deputy, 1664-65, '67, '70-72, '74-77, '84-85, '90; Assistant, 1672, '77-80, '90-91, '96, '98.
Taylor, Mrs. B. Jones.
Wright, Mrs. D. Giraud.

ARNOLD, WILLIAM, 1587-1676. One of the thirteen original proprietors of Providence Plantations, 1636.
Wright, Mrs. D. Giraud.
Taylor, Mrs. B. Jones.

ASHFORDLEY, WILLIAM. Schout Fiscaal for Esopus, New York, 1678-80. High Sheriff Ulster Co., N. Y., 1680-85.
Reed, Mrs. William.
McIlvain, Miss Elizabeth Gunning.

ASHTON, COLONEL HENRY, 1671-1731. County Lieutenant, Westmoreland Co., Va., 1700-1702.
Story, Mrs. B. T.

ATHERTON, MAJOR - GENERAL HUMPHREY, ——1661. Deputy from Dorchester to the General Court, 1638, and nine terms afterwards; Speaker, 1653. Governor's Assistant, 1654-61. Lieutenant, 1645. Captain, 1646. Commander of the Ancient and Honorable Artillery Company, 1650. Commanded expedition against Pesoacus, a Narragansett chief, 1650. Major-General, 1661.
Hall, Miss Elizabeth Ward.
Hall, Miss Mary Stickney.

AVERY, CAPTAIN JAMES, 1620-1700. Ensign, Lieutenant, and Captain of the New London Company. Served throughout King Philip's War in command of forty men from Stonington, New London and Lyme. In 1676 was Captain of one of the four companies which protected the frontier. Was in the Great Swamp Fight. Twelve times Deputy to the General Court, 1656-1680.
Hunter, Mrs. James W.
Stewart, Mrs. David.
Hamilton, Mrs. W. T.

AVERY, CAPTAIN JOHN, ——1682. Commissioned Lieutenant of the Military Forces and President of the Whore Kill, Delaware, 25 June, 1675; Captain, 26 October, 1675. Justice of the Peace and of the Courts, 1678-82.
Poe, Mrs. Neilson, Jr.
Poultney, Mrs. Eugene.
Beasten, Mrs. Charles.

AYLETT, WILLIAM, I. Member of the Virginia House of Burgesses, 1723, '26, '36.
Clark, Mrs. Frank P.
Lyster, Mrs. Henry F. LeH.

AYLETT, WILLIAM, II. Member of the Virginia House of Burgesses, and of the Convention of 1775.
Clark, Mrs. Frank P.

BACON, JOHN, Justice of the Peace, Salem, New Jersey, 1696-1701.
Smith, Mrs. Robert C.

BALL, LIEUTENANT-COLONEL BURGES. 1749-1800. Member of Committee of Lancaster County, Va., 1775. Captain Fifth Virginia Regiment, 10th February, 1776; Lieutenant-Colonel, 1777.
Jenkins, Mrs. Harry S.

BALL, COLONEL WILLIAM, 1615-1680. Member of Virginia House of Burgesses, 1670-77.
Jenkins, Mrs. Harry S.
Hall, Mrs. George W. S.
Buell, Mrs. Daniel H.

BANGS, EDWARD, 1592-1677. One of the recognized Founders of Plymouth Colony. Deputy to the General Court, 1647, and several times subsequently.
Mason, Mrs. John Thomson.

BARBER, CHARLES. Member of Annapolis Convention, 1774.
Iglehart, Mrs. James D.
Stiles, Mrs. Edmund.

BARBER, DR. LUKE, ——1673. Member of Council of Maryland, 1656-60. Deputy-Governor of Maryland, 1657.
Stiles, Mrs. Edmund.
Iglehart, Mrs. James D.

BARNES, MAJOR ABRAHAM, ——1778. Burgess, St. Mary's Co., 1747-54. Delegate to the Albany Congress, 1754.
Rowland, Miss Elizabeth Mason.

BARNEY, COMMODORE JOSHUA, 1759-1818. Commissioned Lieutenant in the Colonial Navy, June 20, 1776. Commissioned by the State of Pennsylvania Captain of the Ship Hyder Aly, 1782. Commissioned by the French Government Captain, 1795, and Commodore, 1796. Captain, U. S. N., 1814.
Thompson, Miss Elizabeth Young.
Gorter, Mrs. Albert L.
Mills, Mrs. Abraham Gilbert.

BARTOW, THOMAS, 1709-1782. Clerk of Supreme and Chancery Courts, New Jersey, 1735; Clerk of Assembly, 1741. Surveyor General of East Jersey, 1762.
Cromwell, Mrs. Kennedy.

BASS, SAMUEL, 1601-1694, Braintree, Mass. Deputy to the General Court, 1641-45, '49, '52, '54, '57, '59, '63-64.
Woods, Mrs. Daniel C.

BASSETT, WILLIAM, (MASS.) —— - 1667. Representative, 1640-48. Marshal of Plymouth Colony. Proprietor of Bridgewater. Original purchaser of Dartmouth.
Huse, Mrs. Harry P.
Johnston, Miss Maria Stith.
Robbins, Mrs. Henry S.

BASSETT, WILLIAM, 1671-1723. Member of the Virginia House of Burgesses, 1692, 1702. Member of Council, 1702. County Lieutenant of New Kent Co., 1709.
Woodruff, Mrs. George C.

BAUMAN, SEBASTIAN, 1739—— 1803. Captain of New York Artillery, 30 March, 1776; Major, 12 September, 1776. Brevet Lieutenant-Colonel, U. S. A., 14 April, 1787. Postmaster of New York, 1789.
Guest, Mrs. William Woodward.

BAYLOR, COLONEL JOHN,

INDEX OF ANCESTORS AND DESCENDANTS.

1725-1795. Member of Virginia House of Burgesses for Caroline Co., 1740-60.
Armistead, Miss Fannie Carter.
Gordon, Mrs. Alexander.
Whiting, Mrs. Clarence.

BAYLY, CAPTAIN RICHARD, —— - 1661. Captain of mounted police organized for protection against Indians, Accomac Co., Va., 1651.
Tiffany, Mrs. L. McLane.
Cator, Mrs. James H.

BEALL, COLONEL NINIAN, 1625-1717. Captain of Calvert County Militia, 1678. Major, before 1688. Colonel, 1694. High Sheriff of Calvert Co., 1692-93.
Boyd, Mrs. Allen Richards.
Beall, Miss Louisa Ogle.

BEALL, SAMUEL, Justice, Frederick Co., 1765. Member of Maryland Convention, 1776.
Mackall, Miss Sally Somervell.

BEARDSLEY, ALEXANDER, —— -1697. Member of Pennsylvania Assembly, 1695.
Huse, Mrs. Harry P.

BEATTY, THOMAS, 1703-1768. Justice Prince George's Co., 1739-48. Justice Frederick Co., 1748-49, '52-60. Burgess, 1757-58.
Reed, Mrs. William.
McIlvain, Miss Elizabeth Gunning.

BEEKMAN, COLONEL, GERARDUS, 1653-1723. Captain of Militia at Flatbush, 1681. Major, 1689. Lieutenant-Colonel of King's County Militia, 1698. Colonel, 1700-03. Member of Leisler's Council, 1705-23. President and Deputy-Governor, 1709-10.
Lürman, Mrs. Gustav W.

BEEKMAN, COLONEL HENRY, I, 1649-1716. Member of the Legislative Assembly, 1691, '92, '95, 1702, '03. Colonel of Militia Province of New York.
Armstrong, Miss Mary Hughes.
Rowley, Mrs. C. W.

BEEKMAN, COLONEL HENRY, II, 1688-1776. Member of the Legislative Assembly, 1724, '28, '30, '59. Judge of Ulster County. Colonel of Militia, Province of New York.
Armstrong, Miss Mary Hughes.
Rowley, Mrs. C. W.

BEEKMAN, LIEUTENANT WILLIAM, 1623-1707. Lieutenant in the Burgher Corps of New Amsterdam, 1652-58. Vice-Director in the South River, 1658-64. Schout at Esopus, 1664. Lieutenant of Militia under the Dutch, 1673. Deputy Mayor of New York, 1681-83.
Morris, Miss Elizabeth M.
Lürman, Mrs. Gustav W.

BENGSTON, ANDREAS, 1640-1706. Member of Pennsylvania Assembly, 1683, '86, '98.
Reed, Mrs. William.
McIlvain, Miss Elizabeth Gunning.

BENNETT, GOVERNOR RICHARD, 1606-1676. Member of Virginia House of Burgesses, 1629, and of the Council, 1642-60. Governor of Virginia, 1652-55. Commissioner to England, where he signed the agree-

ment with Lord Baltimore, 30 November, 1657. Major-General of Virginia Forces, 1662-72.
Woods, Mrs. Daniel C.
Williams, Mrs. Charles Phelps.
Shippen, Mrs. Edward.
Jones, Mrs. George Alphonzo.

BERKELEY, EDMUND, I, ——1718. Member of the Council of Virginia, 1713. County Lieutenant, Middlesex Co., 1715.
Minor, Miss Mary Willis.

BERKELEY, EDMUND, II. Member of the Virginia House of Burgesses, 1736.
Minor, Miss Mary Willis.

BERKELEY, NELSON. Member of Committee of Safety, Hanover Co., Va., 1775, and was High Sheriff in the same year.
Minor, Miss Mary Willis.

BESSON, CAPTAIN THOMAS. Burgess, Anne Arundel Co., 1657, '65. Justice, 1658. Captain of the County Militia, 1661.
McIntire, Mrs. William Watson.
Goldsborough, Mrs. George Robins.

BETHEL, JOHN, ——-1708. Member of Provincial Assembly of Pennsylvania, 1707.
Jenkins, Mrs. T. Meredith.
Brooks, Mrs. Walter B., Jr.
White, Mrs. Miles, Jr.

BETTON, LIEUTENANT SAMUEL DYRE. Commissioned Second Lieutenant, Queen Anne Co. Militia, 31 July, 1777.
Mackenzie, Mrs. George Norbury.
Mackenzie, Miss Mary G. M.

BETTS, CAPTAIN RICHARD, 1613-1713. Member of New York Provincial Assembly, held at Hempstead, L. I., 1665. "High Sheriff of Yorkshire upon Long Island," 1678-81. Captain, 1663.
Hunt, Miss Anita Dunbar.
Thom, Mrs. J. Pembroke.
Duke, Mrs. Basil.

BEVERLY, COLONEL PETER, 1665-1728. Clerk of the Virginia House of Burgesses, 1691-96; Speaker of the same, 1700-14. Surveyor General, 1719-28. Treasurer, 1719-23.
Ramsay, Mrs. Henry Ashton.
Ramsay, Miss Martha Parker.

BIDDLE, COLONEL CLEMENT, 1740-1814. Deputy Quarter Master General, June, 1776. Commissary General, 1777-78. Quarter Master General of Pennsylvania troops in Whiskey Insurrection.
Blackford, Mrs. Eugene.
Poultney, Mrs. Arthur E.

BIDDLE, WILLIAM, I., 1630-1712. Member of the Council of the General Assembly for Province of West Jersey, 1682, and President of the same, 1706-07.
Blackwell Mrs. Josiah Low.
Blackford, Mrs. Eugene.
Poultney, Mrs. Arthur E.

BIDDLE, WILLIAM, II., Commissioner of Lands, New Jersey, 1703.
Blackwell, Mrs. Josiah Low.

BILES (BYLES), WILLIAM, 1650-1710. Signer of Penn's Great Charter. Member of the first Council of the Province of Pennsylvania, held at Philadelphia, 16 March, 1683. Member of

INDEX OF ANCESTORS AND DESCENDANTS.

Assembly from Bucks County, 1686-1710.
Canby, Miss Laura.
Manly, Mrs. L. Tyson.

BLAINE, EPHRAIM, 1741-1804. Commissary Sergeant Pennsylvania Forces, 1763. Sheriff Cumberland Co., Penna., 1771-73. County Lieutenant of Cumberland Co., 5 April, 1777. Commissary-General Continental Army, 19 February, 1778.
Mullikin, Mrs. Richard Oden.
Mullikin, Miss Sophia Margaret.

BLADEN, WILLIAM, 1670-1718. Clerk of House of Burgesses, 1697. Clerk to the Prerogative Office, 1699. Commissary General, 1714.
Brown, Miss Lizinka Campbell.
Roman, Miss Louisa Lowndes.
Lough, Mrs. Ernest St. George.
Lowndes, Mrs. Lloyd.
Lewis, Miss Virginia Tayloe.
Lemmon, Mrs. J. Southgate.
Beall, Mrs. Edward Sinclair.
Beall, Miss Louisa Ogle.
Winn, Miss Mary.
Shawhan, Mrs. Charles S.

BLAIR, ARCHIBALD, 1660-1735. Justice of York Co., Va., 1714. Member of the Virginia House of Burgesses, 1718-1723. Major of Militia.
Keyser, Mrs. R. Brent.
Cary, Miss Jane Margaret.

BLAIR, HONORABLE JOHN, 1687-1771. Member of the Virginia House of Burgesses, 1736. Member of Council from 1745, and its President, 1757-1771. Acting Governor of Virginia, 1757-58, 1768.
Keyser, Mrs. R. Brent.
Cary, Miss Jane Margaret.

BLAY, COLONEL WILLIAM. Burgess Kent Co., 1714-15.
Turnbull, Mrs. John O.
Preston, Mrs. J. Alexander.
Carroll, Miss Sally Wethered.

BLODGETT, HONORABLE SAMUEL, 1724-1807. Served in French Wars. Louisburg, 1745, Crown Point and Lake George. Was Commissary at Fort William Henry, 1755. Judge, Court of Common Pleas, Hillsboro Co., N. H., 1770.
Hall, Miss Elizabeth Ward.
Hall, Miss Mary Stickney.

BLUNSTON, JOHN, ———1723. Member of Pennsylvania Assembly, 1683-84, '87, '95, 1701. Member of Council, 1701.
Smith, Mrs. Robert C.

BOARMAN, MAJOR WILLIAM, 1630-1709. Justice, St. Mary's Co., 1663-78, and Presiding Justice, 1678; High Sheriff, 1678-79, '81; Burgess, 1671-75. Captain, St. Mary's Co. Militia, 1661; Major, 1676. Indian Interpreter, 1678, and rendered valuable services to the Province in its relations with the Indians.
Parran, Mrs. James Bourne.
Howard, Mrs. Charles.

BOGGS, ANDREW,———1765. Ensign in the Associated Regiment of Lancaster Co., Penna., 1747-48.
Cottman, Miss Elizabeth Stewart.

BOLLING, MAJOR JOHN, 1676-1729. High Sheriff of Henrico Co., Va., 1706-7. Burgess, 1714. Major of the County Militia.
Keyser, Mrs. R. Brent.

INDEX OF ANCESTORS AND DESCENDANTS.

Randall, Mrs. Alexander Barton.
Cary, Miss Jane Margaret.

BOLLING, COLONEL ROBERT I., 1646-1709. Member of the Virginia House of Burgesses, 1704. Colonel of Prince George County.
Keyser, Mrs. R. Brent.
Randall, Mrs. Alexander Barton.
Cary, Miss Jane Margaret.

BOLLING, COLONEL ROBERT II., 1682-1749. Member of the Virginia House of Burgesses, 1744.
Hall, Mrs. George W. S.

BOND, WILLIAM, 1625-1697, Massachusetts. Captain Troop of Horse. Member Council of Safety. Member General Court. Speaker Lower House, 1691-95.
Hamilton, Mrs. Levin Mayer.

BORDEN, JOSEPH, 1719-1791. Member of the Stamp Act Congress, 1765. Member of the first New Jersey Convention. Colonel of First New Jersey Regiment. Judge of the Court of Common Pleas, 1776.
Redwood, Mrs. Frank T.
Screven, Mrs. George P.
Sullivan, Mrs. Felix R.

BORDEN, RICHARD, 1601-1671, Rhode Island. Member of the Court of Commissioners, 1654, '56-57; General Treasurer, 1654-55; Assistant, 1653-54; Deputy, 1667, '70.
Taylor, Mrs. B. Jones.
Wright, Mrs. D. Giraud.

BORDEN, THOMAS, ——1676, Rhode Island. Deputy, 1666, '70, '72; Assistant, 1675-76.
Taylor, Mrs. B. Jones.
Wright, Mrs. D. Giraud.

BORDLEY, REVEREND STEPHEN, ——1709. Rector of St. Paul's Parish, Kent Co., 1694-1709.
Chatard, Mrs. Thomas M.

BOUGHTON, RICHARD, ——1706. Secretary of Maryland, 1666; Burgess for Charles Co., 1669; Clerk of the House of Burgesses, 1674-76.
Parran, Mrs. James Bourne.

BOWIE, ALLEN, 1719-1783. Justice, Prince George's County, 1752-54.
Simpson, Mrs. Edward.

BOWIE, CAPTAIN FIELDER, 1745-1794. Commissioned Captain, Prince George's County Militia, February, 1776.
Simpson, Mrs. Edward.

BOWIE, GOVERNOR ROBERT, 1750-1818. Captain Third Maryland Battalion of the Flying Camp, July-December, 1776. Governor of Maryland, 1803-5, 1811-12.
Simpson, Mrs. Edward.

BOWIE, WILLIAM, 1720-1791. Justice, Prince George's Co., 1759-64.
Simpson, Mrs. Edward.

BOWLY, DANIEL, 1745-1807. Member Committee of Observation, 1775. Ensign in Captain John Sterett's Independent Company, Maryland Militia.
Keyser, Mrs. Samuel.
Jackson, Mrs. John J.
Comegys, Mrs. Joseph Parsons.
Thompson, Miss Charlotte de Macklot.
Wilson, Miss Mary Bowly.
Wilson, Miss Ella Chapman.
Wilson, Miss Emma.

INDEX OF ANCESTORS AND DESCENDANTS.

BOWMAN, EDMUND. Justice, Lower Norfolk Co., Va., 1655, '59; Accomac Co., 1663. Major of Accomac Co. Militia. Member of the Virginia House of Burgesses.
Tiffany, Mrs. L. McLane.

BOZMAN, J O H N . Burgess, Somerset Co., 1694.
Markoe, Mrs. Frank.
Sibley, Mrs. Clarence.
Dugan, Mrs. Hammond.

BRANCH, CHRISTOPHER. Member of the Virginia House of Burgesses, 1639. Justice of Henrico Co., 1656, and previously for many years.
Keyser, Mrs. R. Brent.
Buchanan, Miss Esther Sidney.
Randall, Mrs. Alexander Barton.
Cary, Mrs. Wilson Miles.
Cary, Miss Jane Margaret.

BRAXTON, CARTER, 1736-1797. Member of the Virginia House of Burgesses, 1761; Signer of the Declaration of Independence.
Page, Mrs. William C.

BRENT, CAPTAIN GEORGE, of Stafford Co., Va. Captain of a Troop of Horse in 1670; Ranger-General of the Northern neck of Virginia, 1690.
Keyser, Mrs. William.
Hunt, Mrs. Dunbar.
Hunt, Miss Anita Dunbar.
Brent, Miss Nanine Maria.
Brent, Miss Ida S.

BRENT, DEPUTY GOVERNOR GILES. Treasurer of the Province of Maryland. Commander of Kent Island. Deputy Governor and Lieutenant-General of Maryland, 1643-44. Lord of Fort Kent Manor.
Jenkins, Mrs. Michael.
Jenkins, Mrs. Edmund Plowden.
Hinckley, Mrs. Robert.
O'Donnell, Mrs. Columbus.
Lyster, Mrs. Henry F. LeH.

BRENT, WILLIAM., of Richland, Stafford Co., Va. Member of the Virginia House of Burgesses, 1756, 1760. Member of Convention, 1776.
Lyster, Mrs. Henry F. LeH.

BREWER, JOHN. Justice, Anne Arundel Co., 1658-61. Burgess, 1661.
Atkinson, Mrs. Robert.
Gamble, Mrs. Robert Howard.
Calvert, Mrs. Charles Baltimore.
Iglehart, Mrs. C. Iredell.
Robinson, Miss Louisa Hall.
Mackubin, Miss Florence.

BREWSTER, ELDER WILLIAM, 1560-1644. Drafted, in the cabin of the *Mayflower*, the first written Constitution. He served in the early Indian Wars under Captain Miles Standish.
Ridgely, Mrs. John.
Powell, Mrs. William S.
Carroll, Mrs. Mary Randolph.
Clarke, Mrs. Henry F.
Page, Mrs. William C.

BRICE, JUDGE JOHN, 1704-1766. Chief Justice of the Provincial Court of Maryland.
Allen, Mrs. Ethan.

BRISCOE, CAPTAIN JOHN, 1678-1734. Justice of Charles Co., 1720-34.
Parran, Mrs. James Bourne.

BRISCOE, COLONEL PHILIP, ——1724. Justice, Charles County, 1694-1701.
Parran, Mrs. James Bourne.

BRISCOE, SAMUEL, ——1786.

91

INDEX OF ANCESTORS AND DESCENDANTS.

Justice of Charles Co.,
1773-74.
Parran, Mrs. James Bourne.

BROOKE, COLONEL BAKER, 1628-1679. Member of the Council of Maryland, 1658-79; Surveyor - General, 1671-79; Colonel of the Calvert Co. Militia.
Parran, Mrs. James Bourne.

BROOKE, CAPTAIN BENJAMIN, 1753-1834. Lieutenant, Pennsylvania Militia, 1776; Captain, 1777.
Brooke, Mrs. John.

BROOKE, DOCTOR JOHN. Commissioner of Peace. Dorchester Co., Md., 1676. Burgess, 1681.
Dandridge, Miss Anne Spottswood.

BROOKE, MICHAEL. Burgess, Calvert Co., 1657. Commissioned Justice, 1655.
Dandridge, Miss Anne Spottswood.

BROOKE, RICHARD, 1736-1788. Member of the Committees of Correspondence and Observation, Frederick Co., 1774-75. Delegate to Convention, 1775. Captain of Frederick Co. Militia, 1776. Major, 15 August, 1776.
Redwood, Mrs. Frank T.

BROOKE, ACTING GOVERNOR ROBERT, 1602-1655. B. A., 1620; M. A., 1624; Wadleam College, Oxford. Commissioned by Lord Baltimore, 20 September, 1649, Commander of a new county to be erected in Maryland, and Member of Council. Appointed, 29 March, 1652, by Cromwell's Commissioners, President of the Council and Acting Governor.

*Kerfoot, Mrs. Samuel Humes.
Ritchie, Mrs. John.
Pearre, Miss Mary Smith Worthington.
Phenix, Miss Florence.
Blackiston, Mrs. A. Hooton.
Leakin, Miss Margaret Dobbin.
Smith, Miss Clementine.
Smith, Miss Sallie Cox.
Steele, Miss Rosa.
Sioussat, Mrs. Albert Willis.
Penniman, Mrs. George Dobbin.
Thompson, Miss Elizabeth Young.
Manly, Mrs. L. Tyson.
Gorter, Mrs. Albert L.
Boyd, Mrs. Allen Richards.
Denman, Mrs. H. B.
Philpot, Miss Mary Dennison.
Redwood, Mrs. Frank T.
Williams, Miss Elizabeth Chew.
Beall, Miss Louisa Ogle.
Beckwith, Mrs. Franklin H.
Woods, Mrs. Daniel C.
Brent, Miss Ida S.
Keyser, Mrs. William.
Hunt, Mrs. Dunbar.
Hunt, Miss Anita Dunbar.
Williams, Mrs. Charles Phelps.
Parran, Mrs. James Bourne.
Mackenzie, Miss Mary G. M.
Jones, Mrs. George Alphonzo.
Kimball, Mrs. Julius Henry.
Baughman, Mrs. Mary Jane.*

BROOKE, ROGER, 1637-1700. Justice, Calvert Co., 1674-85; of Quorum from 1679. High Sheriff, 1684.
*Penniman, Mrs. George Dobbin.
Brent, Miss Ida S.
Keyser, Mrs. William.
Hunt, Mrs. Dunbar.
Hunt, Miss Anita Dunbar.
Mackenzie, Miss Mary G. M.*

BROOKE, MAJOR THOMAS, 1632-1676. Commissioned Major, Maryland Forces, 11 February, 1660. Served in expedition against In-

INDEX OF ANCESTORS AND DESCENDANTS.

dians, 1667. Member of House of Burgesses for Calvert Co., 1663-76.
Ritchie, Mrs. John.
Williams, Mrs. Charles Phelps.
Pearre, Miss Mary Smith Worthington.
Phenix, Miss Florence.
Blackiston, Mrs. A. Hooton.
Leakin, Miss Margaret Dobbin.
Smith, Miss Clementine.
Smith, Miss Sallie Cox.
Steele, Miss Rosa.
Sioussat, Mrs. Albert Willis.
Thompson, Miss Elizabeth Young.
Gorter, Mrs. Albert L.
Boyd, Mrs. Allen Richards.
Denman, Mrs. H. B.
Philpot, Miss Mary Dennison.
Redwood, Mrs. Frank T.
Williams, Miss Elizabeth Chew.
Beall, Miss Louisa Ogle.
Beckwith, Mrs. Franklin H.
Woods, Mrs. Daniel C.
Kimball, Mrs. Julius Henry.

BROOKE, COLONEL THOMAS, 1659-1730. Member of Council of Maryland, 1691-1707, 1715-24.
Kerfoot, Mrs. Samuel Humes.
Ritchie, Mrs. John.
Pearre, Miss Mary Smith Worthington.
Phenix, Miss Florence.
Blackiston, Mrs. A. Hooton.
Smith, Miss Clementine.
Smith, Miss Sallie Cox.
Steele, Miss Rosa.
Mackall, Miss Sally Somervell.
Boyd, Mrs. Allen Richards.
Beall, Miss Louisa Ogle.
Beckwith, Mrs. Franklin H.

BROOKE, THOMAS, JR., 1683-1744. High Sheriff, Prince George's Co., 1732-33.
Beall, Miss Louisa Ogle.

BROOKS, GOVERNOR JOHN. 1752 - 1825. Captain of Minute Men at Lexington and Concord, 19 April, 1775. Major, Bridge's Massachusetts Regiment, 1775, and of 19th Continental Infantry, 1776. Lieutenant - Colonel, 8th Massachusetts Regiment, 1776. Lieutenant-Colonel commanding 7th Massachusetts Regiment, 1778, and served till 12 June, 1783. Brigadier-General, United States Army, 1792-96. Governor of Massachusetts, 1816.
Mudge, Mrs. Edmund Tileston.

BROOME, JOHN, 1680 - 1738. Burgess, Calvert Co., 1712. High Sheriff, 1714. Justice, 1731-38; of Quorum, 1738.
Penniman, Mrs. George Dobbin.

BROOME, CAPTAIN JOHN, 1703 ———. Captain Calvert Co. Militia, 1754-56.
Penniman, Mrs. George Dobbin.

BROUGHTON, COLONEL THOS. ———1738. Member of Council of South Carolina, 1708. Governor of the Province, 1735-38.
Morris, Miss Elizabeth M.

BROWN, CHAD, ———1650. One of thirteen signers of the first written compact of Providence Plantations.
Wright, Mrs. D. Giraud.
Taylor, Mrs. B. Jones.

BROWN, DR. GUSTAVUS, 1689-1762. Justice, Charles Co., 1726-62; Chief Justice, 1748-62.
Hall, Mrs. George W. S.
Ramsay, Miss Martha Parker.

BUCHANAN, GENERAL AN-

INDEX OF ANCESTORS AND DESCENDANTS.

DREW, 1734-1786. Chief Justice, Baltimore Co. Member of Committees of Correspondence and Observation, 1774-75. One of the five brigadier generals of the Maryland Militia, 1776.
Philpot, Miss Mary Dennison.
Redwood, Mrs. Frank T.
Screven, Mrs. George P.
Sullivan, Mrs. Felix R.

BUCHANAN, DR. GEORGE, 1698-1750. One of the Commissioners for laying out Baltimore Town, 1729. Burgess, Baltimore Co., 1745-50.
Black, Mrs. Charles H.
Sloan, Mrs. Robert Neale.
McIntire, Mrs. William Watson.
Goldsborough, Mrs. George Robins.
Chatard, Mrs. Thomas M.
Philpot, Miss Mary Dennison.
Redwood, Mrs. Frank T.
Screven, Mrs. George P.
Sullivan, Mrs. Felix R.

BUCHANAN, LLOYD, 1729——. Burgess, Baltimore Co., 1751.
McIntire, Mrs. William Watson.
Goldsborough, Mrs. George Robins.

BUCHANAN, COLONEL WILLIAM, 1727-1804. Member of the Maryland Convention, 1775, and of Committee of Observation, 1775-76. Commissioned Colonel of the Baltimore Battalion 25 May, 1776. Appointed, by Congress, Commissary General of the Continental Army, 1777.
Brown, Miss Ellen Sidney.
Buchanan, Miss Esther Sidney.

BUCKNER, MAJOR WILLIAM, ——1716. Justice of York Co., Va., 1694; High Sheriff, 1695-1696; Burgess, 1698-1699.
Johnston, Miss Maria Stith.
Robbins, Mrs. Henry S.

BURFORD, THOMAS, ——1687. Burgess, St. Mary's Co., 1682-87. Attorney-General of Maryland, 1681-86.
Lowndes, Mrs. Lloyd.
Howard, Mrs. Charles.

BURGESS, CAPTAIN EDWARD, ——1722. Commissioned, 4 September, 1689, Captain of Foot, Anne Arundel Co. Militia.
Shippen, Mrs. Edward.

BURGESS, COLONEL WILLIAM, 1622-1686. Justice, Anne Arundel Co., 1664; of Quorum, 1665. Burgess, 1659, 1669-82. Member of Council and Deputy Governor, 1682-86. Colonel, commanding all the military forces of the Province of Maryland.
Leakin, Miss Margaret Dobbin.
Sioussat, Mrs. Albert Willis.
Thompson, Miss Elizabeth Young.
Fuller, Mrs. Olive Clyde.
Gorter, Mrs. Albert L.
Boyd, Mrs. Allen Richards.
Philpot, Miss Mary Dennison.
Redwood, Mrs. Frank T.
Williams, Miss Elizabeth Chew.
Screven, Mrs. George P.
Sullivan, Mrs. Felix R.
Lürman, Mrs. Gustav W.
Beall, Miss Louisa Ogle.
Shippen, Mrs. Edward.
Smith, Mrs. Chandler Price.
Pennington, Miss Elizabeth Lloyd.
Blackiston, Mrs. A. Hooton.
Pearre, Miss Mary Smith Worthington.
McCrackin, Mrs. Alexander.

BURWELL, HONORABLE LEWIS, ———1710. Member of the Council of Virginia, 1702.
Armistead, Miss Fannie Carter.
Smith, Miss Virginia Hope Bryant.
Minor, Miss Mary Willis.

BURWELL, NATHANIEL, 1680-1721. Member of the Virginia House of Burgesses, 1710.
Minor, Miss Mary Willis.

BURWELL, ROBERT CARTER. Member of the Virginia House of Burgesses. Member of Council, 1764.
Minor, Miss Mary Willis.

BUTLER, COLONEL THOMAS, 1748 - 1805. Captain in Pennsylvania Line, 1776, and served through the Revolutionary War. Major United States Army, 1791; Lieutenant-Colonel, 1795; Colonel, 1802.
Chancellor, Mrs. C. W.

BUTLER, CAPTAIN ZEBULON, 1731-1795. Served in the French and Indian War in 1758, on the Canadian frontier, and at Fort Edward, Lake George, Ticonderoga, and Crown Point. Served also in the Havana Expedition, 1762.
Strother, Mrs. Nelson.

BYRD, WILLIAM I., 1652-1704. Member of the Council of Virginia, 1681-1704. Receiver of His Majesty's Revenues for the Colony of Virginia.
Ober, Mrs. Robert.
Minor, Miss Mary Willis.
Randall, Mrs. Alexander Barton.

BYRD, WILLIAM II., 1674-1744. Member of the Council of Virginia, 1707 - 44, and President of the Council. Founder of the City of Richmond. Fellow of the Royal Society.
Poultney, Mrs. Arthur E.
McCandlish, Miss Evelyn Byrd.
Ober, Mrs. Robert.
Minor, Miss Mary Willis.
Randall, Mrs. Alexander Barton.

BYRD, WILLIAM, III., 1729-1777. Colonel of the 2d Virginia Regiment, 1756. Member of the Council of Virginia, 1754-77.
Ober, Mrs. Robert.
Randall, Mrs. Alexander Barton.

CALHOUN, JAMES, 1743-1816. Member of Committee of Observation, Baltimore, 1774-76. Deputy Commissary-General of the Continental Army, 1777. First Mayor of Baltimore, 1797.
Buchanan, Miss Esther Sidney.

CALVERT, HONORABLE BENEDICT, ———1788. Judge of the Land Office. Member of Council, 1770-74. Collector of Customs.
Campbell, Mrs. Duncan.
Campbell, Miss Ella Calvert.
Murray, Mrs. Francis Key.

CALVERT, GOVERNOR CHARLES. Ensign in His Majesty's First Regiment of Foot Guards, 27 November, 1709; Lieutenant and Captain, 4 January, 1718. Governor of Maryland, 1720-27.
Campbell, Mrs. Duncan.
Campbell, Miss Ella Calvert.
Murray, Mrs. Francis Key.

CALVERT, GOVERNOR LEONARD, ———1647. Governor of Maryland from its first

settlement, in 1634, until his death, 9 June, 1647.
Parran, Mrs. James Bourne.

CAMM, REVEREND JOHN, 1718 - 1779. Member of Council of Virginia, 1774. President of William and Mary College, 1771-77.
Atkinson, Mrs Matthew S.
Page, Mrs. William C.

CANBY, THOMAS, 1668-1742. Justice of the Peace, Bucks Co., Penna., 1719-41. Member of Provincial Assembly, 1721-22, '30, '33, '38.
Canby, Miss Laura.
Smith, Mrs. Thomas Marsh.

CARPENTER, WILLIAM. One of the thirteen original proprietors of Providence Plantations, 1636. Commissioner, 1658-63. Assistant, 1665-72.
Wright, Mrs. D. Giraud.
Taylor, Mrs. B. Jones.

CARR, DABNEY, 1743-1773. Member of the Virginia House of Burgesses, for Louisa Co., 1773.
Keyser, Mrs. R. Brent.
Buchanan, Miss Esther Sidney.
Cary, Mrs. Wilson Miles.
Cary, Miss Jane Margaret.

CARROLL, CHARLES, ——1720. Commissioned Attorney-General of Maryland, 18 July, 1688.
Payson, Mrs. Herbert.
Boone, Mrs. Daniel A.
Bayard, Miss Ellen Howard.
Horsey, Mrs. Outerbridge.

CARROLL, DR. CHARLES, 1691-1755. Burgess for Annapolis, 1737, and subsequent years.
Beall, Mrs. Edward Sinclair.
Beall, Miss Louisa Ogle.
Mackubin, Miss Florence.

Allen, Mrs. Ethan.
Turnbull, Mrs. John O.
Washburn, Mrs. Charles W.
Preston, Mrs. J. Alexander.
Carroll, Miss Sally Wethered.
Calvert, Mrs. Charles Baltimore.
Winn, Miss Mary.

CARTER, CHARLES, 1707-1764. Member of the Virginia House of Burgesses, 1748-64.
Minor, Miss Mary Willis.

CARTER, EDWARD. Member of Pennsylvania Assembly, 1688.
Huse, Mrs. Harry P.

CARTER, COLONEL JOHN, —— 1669. Member of the Virginia House of Burgesses, 1642 - 49, '53 - 59. Commanded against Rappahannock Indians, 1654. Member of Council, 1659-69. Colonel of Lancaster Co., 1656.
Hoffman, Mrs. R. Curzon.
McLean, Mrs. Thomas Chalmers.
Poultney, Mrs. Arthur E.
Lyster, Mrs. Henry F.
Gordon, Miss Margaret.
Ober, Mrs. Robert.
Lemmon, Mrs. J. Southgate.
Minor, Miss Mary Willis.
Carter, Miss Mary Coles.
Nicholas, Miss Cary Ann.
Nicholas, Miss Elizabeth Cary.
Page, Mrs. William C.
Randall, Mrs. Alexander Barton.

CARTER, HONORABLE JOHN, 1690-1743. Member of the Council of Virginia, 1724.
Carter, Miss Mary Coles.

CARTER, LANDON (Sabine Hall). Member of the Virginia House of Burgesses, 1748-65. Chairman Committee of Safety, Richmond Co., 1775.

Minor, Miss Mary Willis.
Lyster, Mrs. Henry F. LeH.

CARTER, HONORABLE ROBERT, 1663-1732. Speaker of the Virginia House of Burgesses, 1695-99. Treasurer, 1694-1732. President of the Council and Acting Governor, 1726-27. Member of Council, 1699-1732.
McLean, Mrs. Thomas Chalmers.
Poultney, Mrs. Arthur E.
Lyster, Mrs. Henry F. LeH.
Gordon, Miss Margaret.
Ober, Mrs. Robert.
Lemmon, Mrs. J. Southgate.
Minor, Miss Mary Willis.
Carter, Miss Mary Coles.
Nicholas, Miss Cary Ann.
Nicholas, Miss Elizabeth Cary.
Page, Mrs. William C.
Randall, Mrs. Alexander Barton.

CARTER, ROBERT. Member of Pennsylvania Assembly, 1698-99. Member of the House of Representatives, 1703.
Huse, Mrs. Harry P.

CARTER, ROBERT WORMLEY. Member of the Virginia House of Burgesses, 1769-74. Member of Convention, 1775.
Lyster, Mrs. Henry F. LeH.

CARY, ARCHIBALD, 1720-1787. Member of the Virginia House of Burgesses, 1748-74. Colonial Committee of Correspondence, 1773-74. Member of Convention, 1775. Speaker of Virginia Senate, 1776-87.
McLean, Mrs. Thomas Chalmers.
Gordon, Miss Margaret.
Keyser, Mrs. R. Brent.
Randall, Mrs. Alexander Barton.
Cary, Miss Jane Margaret.

CARY, COLONEL MILES I., 1620-1667. Member of the Virginia House of Burgesses, 1659-63. Member of Council, 1663-67. Major of Militia, Warwick Co., 1654; Lieutenant-Colonel, 1657; Colonel and County Lieutenant, 1659. Killed in action with the Dutch; died, 10 June, 1667.
Carter, Miss Mary Coles.
Nicholas, Miss Cary Ann.
Nicholas, Miss Elizabeth Cary.
Keyser, Mrs. R. Brent.
Randall, Mrs. Alexander Barton.
Cary, Miss Jane Margaret.

CARY, COLONEL MILES II., 1655-1709. Justice of Warwick Co., Va., 1680; Captain of the County Militia, 1691; Lieutenant-Colonel, 1701; Colonel, 1704. Member of the Virginia House of Burgesses, 1692-93, 1699-1704. Charter Trustee of William and Mary College, 1693, and Rector, 1706. Surveyor-General of Virginia, 1699-1709. Naval Officer of York River, 1699-1709.
Cary, Miss Jane Margaret.
Carter, Miss Mary Coles.
Nicholas, Miss Cary Ann.
Nicholas, Miss Elizabeth Cary.
Keyser, Mrs. R. Brent.
Randall, Mrs. Alexander Barton.

CARY, COLONEL WILSON, 1703-1772. Major of Militia, Elizabeth City Co., Va., 1740; Colonel and County Lieutenant, 1751. Naval Officer of Lower James River, 1726, and for thirty-five years thereafter.
Carter, Miss Mary Coles.
Nicholas, Miss Cary Ann.
Nicholas, Miss Elizabeth Cary.
Keyser, Mrs. R. Brent.
Randall, Mrs. Alexander Barton.
Cary, Miss Jane Margaret.

INDEX OF ANCESTORS AND DESCENDANTS.

CARY, COLONEL WILSON MILES, 1734-1817. Member of the Virginia House of Burgesses, 1759, 1766-68. Lieutenant-Colonel of Warwick Co., 1758; County Lieutenant and Colonel of Eliazbeth City Co., 1762. Visitor of William and Mary College. Member of Virginia Convention, 1776. Naval Officer of Lower James, 1760-76.
Keyser, Mrs. R. Brent.
Cary, Miss Jane Margaret.

CATTELL, CAPTAIN BENJAMIN, 1749-1782. Commissioned Captain in 1st South Carolina Regiment, 5 June, 1775.
Iglehart, Mrs. C. Iredell.
Robinson, Miss Louisa Hall.
Whitridge, Mrs. Horatio L.
Taylor, Mrs. Winfield J.
Turnbull, Mrs. Alexander Nisbet.
Garrett, Mrs. T. Harrison.

CATTELL, HONORABLE WILLIAM, 1682-1752. Member of the Council of South Carolina, 1724.
Iglehart, Mrs. C. Iredell.
Robinson, Miss Louisa Hall.
Whitridge, Mrs. Horatio L.
Taylor, Mrs. Winfield J.
Turnbull, Mrs. Alexander Nisbet.
Garrett, Mrs. T. Harrison.

CHAMBERLAINE, SAMUEL, 1697-1773. Burgess, Talbot Co., 1731. Member of Council, 1740-50.
Merritt, Mrs. J. Alfred.
Earle, Miss Mary Isobel.
Stokes, Miss Eliza Hughes.

CHANDLER, JOB, ——1659. Receiver-General of Maryland, 1651. Member of Council, 1651-54, '56-59.
Milnor, Miss Mary Worthington.

CHASE, HONORABLE SAMUEL, 1741-1811. Member of House of Burgesses. Delegate, from Maryland, to Continental Congress, 1774-78. Signer of the Declaration of Independence. Chief Justice of Maryland. Justice of the Supreme Court of the United States.
Mills, Mrs. Abraham Gilbert.

CHASE, REVEREND THOMAS, 1703-1779. Rector of St. Paul's Church, Baltimore Co., 1745-79.
Mills, Mrs. Abraham Gilbert.

CHECKLEY, COLONEL SAMUEL, 1653-1738. Captain of Ancient and Honorable Artillery Company. Colonel, 1715. Representative to General Court, 1702-17.
Jones, Mrs. E. Bradley.

CHEESEBOROUGH, SAMUEL, 1627-1673. Representative, 1657, '65-66, '70-73, Colony of Connecticut.
Mason, Mrs. John Thomson.

CHEESEBOROUGH, WILLIAM, 1594-1667. Deputy, 1640, '42, Colony of Massachusetts Bay; Representative, 1653, '55, '57, 64, Colony of Connecticut.
Mason, Mrs. John Thomson.

CHEW, BENJAMIN, 1722-1810. Attorney-General of Pennsylvania, 1755-67. Member of Governor's Council, 1755. Speaker of Assembly of Lower Counties, 1756. Chief Justice, Supreme Court of Pennsylvania, 1774.
Sibley, Mrs. Clarence.
Keyser, Mrs. R. Brent.
Dugan, Mrs. Hammond.
Bayard, Miss Ellen Howard.
Howard, Miss Marian Gilmor.
Bayard, Mrs. Richard Bassett.

INDEX OF ANCESTORS AND DESCENDANTS.

King, Mrs. Joseph.
Marshall, Mrs. Edward Athelstan.

CHEW, JOHN, ——1668. Member Virginia House of Burgesses, 1623-29, '42-44. Justice, York Co., Va., 1634-52.
Williams, Miss Elizabeth Chew.
Keyser, Mrs. R. Brent.
Paca, Miss Juliana Tilghman.
Bayard, Miss Ellen Howard.
Howard, Miss Marian Gilmor.
Bayard, Mrs. Richard Bassett.
King, Mrs. Joseph.
Marshall, Mrs. Edward Athelstan.
Philpot, Miss Mary Dennison.
Milnor, Miss Mary Worthington.

CHEW, SAMUEL, ——1677. Burgess, Anne Arundel Co., 1659. Member of Council and Justice of the Provincial Court, 1669-77.
Keyser, Mrs. R. Brent.
Williams, Miss Elizabeth Chew.
Bayard, Miss Ellen Howard.
Howard, Miss Marian Gilmor.
Bayard, Mrs. Richard Bassett.
King, Mrs. Joseph.
Marshall, Mrs. Edward Athelstan.
Ridgely, Mrs. Charles.
Ridgely, Mrs. John.
Philpot, Miss Mary Dennison.
Milnor, Miss Mary Worthington.

CHEW, SAMUEL, M. D., 1693-1743. Chief Justice of the three lower counties of Delaware, 1741-43.
Bayard, Miss Ellen Howard.
Howard, Miss Marian Gilmor.
Bayard, Mrs. Richard Bassett.
King, Mrs. Joseph.
Marshall, Mrs. Edward Athelstan.
Keyser, Mrs. R. Brent.

CLAGETT, CAPTAIN THOMAS, ——1703. Captain Calvert Co. Militia, 1683.
Williams, Miss Elizabeth Chew.
Boyd, Mrs. Allen Richards.
Bass, Mrs. John M.
Cheatham, Mrs. Richard.

CLAPP, CAPTAIN ROGER, 1609-1692. Lieutenant, 1644. Member Ancient and Honorable Artillery Company, 1646. Lieutenant in same, 1655. Captain at the Castle (Fort Independence), 1665-86. Deputy, 1652, thirteen years.
Currie, Mrs. C. George.

CLARK, LIEUTENANT WILLIAM, 1609-1690. Elected to General Assembly, 1663. Lieutenant in King Philip's War, 1676.
Currie, Mrs. C. George.

CLARKE, GENERAL ELIJAH, ——1799. Captain of Georgia Militia, 1776; later Colonel. Took part in the Capture of Augusta, 1781.
Williams, Miss Sue Campbell.

CLARKSON, MATTHEW, ——1702. Commissioned, in 1689, by William III., Secretary of the Colony of New York, and held office until his death.
Whitelock, Mrs. George.

CLAYPOOLE, JAMES, 1634-1687. Member of Legislative Assembly of Pennsylvania, 1686. Member of Provincial Council, 1687. Commissioner to Sign Patents and Grant Warrants, 1686. Register-General, 1686.
Cook, Mrs. George Hamilton.

CLOWES, JOHN,——1687. Member Pennsylvania Assembly, 1683-1687.
Hough, Miss Ethel.

INDEX OF ANCESTORS AND DESCENDANTS.

COCKE, WILLIAM, 1672-1720. Member of Council of Virginia, 1712. Secretary of State and Judge of the General Court.
Latané, Miss Lucy Temple.

COFFIN, TRISTRAM, I., 1609-1681, Nantucket, Mass. Chief Magistrate of General Court, 1671, '77-78.
Stewart, Mrs. David.
Hamilton, Mrs. W. T.

COFFIN, TRISTRAM, II., 1632-1704, Newbury, Mass. Lieutenant, 1668. Deputy, 1695, 1700-1702.
Stewart, Mrs. David.
Hamilton, Mrs. W. T.

COLDEN, HONORABLE CADWALADER, 1688-1776. Surveyor-General of New York. Master in Chancery, 1718. Member of Council from 1720, and its President in 1760. Lieutenant-Governor of New York, 1761-76.
Morris, Miss Elizabeth M.

COLE, ROBERT. One of the thirteen original proprietors of Providence Plantations, 1636.
Hodges, Mrs. J. S. B.
Milnor, Miss Mary Worthington.

COLE, COLONEL WILLIAM, 1637-1693. Member of the Council of Virginia, 1675-94. Secretary of State, 1690-91. One of the original trustees of William and Mary College, 1693. County Lieutenant, Warwick Co., 1680.
Tiffany, Mrs. L. McLane.
Randall, Mrs. Alexander Barton.

COLEGATE, COLONEL RICHARD, 1676-1721. Burgess from Baltimore Co., 1709-21. Colonel of Militia.
Christopher, Mrs. John G.
Burleson, Mrs. Albert Sidney.
Johns, Mrs. Claude Douglas.

COLEMAN, WILLIAM, 1643——. Member of the Ancient and Honorable Artillery Company of Boston, 1676. Ensign, 1692.
Hall, Miss Elizabeth Ward.
Hall, Miss Mary Stickney.

COLLIER, WILLIAM, ——1670. Assistant, 1634-65, Plymouth Colony. Member of the Council of War. Commissioner for the United Colonies, 1643.
Ridgely, Mrs. John.

COLLINS, FRANCIS, 1635-1720. Member of New Jersey Assembly, 1683-84. Member of Governor Jennings' Council, 1683. Judge of West Jersey Court, 1684, and of Gloucester Co. Court, 1684, etc.
Huse, Mrs. Harry P.
Griswold, Miss Ellen Howell.

COLSTON, WILLIAM. Member of the Virginia House of Burgesses, 1692.
Carroll, Mrs. Mary Randolph.
Page, Mrs. William C.

COLT, JOHN, 1658-1751. Lieutenant of Lynn (Mass.) Company, 1717, and Captain, 1723. Member of Assembly from Lynn, 1718-31.
Fowler, Miss Amélie de Pau.

COLT, PETER, 1744-1824. Assistant Commissary to General Fitch, 1775. At siege of Boston, 1777. Deputy Commissary-General for territory East of the Hudson River, and for New York and New Jer-

sey, until 1780. Treasurer of Connecticut, 1789-93.
Fowler, Miss Amélie de Pau.

CONTEE, ALEXANDER, 1691-1740. Burgess for Charles Co., 1724.
Ritchie, Mrs. John.
Boyd, Mrs. Allen Richards.
Carroll, Mrs. Mary Randolph.

CONWAY, COLONEL EDWIN, 1681-1763. Member of the Virginia House of Burgesses, 1710-42.
Hall, Mrs. George W. S.

COOK, MAJOR AARON, 1610-1690. Westfield, Mass. Deputy to the General Court, 1668. Ensign, 1676. Captain of a garrison in King Philip's War. Major of Hartford Troop, 1658.
Stockbridge, Mrs. Henry, Jr.

COOPER, JOSEPH, 1666-1749. Member of New Jersey Assembly for nineteen years. Member of Council, 1703.
Smith, Mrs. Robert C.

COOPER, WILLIAM, 1632-1710. Member of New Jersey Assembly, 1685, '88, '97. Justice of the Peace, 1682-86. Judge of Gloucester Co. Court, 1686. Member of the Proprietors' Council, 1689.
Huse, Mrs. Harry P.
Smith, Mrs. Robert C.

COPPOCK, HONORABLE BARTHOLOMEW, ——1720. Member Penn's Council, 1688-1690. Member Assembly, Chester Co., 1686-87, '92, '95, '97.
Mackenzie, Miss Mary G. M.

CORBIN, HENRY, ——1676. Member of Virginia House of Burgesses, 1658-59. Member of Council, 1663-67.
Pitts, Mrs. Sullivan.
Tilton, Miss Elizabeth.
Colvin, Mrs. Alexander B.
Reynolds, Mrs. William.
Tarleton, Mrs. Robert.
Lewis, Miss Virginia Tayloe.
Lyster, Mrs. Henry F. LeH.
Emory, Mrs. Campbell D.
Screven, Mrs. George P.
Trimble, Mrs. David C.
Sullivan, Mrs. Felix R.
Magruder, Mrs. John Read.
Shippen, Mrs. Edward.
Pennington, Miss Elizabeth Lloyd.
Howard, Mrs. Charles.
Calvert, Mrs. Charles Baltimore.
Lowndes, Mrs. Lloyd.
Dandridge, Miss Anne Spottswood.
Shawhan, Mrs. Charles S.

CORNELL, HONORABLE GIDEON, 1710-1765. Lieutenant-Governor and Chief Justice of Rhode Island.
Blackford, Mrs. Eugene.
Poultney, Mrs. Arthur E.

COURSEY, WILLIAM, ——1684. High Sheriff, Calvert Co., 1659-60. Justice, Kent Co., 1661, and of Talbot Co. in the same year. Burgess, Talbot Co., 1666-68.
Orrick, Mrs. Henry Abert.

COURTS, COLONEL JOHN, 1655-1702. Justice, Charles Co., 1685-89; Captain of Horse, Charles Co. Militia, 1689; Lieutenant-Colonel, 1694; Colonel, 1695. Member of Council, 1692-97.
Parran, Mrs. James Bourne.

COURTS, JOHN, 1691-1748. Burgess, Charles Co., 1728-48.
Parran, Mrs. James Bourne.

COUYN, CASPARUS, I., 1693-——. Ensign of Foot,

New York Militia, 8 January, 1735. First Lieutenant, 30 November, 1743.
Bond, Mrs. Hugh Lennox, Jr.

COUYN, CASPARUS, II., 1725-1805. Member Committee of Safety, Clavrack District, New York, 1775. Commissioned Captain 8th Regiment, New York Volunteers, 20 October, 1775.
Bond, Mrs. Hugh Lennox, Jr.

COWPLAND, HONORABLE CALEB, ———1758. Member Pennsylvania Provincial Assembly, 1729-36. Justice of the Peace, 1733, '38, '41, '49. Trustee of Loan Office, 1738-43. Puisne Judge, 1750-58.
Gill, Mrs. William Harrison.

COWPLAND, CAPTAIN JONATHAN, 1724———. Captain of the armed boat *Fame*, 17 October, 1776.
Gill, Mrs. William Harrison.

CRASKE, CAPTAIN EDMUND, 1640-1683. Captain, Rappahannock Co., Virginia Militia, 1676, in Bacon's Rebellion.
Wilson, Mrs. William B.
Wilson, Miss Emma.

CRASKE, CAPTAIN JOHN, 1668-1706. Captain of Richmond Co. Virginia Militia, in active service against Indians, 1704.
Wilson, Mrs. William B.
Wilson, Miss Emma.

CRAUFURD, DAVID, 1736-1800. Justice, Prince George's Co., 1773. Member of Maryland Convention, 1774-75.
Henry, Mrs. James L.

CRESAP, DANIEL, I., 1727-1798. Member Committee of Safety, Frederick County, 1775.
Holladay, Mrs. Samuel W.

CRESAP, DANIEL, II., 1753-1794. First Lieutenant Smallwood's Battalion, 1775. Lieutenant-Colonel of Militia, Alleghany Co., 1794, and commanded a regiment in the Whiskey Insurrection.
Holladay, Mrs. Samuel W.

CRESAP, THOMAS, 1702-1788. Surveyor of Western Maryland, 1737-50. Captain of Riflemen, 1754, and served with distinction in the French and Indian War. Burgess, Frederick Co., 1765, and several times subsequently. Colonel of Maryland Forces.
Holladay, Mrs. Samuel W.

CROPPER, GENERAL JOHN, 1755-1821. Captain of Virginia Minute Men, 1775, and later his company was attached to the 9th Virginia Regiment. Brigadier-General, 21st Virginia Brigade, 1815.
Tiffany, Mrs. L. McLane.

CROPPER, CAPTAIN SEBASTIAN, 1731-1776. Commissioned Captain, Accomac Co. Militia, 30 September, 1773.
Tiffany, Mrs. L. McLane.

CROSHAW, MAJOR JOSEPH, ———1667. Justice of York Co., Va., 1655, and subsequently Major of the County Militia. Member of the Virginia House of Burgesses, 1659-60.
Clark, Mrs. Frank P.
Dandridge, Miss Anne Spottswood.

CUSHING, HONORABLE JOHN, I., 1627-1708. Deputy to

General Court, 1674, and for many years after. Assistant, 1689, '90, '91, Plymouth Colony. Deputy to General Court, Massachusetts, 1692.
Thomas, Mrs. Douglas H.
Turnbull, Mrs. Alexander Nisbet.
Garrett, Mrs. T. Harrison.

CUSHING, HONORABLE JOHN, II., 1660-1738. Member of the Governor's Council of Massachusetts, 1710-28.
Thomas, Mrs. Douglas H.
Turnbull, Mrs. Alexander Nisbet.
Garrett, Mrs. T. Harrison.

CUSHING, HONORABLE JOHN, III., 1695-1778. Representative from Scituate, Mass., 1721, and several succeeding years. Member of the Governor's Council, 1746-63.
Thomas, Mrs. Douglas H.
Turnbull, Mrs. Alexander Nisbet.
Garrett, Mrs. T. Harrison.

CUSTIS, MAJOR-GENERAL JOHN, 1630-1696. Member of Council of Virginia, 1680. Major-General of Virginia Forces.
von Kapff, Mrs. Frederick.
Custis, Miss Lena Wise.
Custis, Miss Sarah Horsey.
Custis, Miss Clara Douglas.
Bayard, Miss Ellen Howard.
Wilson, Mrs. James W.
Howard, Miss Marian Gilmor.
Bayard, Mrs. Richard Bassett.
King, Mrs. Joseph.
Marshall, Mrs. Edward Athelstan.
Goldsborough, Mrs. George Robins.
Whitridge, Mrs. William H.
Floyd, Miss Nannie Teackle.

CUSTIS, COLONEL JOHN, 1653-1713. Member of Council of Virginia, 1699. Colonel and Commander-in-Chief of Militia on Eastern Shore of Virginia.
Von Kapf, Mrs. Frederick.
Bayard, Miss Ellen Howard.
Wilson, Mrs. James W.
Howard, Miss Marian Gilmor.
Bayard, Mrs. Richard Bassett.
King, Mrs. Joseph.
Marshall, Mrs. Edward Athelstan.
Whitridge, Mrs. William H.
Floyd, Miss Nannie Teackle.

CUTT, JOHN, ——1681. President of the Council of New Hampshire, 1679-81.
Hall, Miss Elizabeth Ward.
Hall, Miss Mary Stickney.

DANDRIDGE, COLONEL WILLIAM, ——1743. Member of the Council of Virginia, and Commissioner on the boundary of Virginia and North Carolina, 1727. Captain in the Royal Navy, 1737-43.
Clark, Mrs. Frank P.
Dandridge, Miss Anne Spottswood.

DARNALL, COLONEL HENRY, ——1711. Member of Council of Maryland and Deputy Governor, 1684-89.
Payson, Mrs. Herbert.
Boone, Mrs. Daniel A.
Bayard, Miss Ellen Howard.
Lyster, Mrs. Henry F.
Horsey, Mrs. Outerbridge.

DAVES, CAPTAIN JOHN, 1748-1804. Ensign, 1776; Lieutenant, 1777; Captain, 1781, North Carolina Line.
Daves, Miss Jennie Haywood.

DAVIS, CAPTAIN JAMES, of Gloucester, Mass., 1664-1715. Representative, 1695-99, 1701-1703, 1708-9. Ensign, 1681, and Captain, 1689, in Massachusetts Bay Colony Militia.
Belknap, Mrs. Charles.

INDEX OF ANCESTORS AND DESCENDANTS.

Browne, Mrs. Samuel Tracy.
Asshcton, Mrs. William Herbert.

DE HAES, JOANNES, ——1694. Justice, New Castle, Del., 1680. Member of Assembly, 1683, '87, '88, '90.
Mullikin, Mrs. Richard Oden.
Mullikin, Miss Sophia Margaret.

DE LANCY, PETER. Member of Assembly, Province of New York, 1756-1768.
Morris, Miss Elizabeth Manigault.

DEMING, JOHN, 1615-1705, Wethersfield, Conn. Deputy, 1649-61. Named as one of the Patentees of Connecticut, by Charles II., in the Royal Charter, 1662.
Chatard, Mrs. Thomas M.
Williams, Miss Rebecca Dalrymple.
Mackenzie, Miss Mary G. M.

DENISON, CAPTAIN GEORGE, 1620-1694. Captain, 26 May, 1676. Provost of Stonington, 12 February, 1676. Deputy, 1676-87. Commissioner to Court, 1675-94.
Powell, Mrs. William S.
Hamilton, Mrs. Levin Mayer.

DENNING, WILLIAM, 1740-1819. Member of the Committee of One Hundred, New York, 1775.
Hodges, Mrs. J. S. B.

DENNIS, DONNACK, ——1716. High Sheriff, Somerset Co., 1685.
Cook, Mrs. Harry C.
Snead, Mrs. Charles W.
Rogers, Mrs. Henry W.

DENNIS, JOHN, 1704-1766. Burgess, Somerset Co., 1755.
Cook, Mrs. Harry C.
Snead, Mrs. Charles W.
Rogers, Mrs. Henry W.

DENT, THOMAS, ——1676. Justice, St. Mary's Co., 1661-68. High Sheriff, 1664-65. Burgess, 1669, '74-76.
Boyd, Mrs. Allen Richards.

DE PEYSTER, COLONEL ABRAHAM, 1657-1728. Colonel of the New York Regiment of Foot, 1695. Chief Justice and member of the Royal Council, 1698. Acting Governor, 1 7 0 0. Treasurer of the Provinces of New York and New Jersey, 1706-21.
Whitelock, Mrs. George.

DERBY, RICHARD, 1712-1783. Member General Court of Massachusetts Bay, 1769-1773. Member Governor's Council, 1774-76.
Moore, Mrs. Benjamin P.

DE SILLE, NICASIUS. Member of Council, 1653-60. Schout Fiscal, New Netherland, 1658-60.
Hoffman, Mrs. R. Curzon.

DICK, JAMES, 1710——. Justice, Anne Arundel Co., 1756.
Cushman, Mrs. Charles D.

DICKINSON, SAMUEL, 1689-1760. Presiding Judge, Court of Common Pleas, Kent Co., Del., 1740. Associate Judge, Supreme Court of Delaware, 1754.
Pitts, Mrs. Sullivan.

DICKINSON, WALTER, 1621-1681. Justice, Talbot Co., 1679.
Pitts, Mrs. Sullivan.
Dandridge, Miss Anne Spottswood.

DIGGES, HONORABLE COLE, 1692-1744. Member of the

INDEX OF ANCESTORS AND DESCENDANTS.

Virginia House of Burgesses. Member of Council, 1719-44. County Lieutenant of Elizabeth City, Warwick and York Counties, 1728.
Randall, Mrs. Alexander Barton.

DIGGES, SIR DUDLEY, 1583-1639. Member of Council of the Virginia Company, 1609. Patented land in Virginia, 1620.
Randall, Mrs. Alexander Barton.

DIGGES, HONORABLE DUDLEY, 1665-1710. Member of the Council of Virginia, 1698-1710. Auditor-General.
Randall, Mrs. Alexander Barton.

DIGGES, GOVERNOR EDWARD, 1620-1675. Member of Council of Virginia, 1654-75. Governor of Virginia, 1656-58.
Steuart, Miss Mary Elizabeth.
Steuart, Miss Henrietta.
Denman, Mrs. H. B.
Tiffany, Mrs. L. McLane.
Williams, Mrs. Charles Phelps.
Randall, Mrs. Alexander Barton.
Hill, Mrs. Richard S.
Baughman, Mrs. Mary Jane.
Jones, Mrs. George Alphonzo.

DIGGES, COLONEL WILLIAM, ———1698. Captain of Horse, 1674. Sheriff of York Co., Va., 1679. Member of Council of Maryland and Deputy Governor, 1681-89.
Steuart, Miss Mary Elizabeth.
Steuart, Miss Henrietta.
Denman, Mrs. H. B.
Williams, Mrs. Charles Phelps.
Jones, Mrs. George Alphonzo.
Baughman, Mrs. Mary Jane.

DILL, CAPTAIN MATTHEW, ——1776. Commissioned Captain in Colonel Benjamin Chambers' Regiment, 1743. Commissioned Justice of the Peace and Court of Common Pleas, York Co., Penna., 10 March, 1749.
Morris, Mrs. Charles Manigault.
Morris, Miss Elizabeth M.

DORSEY, COLONEL EDWARD, ———1705. Justice, Anne Arundel Co., 1686-89. Associate Judge of High Court of Chancery, 1694-96. Commissioned Major, 1694. Burgess, 1692-97, 1700-1705.
Keyser, Mrs. William.
Fisher, Mrs. Charles D.
Mitchell, Miss Elizabeth Farnandis.
Harrison, Mrs. Edmund Pitts.
Hunt, Mrs. Dunbar.
Hunt, Miss Anita Dunbar.
Brent, Miss Ida S.
Gill, Mrs. Martin Gillet.
Dorsey, Miss Ella Loraine.
Parsons, Mrs. Joel Burton.
Smith, Mrs. Chandler Price.
Kerfoot, Mrs. Samuel Humes.

DORSEY, COLONEL JOHN, ——— 1714. Justice of Anne Arundel Co., 1694. Burgess, 1692, 1700-1703. Member of Council, 1710-14.
Smith, Mrs. Benjamin Franklin.
Moore, Mrs. Henry.
Fisher, Mrs. Charles D.
McBlair, Miss Emily.
Penniman, Mrs. Nicholas G.
Smith, Mrs. Virginia McBlair.
Simpson, Mrs. Edward.
Williams, Miss Elizabeth Chew.
Beall, Mrs. Edward Sinclair.
Beall, Miss Louisa Ogle.
Penniman, Miss Rebecca.
Turnbull, Mrs. John O.
Thompson, Miss Elizabeth Young.

INDEX OF ANCESTORS AND DESCENDANTS.

Washburn, Mrs. Charles W.
Preston, Mrs. J. Alexander.
Gorter, Mrs. Albert L.
Carroll, Miss Sally Wethered.
Ligon, Miss Elizabeth Worthington Dorsey.
Ridgely, Mrs. Charles.
Chatard, Mrs. Thomas M.
Smith, Mrs. Chandler Price.
Bass, Mrs. John M.
Cheatham, Mrs. Richard.
Winn, Miss Mary.
Goodwin, Miss E. Taylor.

DOUGLAS, MAJOR WILLIAM, 1723-1776. Major in the Royal Army. Served in America from 1745.
Cottman, Mrs. Clarence.
Powell, Miss Sarah Harrison.

DOW, CAPTAIN HENRY, 1634-1707, Hampton, N. H. Ensign, Hampton Company, 1689; Captain, 1692. Marshal of Norfolk Co., 1673, '80. Representative, 1693, '97-99. Mandamus Councillor, 1702-1707. Justice, Inferior Court of Common Pleas, 1695; reappointed, 1697; Senior Justice, 1699-1707.
Stewart, Mrs. David.
Hamilton, Mrs. W. T.

DOYNE, JOSHUA, ——1698. High Sheriff St. Mary's Co., 1683.
Keyser, Mrs. William.
Hunt, Mrs. Dunbar.
Hunt, Miss Anita Dunbar.
Brent, Miss Nanine Maria.
Brent, Miss Ida S.
Milnor, Miss Mary Worthington.

DUKE, JAMES, ——1754. Justice, Calvert Co., 1731-54; of Quorum, from 1736.
Penniman, Mrs. George Dobbin.

DULANY, DANIEL I., 1685-1753. Commissary-General of Maryland, 1721-27, 1734-53. Attorney-General from 1722. Burgess for Annapolis, 1728-38. Member of Council. Judge of the Court of Admiralty, Receiver-General, and Recorder of Annapolis.
Batré, Mrs. Alfred.
Lemmon, Mrs. J. Southgate.
Calvert, Mrs. Charles Baltimore.
Beall, Mrs. Edward Sinclair.
Beall, Miss Louisa Ogle.
Winn, Miss Mary.

DULANY, DANIEL II., 1721-1797. Mayor of Annapolis, 1764. Member of Council from 1757. Secretary of Maryland from 1761.
Lemmon, Mrs. J. Southgate.
Beall, Mrs. Edward Sinclair.
Beall, Miss Louisa Ogle.
Winn, Miss Mary.

DULANY, WALTER, 1721-1773. Member of Council and Commissary-General.
Batré, Mrs. Alfred.

DURAND, REVEREND LEVI, ——1765. Missionary sent by the "Society for the Propagation of the Gospel in Foreign Ports" to South Carolina, 1740. Rector of Christ Church Parish, 1741-51, and of St. John's Parish, 1751-65.
Wright, Mrs. D. Giraud.
Taylor, Mrs. B. Jones.

DUVAL, JOHN, 1713——. Member Committee of Observation, Prince George's Co., 1775. Captain, Prince George's Co. Militia, 5 September, 1777.
Duval, Miss Mary Rebecca.

DUVAL, MARSH MAREEN, 1741——. Member of Committee to carry out resolves of Congress, 1774.
Duval, Miss Mary Rebecca.

INDEX OF ANCESTORS AND DESCENDANTS.

DWIGHT, CAPTAIN TIMOTHY, 1639-1718, of Dedham, Mass. Colonel of Horse and Captain of Foot. Served in ten Indian expeditions, and was Deputy to the General Court of Massachusetts.
Jacobs, Mrs. Jesse Elliott.
Wood, Mrs. Joseph C.

DWIGHT, COLONEL TIMOTHY, 1694-1771. Served as Captain in the old French War in 1724. He built Fort Dummer and was its first commander. He was Colonel of a regiment, Chief Justice of Hampshire County, and Deputy to the General Court.
Jacobs, Mrs. Jesse Elliott.
Wood, Mrs. Joseph C.

EARLE, JAMES, 1694-1739. Burgess, Talbot Co., 1719, '21.
Earle, Miss Mary Isabel.

EARLE, RICHARD TILGHMAN, 1728-1778. Member Committee of Safety, Queen Anne's Co., 1774, and of the Maryland Assembly, 1774-76. Colonel of the County Militia, 1776.
Earle, Miss Mary Isabel.

EASTOW, WILLIAM, ——1655, Hampton, N. H. Representative, 1644, '48, '49.
Stewart, Mrs. David.
Hamilton, Mrs. W. T.

EATON, COLONEL WILLIAM. Member of North Carolina Assembly, 1746-53. Member Committee of Safety, 1775. Colonel of Militia, Northampton Co., N. C., 1776.
Daves, Miss Jennie Haywood.

EDMONDSON, POLLARD. Burgess, Talbot Co., 1759-63. Commissioned 3d Lieutenant, Talbot Co. Militia, 22 January, 1776. Represented Talbot Co. in Constitutional Convention of 1776.
Giffen, Mrs. James Fortescue.
Giffen, Miss Lilian.
Giffen, Miss Louise.

EDMONSTONE, JAMES, 1699——. Justice, Prince George's Co., 1741-51.
Boyd, Mrs. Allen Richards.

ELLYSON, CAPTAIN ROBERT. Member of the Virginia House of Burgesses, 1657-63.
Cottman, Miss Elizabeth Stewart.
Cottman, Mrs. J. Hough.

EMORY, ARTHUR, 1663-1747. Justice Kent Co., 1706; Justice Queen Anne Co., 1708-30.
Mackenzie, Mrs. George Norbury.
Mackenzie, Miss Mary G. M.

ENNALLS, BARTHOLOMEW, 1643-1688. Burgess, Dorchester Co., 1678-82.
Steuart, Miss Henrietta.
Steuart, Miss Mary Elizabeth.
Nicholson, Mrs. Charles G.
Presstman, Mrs. Benjamin.
Pitts, Mrs. Sullivan.
Dandridge, Miss Anne Spottswood.

ENNALLS, COLONEL HENRY, 1675-1734. Burgess, Dorchester Co., 1712-13. Justice, 1726.
Steuart, Miss Mary Elizabeth.
Steuart, Miss Henrietta.
Pitts, Mrs. Sullivan.
Dandridge, Miss Anne Spottswood.

ENNALLS, JOSEPH. Burgess, Dorchester Co., 1704.
Nicholson, Mrs. Charles G.
Pitts, Mrs. Sullivan.
Dandridge, Miss Anne Spottswood.

EPPES, COLONEL FRANCIS, I., ——1652. Member of the Virginia House of Burgesses, 1625, '31-32, '45. Member of Council, 1652.
Randall, Mrs. Alexander Barton.

EPPES, COLONEL FRANCIS, II., 1628-1678. Justice of Henrico Co., Va., 1677, and many years previously. Lieutenant-Colonel of the County.
Randall, Mrs. Alexander Barton.

EPPES, COLONEL FRANCIS, III., 1659-1720. Justice of Henrico Co., Va., 1683, and High Sheriff, 1685-86, 1700-1701, 1710-12. Member of the Virginia House of Burgesses, 1691-93, 1704.
Randall, Mrs. Alexander Barton.

EPPES, COLONEL FRANCIS, IV., 1685-1734. Member of the Virginia House of Burgesses, 1712-14. High Sheriff of Henrico Co., 1725-28.
Randall, Mrs. Alexander Barton.

ESTE, CAPTAIN MOSES, 1752-1836. Lieutenant of Militia, Huntedon Co., N. J., 1774; Captain, 1778: severely wounded at battle of Monmouth.
Fisher, Mrs. William A.
Woodruff, Mrs. George C.

FARMER, EDWARD, 1670-1745. Member of General Assembly of Pennsylvania, 1710-24.
Tyson, Mrs. John Snowden.
Martin, Mrs. Frank.
Coates, Mrs. Charles Edward.

FAUNTLEROY, COLONEL MOORE, ——1664. Member of the Virginia House of Burgesses, 1644-47, 1653, 1656-59; Colonel of Militia, Rappahannock Co., 1656.
Page, Mrs. William C.

FAY, CAPTAIN JOSIAH, 1732-1776. Captain of Massachusetts Volunteers, 5 September, 1774; 21st Continental Infantry, 1 January, 1776.
Mackubin, Miss Florence.

FENNER, ARTHUR, 1622-1703. Providence, R. I., Assistant at various times between 1657 and 1690. Deputy a number of times between 1664 and 1700. Justice of Quarter Sessions, and Court of Common Pleas, 1653. Commander of the garrison at Providence, 1676.
Wright, Mrs. D. Giraud.
Taylor, Mrs. B. Jones.

FENNER, THOMAS, 1652-1718, Rhode Island. Deputy seven years, 1683, '91, '95, '99, 1704-05. Assistant ten years, 1707-13, 1715-17. Major for the Main, 1712-1713.
Taylor, Mrs. B. Jones.
Wright, Mrs. D. Giraud.

FENWICK, CUTHBERT, 1614-1655. Member of Assembly, 1638. Justice, St. Mary's Co., 1644.
Denman, Mrs. H. B.
Brent, Miss Ida S.
Keyser, Mrs. William.
Hunt, Mrs. Dunbar.
Hunt, Miss Anita Dunbar.
Jones, Mrs. George Alphonzo.

FENWICK, COLONEL IGNATIUS. Member of Maryland Convention, 1774-76.
Hunt, Miss Anita Dunbar.
Hunt, Mrs. Dunbar.

Brent, Miss Ida S.
Keyser, Mrs. William.

FIELD, MAJOR PETER, 1647-1707. High Sheriff of Henrico Co., Va., 1682, and Captain in the County Militia, 1693. Major, New Kent Co., 1705. Member of the Virginia House of Burgesses, 1693.
Keyser, Mrs. R. Brent.
Buchanan, Miss Esther Sidney.
Randall, Mrs. Alexander Barton.
Cary, Mrs. Wilson Miles.
Cary, Miss Jane Margaret.

FITZHUGH, COLONEL HENRY, 1687——. Member of the Virginia House of Burgesses, 1736-40.
Tiffany, Mrs. L. McLane.

FITZHUGH, COLONEL WILLIAM, 1651-1701. Lieutenant-Colonel, Westmoreland Co., Va., 1683. Member of House of Burgesses, 1678-87. Colonel of Stafford County Forces, 1690.
Armistead, Miss Fannie Carter.
Whiting, Mrs. Clarence.
McLean, Mrs. Thomas Chalmers.
McCrackin, Mrs. Alexander.
Fuller, Mrs. Oliver Clyde.
Hayes, Mrs. John S.
Blackford, Mrs. Eugene.
Poultney, Mrs. Arthur E.
Gordon, Miss Margaret.
Gordon, Mrs. Alexander.
Calvert, Mrs. Charles Baltimore.
Tiffany, Mrs. L. McLane.

FITZHUGH, COLONEL WILLIAM (Maryland). Captain in the British Army, serving in America in 1754. Resigned as half-pay Captain, June, 1776. Colonel in the Revolution. Member of Maryland Constitutional Convention, 1776.

McCrackin, Mrs. Alexander.
Fuller, Mrs. Oliver Clyde.
Calvert, Mrs. Charles Baltimore.

FITZ RANDOLPH, LIEUTENANT EDWARD, 1754-1837. First Lieutenant, 4th Regiment, Pennsylvania Line.
Smith, Mrs. Thomas Marsh.

FITZ RANDOLPH, NATHANIEL, 1642-1713. Member of New Jersey General Assembly, 1693-94. High Sheriff of Middlesex Co., 1699.
Smith, Mrs. Thomas Marsh.

FLOYD, CHARLES, ——1718, of Northampton Co., Va. Member of the Virginia House of Burgesses, 1704, 1711, 1714.
Floyd, Miss Nannie Teackle.

FORBES, HONORABLE JOHN, 1731-1780. Second Lieutenant, 3d Maryland Battalion, June-December, 1776; Member of Congress from Maryland, 1778-80.
Haughton, Mrs. Henry Osburne.
Brown, Mrs. Arthur George.

FOWKE, COLONEL GERARD, ——1669. Burgess, Westmoreland Co., Va., 1663. Burgess, Charles Co., Md., 1666.
Rowland, Miss Elizabeth Mason.
Story, Mrs. B. T.
Hall, Mrs. George W. S.
Calvert, Mrs. Charles Baltimore.

FOWLER, WILLIAM, 1598-1660. Magistrate of New Haven, Conn., 1637.
Fowler, Miss Amélie de Pau.

FRANCIS, TENCH, 1701——. Attorney-General of Pennsylvania, 1744-52. Re-

corder of Philadelphia, 1750-54.
Coolidge, Mrs. Charles Austin.
Sibley, Mrs. Clarence.
Dugan, Mrs. Hammond.
Markoe, Mrs. Frank.
Bateman, Mrs. James M. H.

FREEBORN, GIDEON, ——1720, Portsmouth, R. I. Deputy, 1675, '90, 1703-04, '13.
Blackford, Mrs. Eugene.
Poultney, Mrs. Arthur E.

FREEBORN, WILLIAM. 1594-1670. One of the original proprietors of Aquidneck who settled Pocasset (later Portsmouth, R. I.), 1638.
Blackford, Mrs. Eugene.
Poultney, Mrs. Arthur E.

FREEMAN, EDMUND, 1590-1682. Assistant, Plymouth Colony, 1640-45.
Huse, Mrs. Harry P.

FRISBY, JAMES, 1676-1719. Burgess, Cecil Co., 1715-19.
Allen, Mrs. Ethan.

FRISBY, CAPTAIN PEREGRINE, ——1738. Burgess, Cecil Co., 1713.
Fuller, Mrs. Oliver Clyde.
Earle, Miss Mary Isabel.
Lürman, Mrs. Gustav W.
Beall, Miss Louisa Ogle.

FROST, MAJOR CHARLES (of Kittery, Me.), 1632-1697. Member Provincial Council, New Hampshire, 1681. Major of the Maine Regiment. Killed by Indians, 1697.
Belknap, Mrs. Charles.
Browne, Mrs. Samuel Tracy.
Assheton, Mrs. William Herbert.

GARDINER, CAPTAIN LUKE, 1622-1674. Burgess, St. Mary's Co., 1660-62, '71; Justice, 1661, '64-66; High Sheriff, 1672-74. Lieutenant, St. Mary's Co. Militia, 1660; Captain, 1664.
Parran, Mrs. James Bourne.
Howard, Mrs. Charles.

GARDINER, RICHARD, ——1687. Justice and of the Quorum, St. Mary's Co., Md., 1677-86. Burgess, 1681-87.
Howard, Mrs. Charles.

GASKINS, COLONEL THOMAS. Lieutenant-Colonel, 3d Virginia Line, 1778-81.
Hall, Mrs. George W. S.

GASSAWAY, COLONEL NICHOLAS, ——1700. Justice of Anne Arundel Co., 1686, '92. Colonel Anne Arundel Co. Militia.
Gill, Mrs. Martin Gillet.

GAYLORD, WILLIAM, 1585-1673. Representative, Dorchester, Mass., 1635-38, and for Windom, Conn., 1639-64.
Franklin, Mrs. Fabian.

GERARD, THOMAS, 1600-1673. Member of Assembly from St. Mary's Hundred, 1641. Member of Council of Maryland. Lord of St. Clement's Manor.
Jenkins, Mrs. Michael.
Jenkins, Mrs. Edmund Plowden.
Hinckley, Mrs. Robert.
O'Donnell, Mrs. Columbus.

GHISELIN, REVERDY, 1727-1775. Justice, Anne Arundel Co., 1760——; Chief Judge of the County Court, 1764-75.
Simpson, Mrs. Edward.

GHISELIN, WILLIAM, 1700-1743. Justice, Anne Arundel Co., 1742.
Simpson, Mrs. Edward.

GIBBONS, AMBROSE, 1600-1657. Deputy Governor of New Hampshire, 1630; Assistant, 1640. Captain, Portsmouth Colony Alarm, 1643.
Stewart, Mrs. David.
Hamilton, Mrs. W. T.

GILMAN, HONORABLE JOHN, 1624-1708. Lieutenant of the Militia at Exeter, 1669. Member of the first Council of the Province of New Hampshire, 1680. Member of Assembly, 1693-97. Speaker of the House, 1695.
Franklin, Mrs. Fabian.

GIST, RICHARD, 1684-1741. Justice, Baltimore Co., 1727-41, and Presiding Justice from 1735. One of the Commissioners to lay out Baltimore Town, 1729.
Iglehart, Mrs. C. Iredell.
Robinson, Miss Louisa Hall.
Whitridge, Mrs. Horatio L.
Buchanan, Miss Esther Sidney.
Turnbull, Mrs. Alexander Nisbet.
Garrett, Mrs. T. Harrison.

GITTINGS, JAMES, ——1823. Justice, Baltimore Co., 1768-75. Member Committee of Correspondence, Baltimore Co., 1774, and of Committee of Observation, 1775. Captain, Baltimore Co. Militia, 1775; Major, 1776.
Sloan, Mrs. Robert Neale.
Chatard, Mrs. Thomas M.

GODFREY, COLONEL JOHN. Member of the Council of South Carolina, 1684.
Iglehart, Mrs. C. Iredell.
Robinson, Miss Louisa Hall.
Whitridge, Mrs. Horatio L.
Taylor, Mrs. Winfield J.
Turnbull, Mrs. Alexander Nisbet.
Garrett, Mrs. T. Harrison.

GOLDSBOROUGH CHARLES, 1707-1767. Clerk of Dorchester Co., 1728. Burgess, 1752, '63. Member of Council and Commissary-General.
Nicholson, Mrs. Charles G.
Pitts, Mrs. Sullivan.
Dandridge, Miss Anne Spottswood.

GOLDSBOROUGH, JOHN, 1711-1778. Burgess, Talbot Co., 1745-66.
Markoe, Mrs. Frank.
Dugan, Mrs. Hammond.
Sibley, Mrs. Clarence.

GOLDSBOROUGH, NICHOLAS, 1687-1766. Burgess for Talbot Co., 1732-35, 1745-1750.
Bateman, Mrs. James M. H.

GOLDSBOROUGH, ROBERT, 1660-1746. Burgess, Talbot Co., 1706-7.
Markoe, Mrs. Frank.
Sibley, Mrs. Clarence.
Dugan, Mrs. Hammond.
Nicholson, Mrs. Charles G.
Pitts, Mrs. Sullivan.
Dandridge, Miss Anne Spottswood.

GOLDSBOROUGH, HONORABLE ROBERT, 1733-1788. Burgess, Dorchester Co.,1765. Attorney-General of Maryland, 1776. Member Maryland Convention, 1774. Delegate to Continental Congress, 1774-75. Member of Maryland Constitutional Convention, 1776.
Nicholson, Mrs. Charles G.
Pitts, Mrs. Sullivan.
Dandridge, Miss Anne Spottswood.

GOLDTHWAITE, COLONEL THOMAS, 1718-1799. Commandant of Fort Pownal, on the Penobscot, 1763. Judge of the Court of

INDEX OF ANCESTORS AND DESCENDANTS.

Common Pleas. Colonel of Militia.
Campbell, Miss Ella Calvert.

GOOCH, MAJOR WILLIAM, —— 1655. Member of the Council of Virginia, 1655.
Page, Mrs. William C.

GOOKIN, CAPTAIN JOHN, —— 1643. Member of Grand Assembly for Lower Norfolk, 1639.
Smith, Miss Virginia Hope Bryant.

GRAFTON, RICHARD, 1683-1743. Judge of the Supreme Court for the three lower counties of Delaware, 1727.
Batre, Mrs. Alfred.

GRAHAM, COLONEL JAMES, ——1701. Attorney-General, Province of New York, 1685-87, and 1691-1701. Member and Speaker of the Provincial Assembly of New York. First Recorder of New York, 1683-1700.
Morris, Miss Elizabeth M.

GREEN, THOMAS, ——1650. Governor of Maryland, 1647, '49.
Heighe, Mrs. John M.
Littig, Mrs. John Merryman.
Sloan, Mrs. Robert.

GREENBERRY, COLONEL NICHOLAS, 1627-1697. Justice, Anne Arundel Co., 1686,'89. Member of Council, 1692-97. President of Council, and Chancellor of Maryland, 1693-94. Acting Governor, 1693. Commissioned Captain of Foot, Militia of Anne Arundel Co., 4 September, 1689; Colonel, 9 October, 1694. Commissioned Judge of High Court of Chancery, 2 March, 1695-6.
Fisher, Mrs. Charles D.
Carrington, Miss Henrietta Penniman.
Harrison, Mrs. Edmund Pitts.
Early, Mrs. Alexander R.
Slingluff, Mrs. Fielder C.
Gill, Mrs. Martin Gillet.
Penniman, Miss Rebecca.
Nicholson, Mrs. Charles G.
Dorsey, Miss Ella Loraine.
Marshall, Mrs. Charles.
Nicholas, Mrs. Wilson Cary.
Parsons, Mrs. Joel Burton.
Calvert, Mrs. Charles Baltimore.
Pitts, Mrs. Sullivan.
Mercein, Mrs. Thomas R.
Smith, Mrs. Chandler Price.
Dandridge, Miss Anne Spottswood.

GREENLEAF, CAPTAIN EDMUND, 1600-1671, Newbury, Mass. Ensign of the Newbury Company, 1639; Lieutenant, 1642; Captain, 1645.
Stewart, Mrs. David.
Hamilton, Mrs. W. T.

GRIFFITH, COLONEL HENRY, 1720-1794. Justice, Frederick Co., 1755-60; Burgess, 1773-75. Member Commitee of Observation, 1775. Justice, Frederick Co., 1777.
Carrington, Miss Henrietta Penniman.
Harrison, Mrs. Edmund Pitts.
Penniman, Miss Rebecca.
Parsons, Mrs. Joel Burton.

GRISWOLD, LIEUTENANT EBENEZER, 1702-1779. Lieutenant, First Company 3d Connecticut Regiment, Crown Point Campaign, 1755.
Griswold, Miss Ellen Howell.

GRISWOLD, EDWARD, 1608-1671. Representative for Windsor, Conn., 1658-61, and frequently later for Kenilworth.
Franklin, Mrs. Fabian.

GRUNDY, ROBERT, ———1720. High Sheriff, Talbot Co., 1698-99; Justice, 1702; of Quorum, 1705.
Coolidge, Mrs. Charles Austin.
Lürman, Mrs. Theodor G.
Tilghman, Miss Mary.
Pitts, Mrs. Sullivan.
Norris, Mrs. Owen.
Dandridge, Miss Anne Spottswood.

GRYMES, HONORABLE JOHN, 1691-1748. Member of the Virginia House of Burgesses, 1718. Member of Council and Receiver-General, 1725.
Minor, Miss Mary Willis.

HAGER, JONATHAN, 1719-1775. Founder of Hagerstown, 1750. Burgess, 1771-73. Member of Committee for raising money for the Revolution and of the Committee of Correspondence and Observation, 1775.
Keyser, Mrs. William.
Hunt, Mrs. Dunbar.
Hunt, Miss Anita Dunbar.
Brent, Miss Ida S.

HALDEMAN, JACOB, 1722-1783. Member of the Committee of Safety, Rapho Township, Lancaster Co., Pa. 1775.
Lowndes, Mrs. Lloyd.

HALL, AQUILLA CARVIL, 1728-1779. High Sheriff, Baltimore Co., 1761, and Burgess, 1773. Lieutenant-Colonel of the County Militia. Colonel of the Upper Battalion, Harford Co., 1775.
Ringgold, Mrs. James T.

HALL, B E N J A M I N, Prince George's Co., Md. Member of the Maryland Convention, 1775.
Woods, Mrs. Daniel C.

HALL, REVEREND HENRY, 1676———. Rector of St. James' Parish, Anne Arun- Co., 1698.
Duval, Miss Mary Rebecca.

HALL, CAPTAIN JOHN, 1658-1737. High Sheriff, Baltimore Co., 1693. Captain of the County Militia.
Iglehart, Mrs. C. Iredell.
Robinson, Miss Louisa Hall.
Ringgold, Mrs. James T.
Whitridge, Mrs. Horatio L.
Turnbull, M r s. Alexander Nisbet.
Garrett, Mrs. T. Harrison.

HALL, COLONEL JOHN, 1701-1774. High Sheriff, Baltimore Co., 1730. Burgess, 1745-48. Colonel of the County Militia, 1735.
Iglehart, Mrs. C. Iredell.
Robinson, Miss Louisa Hall.
Whitridge, Mrs. Horatio L.
Turnbull, M r s. Alexander Nisbet.
Garrett, Mrs. T. Harrison.

HALL, COLONEL JOSIAS CARVIL, 1746-1814. Colonel of the 4th Regiment, Maryland Line, 1775-83.
Iglehart, Mrs. C. Iredell.
Robinson, Miss Louisa Hall.
Whitridge, Mrs. Horatio L.
Turnbull, M r s. Alexander Nisbet.
Garrett, Mrs. T. Harrison.

HALL, RICHARD, ———1688. Burgess, Calvert Co., 1666-70, '74-85. Commissioner for laying o u t towns and ports in Calvert Co., November, 1683.
Harrison, Mrs. Edmund Pitts.
Van Antwerp, Mrs. Thomas C.
Thompson, M i s s Elizabeth Young.
Gorter, Mrs. Albert L.
Parsons, Mrs. Joel Burton.
Chatard, Mrs. Thomas M.
Lemmon, Mrs. J. Southgate.
Philpot, Miss Mary Dennison.

INDEX OF ANCESTORS AND DESCENDANTS.

Redwood, Mrs. Frank T.
Beall, Mrs. Edward Sinclair.
Beall, Miss Louisa Ogle.
Winn, Miss Mary.
Blackiston, Mrs. A. Hooton.
Pearre, Miss Mary Smith Worthington.
Woods, Mrs. Daniel C.
Williams, Miss Elizabeth Chew.
Sullivan, Mrs. Felix R.
Screven, Mrs. George P.

HAMMOND, MAJOR - GENERAL JOHN, 1643-1707. Commissioned Colonel, 4 October, 1699. Burgess, Anne Arundel Co., 1692. Justice of Provincial Court and Member of Council, 1698-1707. Judge of the Vice-Admiralty, 1702. Major-General of the Western Shore.
Conrad, Mrs. Lawrence Lewis.
Belt, Mrs. Alfred McGill.
Early, Mrs. Alexander R.
Slingluff, Mrs. Fielder C.
Ligon, Miss Elizabeth Worthington Dorsey.
Nicholas, Mrs. Wilson Cary.
Milnor, Miss Mary Worthington.

HAMMOND, COLONEL WILLIAM, 1711-1752. One of the Commissioners appointed to lay off Baltimore Town, 1729. High Sheriff, Baltimore Co., 1736. Colonel of the County Militia.
Redwood, Mrs. Frank T.

HANCE, CAPTAIN JOHN, —— 1709. Justice, Calvert Co., 1689. Captain, Indian War, 1697.
Mackenzie, Miss Mary G. M.

HANSON, JUDGE FREDERICK, 1693-1738. Presiding Justice, Kent Co. Court, 1732.
Jenkins, Mrs. E. Austin.
Polk, Miss Anna Maria.
Gorter, Mrs. Gosse Onno.

HANSON, COLONEL HANS, 1646-1703. Justice, Kent Co., 1685-87; Burgess, Kent Co., 1694-97; Burgess, Cecil Co., 1699.
Jenkins, Mrs. E. Austin.
Merritt, Mrs. J. Alfred.
Polk, Miss Anna Maria.
Gorter, Mrs. Gosse Onno.

HANSON, JOHN, ——1714. Justice, Charles Co., 1694-96.
Dorsey, Miss Ella Loraine.
Parran, Mrs. James Bourne.

HANSON, HONORABLE JOHN, 1715-1783. Member of the House of Burgesses, 1757-58, '65, '66, '68, and of House of Delegates, 1777-79; President of Continental Congress, 1781-82.
Carroll, Mrs. Mary Randolph.

HANSON, SAMUEL, ——1740. Burgess, Charles Co., 1728-31.
Mitchell, Miss Elizabeth Farnandis.
Dorsey, Miss Ella Loraine.
Carroll, Mrs. Mary Randolph.
Parran, Mrs. James Bourne.

HANSON, JUDGE WALTER, 1711-1794. Justice, Charles Co., 1741; of Quorum, from 1748; Chief Judge, 1774-86.
Mitchell, Miss Elizabeth Farnandis.
Parran, Mrs. James Bourne.

HARRIS, WILLIAM, 1610-1680. One of the five associates of Roger Williams, and one of the thirteen original proprietors of Providence Plantations, 1636. Commissioner, 1660-63. Assistant, 1666-76.
Wright, Mrs. D. Giraud.
Taylor, Mrs. B. Jones.

HARRISON, BENJAMIN, I. Clerk of the Council of Virginia, 1634. Member

of the House of Burgesses, 1642.
Lyster, Mrs. Henry F. LeH.
Woodruff, Mrs. George C.
Minor, Miss Mary Willis.
Tiffany, Mrs. L. McLane.
Randall, Mrs. Alexander Barton.

HARRISON, BENJAMIN, II., 1645-1712. Member of the Council of Virginia, 1699-1712.
McLean, Mrs. Thomas Chalmers.
Gordon, Miss Margaret.
Woodruff, Mrs. George C.
Minor, Miss Mary Willis.
Randall, Mrs. Alexander Barton.
Lyster, Mrs. Henry F. LeH.

HARRISON, BENJAMIN, III., 1673-1710. Attorney-General and Treasurer of Virginia. Speaker of the House of Burgesses.
Woodruff, Mrs. George C.

HARRISON, BENJAMIN, IV., ———-1744. Member of the Virginia House of Burgesses.
Woodruff, Mrs. George C.

HARRISON, BENJAMIN, V., 1726-1791. Member of the Virginia House of Burgesses, 1764. Member of Congress, 1774-78. Governor of Virginia. Signer of the Declaration of Independence.
Woodruff, Mrs. George C.

HARRISON, BURR, 1637-1710. Member of the Virginia House of Burgesses, 1699.
Cottman, Mrs. Clarence.
Powell, Miss Sarah Harrison.

HARRISON, HONORABLE NATHANIEL, 1677-1727. Member of the Virginia House of Burgesses, 1706. Member of Council, 1713-27. County Lieutenant, Surrey and Prince George counties, 1715. Auditor-General, Naval officer for the Lower James, 1713.
Randall, Mrs. Alexander Barton.

HARTSHORNE, RICHARD, 1641-———. One of the proprietors of East Jersey, 1682. A Deputy in Governor Lawrie's Council, 1684. Member of the Assembly from Middletown, 1685. Speaker of the Assembly, 1687-98. Member of Governor Basse's Council from 1698 to the surrender of the Government to the Crown.
Smith, Mrs. Thomas Marsh.

HATTON, WILLIAM, 1630-1713. Burgess, St. Mary's Co., 1671-75.
Leakin, Miss Margaret Dobbin.
Sioussat, Mrs. Albert Willis.

HAWKINS, CAPTAIN HENRY, ———-1699. Justice, Charles Co., 1687-1694; Burgess, 1688-1692; Commissioned Captain of Horse, Charles Co. Militia, 30 July, 1694.
Jenkins, Mrs. E. Austin.

HAWKINS, JOHN, 1656-1717. Justice, Talbot Co., 1694. Justice of the Provincial Court, 1698. Burgess, Queen Anne's Co., 1714-17.
Chatard, Mrs. Thomas M.

HAWKINS, PHILEMON, ———-1801. High Sheriff, Granville Co., N. C., 1752.
Brown, Miss Lizinka Campbell.

HAWKINS, THOMAS. Member of Frederick Co. Com-

INDEX OF ANCESTORS AND DESCENDANTS.

mittee of Observation, 1775.
Atkinson, Mrs. Isaac Edmondson.

HAZARD, JONATHAN. Magistrate of Newtown, L. I., 1673; member of the Court of Overseers, 1675-77; Commissioner of the Town Court 1684-87.

HAZARD, THOMAS. Schepen of Middleborough, Delegate to the Convention at New Amsterdam, 1653.
Thom, Mrs. J. Pembroke.
Duke, Mrs. Basil.

HAZARD, THOMAS, 1610-1680. One of the nine who settled Newport, R. I., 1639. Member of the General Court of Elections, 1640.
Blackford, Mrs. Eugene.
Poultney, Mrs. Arthur E.

HENDERSON, SAMUEL, 1700-1784. High Sheriff of Granville Co., N. C. 1750.
Mercer, Mrs. Carroll.

HENLEY, CAPTAIN ROBERT. ——-1684. Justice, Charles Co., 1659; Burgess, 1676.
Parran, Mrs. James Bourne.

HERKIMER, LIEUTENANT HANSYOOST. —1775. Lieutenant, New York Provincial Forces, 1733.
Christopher, Mrs. John G.

HERMAN, COLONEL AUGUSTINE, 1605-1686. First Lord of Bohemia Manor, Cecil Co. One of the "Nine Men" of New Amsterdam. 1647-50. Ambassador from New Amsterdam to Rhode Island, 1652, and to Maryland and Virginia, 1659. Member of the Council of Maryland, and Colonel of Militia. Commissioner to treat with the Indians, 1678.
Allen, Mrs. Ethan.
Bayard, Miss Ellen Howard.

HERTER, CAPTAIN HENRY, 1730-1822. Served in the French and Indian Wars. Was made captive by the Indians and carried to Canada.
Christopher, Mrs. John G.

HEYWARD, CAPTAIN THOMAS, 1700-1738. Captain in the Provincial service, and Commander of Fort Johnson, South Carolina.
Taylor, Mrs. Winfield J.

HEYWARD, JUDGE THOMAS, 1746-1809. Captain of the Charleston Ancient Battalion of Artillery. Member of the Council of Safety, 1775. Member of the first Revolutionary Assembly in the Province. Signer of the Declaration of Independence.
Taylor, Mrs. Winfield J.

HILL, COLONEL EDWARD, 1632-1700. Member of the Virginia House of Burgesses, 1676. Member of Council, 1688.
Carter, Miss Mary Coles.

HILL, CAPTAIN RICHARD. Burgess, Anne Arundel Co., 1681-89, '94-99, and Chief Judge of the County Court, 1686. Captain of Anne Arundel Co. Militia until 1689.
Winn, Miss Mary.
Penniman, Mrs. Nicholas G.
Penniman, Miss Rebecca.
Turnbull, Mrs. John O.
Washburn, Mrs. Charles W.
Preston, Mrs. J. Alexander.
Carroll, Miss Sally Wethered.
Ridgely, Mrs. Charles.

INDEX OF ANCESTORS AND DESCENDANTS.

Beall, Mrs. Edward Sinclair.
Beall, Miss Louisa Ogle.

HOBART, EDMUND, 1570-1646, Hingham, Mass. Representative, 1639-42.
Johnston, Miss Maria Stith.
Robbins, Mrs. Henry S.

HOLLIDAY, JOHN ROBERT, 1747-1801. High Sheriff, Baltimore Co., 1770.
Semmes, Mrs. John E.

HOLLIDAY, COLONEL THOMAS, —— -1703. Justice, Calvert Co., 1690-94.
Zunts, Miss Sue Howard.

HOLLYDAY, JAMES, 1695-1747. Treasurer Eastern Shore. Md., 1726-1739; of Council, 1735. Naval Officer Port of Oxford.
Semple, Mrs. Percy.

HOLLINGSWORTH, HENRY, 1664-1721. Member of Assembly, New Castle Co., Del., 1695. Deputy Master of the Rolls, 1700. Surveyor of Cecil Co., Md., 1712.
Simpson, Mrs. Edward.
Manly, Mrs. L. Tyson.

HOLLINGSWORTH, VALENTINE. Member of the Assembly, New Castle Co., Del., 1683, '87, '95. Justice, 1695.
Simpson, Mrs. Edward.
Manly, Mrs. L. Tyson.

HOOPER, GENERAL HENRY, —— -1790. Member of Assembly, Dorchester Co., 1775. Member of Council of Safety, 1775. Brigadier-General, Lower District, Eastern Shore of Maryland, 1776.
Presstman, Mrs. Benjamin.

HOOPER, HONORABLE JOHN, 1695- ——. Representative and Speaker of Colonial Assembly of Connecticut, member of Colonial Council. Judge of Supreme Court.
Goddard, Mrs. Henry P.

HOOKER, REV. THOMAS, 1586-1647. Pastor of Church at Newtown, Mass., 1633; removed, 1636, to Hartford. One of founders of Connecticut.
Goddard, Mrs. Henry P.

HOPKINSON, THOMAS, 1709-1751. Member of Council, Province of Pennsylvania, 1747. First President of the American Philosophical Society, 1743.
Smith, Miss Josephine Hopkinson.
Redwood, Mrs. Frank T.

HORSMANDEN, WARHAM. Member of the Virginia House of Burgesses, 1657-58, and member of Council, 1658.
Poultney, Mrs. Arthur E.
McCandlish, Miss Evelyn Byrd.
Minor, Miss Mary Willis.
Randall, Mrs. Alexander Burton.

HOSMER, STEPHEN, 1645-1693. Hartford, Conn. Deputy to the General Court, 1692, and for many years previously.
Winchester, Mrs. H. Carroll.

HOSMER, THOMAS, 1602-1687. One of the founders of Hartford, 1636, and left money towards the founding of the first free school there. Deputy to the General Court for several terms.
Winchester, Mrs. H. Carroll.

HOSMER, CAPTAIN THOMAS, 1675-1732. Commission-

117

INDEX OF ANCESTORS AND DESCENDANTS.

ed Captain of the South Side Company, in the town of Hartford, May, 1721.
Winchester, Mrs. H. Carroll.

HOSMER, HONORABLE TITUS, 1737-1780. Representative in the General Assembly, 1773-78. Speaker of the House, 1777. Member of Congress and signed the Articles of Confederation, 1778. One of the three Judges of the U. S. Court of Appeals, 1780.
Winchester, Mrs. H. Carroll.

HOUCHIN, JEREMY, ——1670. Representative from Hingham, Mass., 1651-59; from Salisbury, 1663.
Belknap, Mrs. Charles.
Browne, Mrs. Samuel Tracy.
Assheton, Mrs. William Herbert.

HOUGH, RICHARD, ——1705. Member of Assembly, 1684, '88, '90, '97, '99, 1700, 1704. Member of Council, 1692-1700.
Hough, Miss Ethel.

HOWARD EDMUND, ——-1713. Justice, Somerset Co., 1689. Clerk of Charles Co.
Zunts, Miss Sue Howard.

HOWARD, COLONEL JOHN EAGER, 1752-1827. Captain, 2d Battalion, Maryland Flying Camp, June, 1776. Major of 4th Maryland Regiment, 1778. Lieutenant-Colonel, 5th Maryland, 1778. Awarded a medal by Congress for gallant conduct at the battle of Cowpens, 1781. Member of Congress. Governor of Maryland. U. S. Senator.
Bayard, Miss Ellen Howard.
Howard, Miss Marian Gilmor.
Bayard, Mrs. Richard Bassett.
King, Mrs. Joseph.
Marshall, Mrs. Edward Athelstan.
Ridgely, Mrs. Charles.
Keyser, Mrs. R. Brent.

HOWE, THOMAS. Burgess, Calvert Co., 1704-08.
Penniman, Mrs. George Dobbin.

HOWELL, EDWARD, 1584-1656. Lynn, Mass. Removed to Southampton, L. I., 1639. Assistant, 1647-53, Connecticut Colony.
Chatard, Mrs. Thomas M.
Williams, Miss Rebecca Dalrymple.
Mackenzie, Miss Mary G. M.

HOWELL, JACOB, 1687-1768. Delegate to Provincial Assembly of Pennsylvania, 1752.
Griswold, Miss Ellen Howell.

HOWELL, MAJOR JOHN, 1625-1696, Southampton, L. I. Deputy, 1662-64. In command against the Dutch. Major of Horse, 1684.
Chatard, Mrs. Thomas M.
Williams, Miss Rebecca Dalrymple.
Mackenzie, Miss Mary G. M.

HOWELL, MAJOR JOSEPH, 1750-1798. Captain in Atlee's Battalion, Wayne's Brigade, Pennsylvania Line, 1776. Wounded and taken prisoner at battle of Long Island. Subsequently Paymaster and Major, U. S. A.
Griswold, Miss Ellen Howell.

HUMFREY, HONORABLE JOHN, 1595-1661. One of the original patentees Colony of Massachusetts Bay, 1627; Deputy Governor, 1630. Member of the Ancient and Honorable Artillery

Company, 1641. First Major-General of the Colony. With the Governor and others, appointed by the Court "to take order for a college" at Cambridge.
Stewart, Mrs. David.
Hamilton, Mrs. W. T.

HUNT, LIEUTENANT-COLONEL ABRAHAM, 1739-1821. Lieutenant-Colonel of Colonel Isaac Smith's First Regiment, Hunterdon Co., N. J., militia.
Thom, Mrs. J. Pembroke.
Duke, Mrs. Basil.

HUNT, LIEUTENANT RALPH, 1640-1677. Commissioned Lieutenant of Long Island Militia, 21 April, 1665. Patentee of Newtown, L. I.; Magistrate, Surveyor, Indian Lands, 1663-64.
Hunt, Miss Anita Dunbar.
Thom, Mrs. J. Pembroke.
Duke, Mrs. Basil.

HUNTER, CAPTAIN JAMES, 1711-1782. Captain, Chester Co., Pennsylvania Associators, 1747-48. Justice of the Peace, and Judge of the Common Pleas, Chester Co., 1764-70.
Brooke, Mrs. John.

HUTCHINS, CAPTAIN FRANCIS, ——-1698. Justice for Calvert Co., 1689. Burgess, 1682-85, '94-97.
Fisher, Mrs. Charles D.
Simpson, Mrs. Edward.
Roberts, Mrs. John B.
Manly, Mrs. L. Tyson.
Hough, Miss Ethel.
Mackenzie, Miss Mary G. M.

HYNSON, COLONEL JOHN, ——-1705. Justice, Kent Co., 1674; Burgess, 1681-83, 1694-97; High Sheriff, 1670.
Shippen, Mrs. Edward.

HYNSON, THOMAS, 1620-1667. Clerk of Kent Co., 1652; Burgess, 1654-1660; High Sheriff of the County, 1655.
Shippen, Mrs. Edward.

ISHAM, CAPTAIN HENRY. Captain of Militia, and High Sheriff of Henrico Co., Va., 1668-69.
Keyser, Mrs. R. Brent.
Buchanan, Miss Esther Sidney.
Randall, Mrs. Alexander Barton.
Cary, Mrs. Wilson Miles.
Cary, Miss Jane Margaret.

IZARD, HONORABLE RALPH. Member of South Carolina Assembly, 1716-20. Member of Proprietary Council, 1719. Attorney-General, 1737.
Morris, Miss Elizabeth M.

JACKSON, EDWARD, 1605-1681. Deputy from Cambridge to the General Court, Colony of Massachusetts Bay, 1647-1662. Left by his will a large gift of land to Harvard College.
Hall, Miss Elizabeth Ward.
Hall, Miss Mary Stickney.

JACQUETT, GOVERNOR JEAN PAUL, 16——-17——, New Castle, Del. Governor of New Sweden under General-Governor Peter Stuyvesant, 1655-57. Justice of New Castle, 1676-78.
Reed, Mrs. William.
McIlvain, Miss Elizabeth Gunning.

JAMES, CAPTAIN JOHN, 1720-1778. Captain of Militia, Prince William Co., Va.,

INDEX OF ANCESTORS AND DESCENDANTS.

1755 ; Captain, Fauquier Co. Militia, 1759.
Wilson, Mrs. William B.
Wilson, Miss Emma.
Wilson, Miss Ella C.

JANNEY, THOMAS, ——-1696. Member of the Council of Pennsylvania, 1684-86.
Manly, Mrs. L. Tyson.

JARBOE, COLONEL JOHN, 1619-1674. Justice, St. Mary's Co., 1663-65; High Sheriff, 1667-68, '70-72; Burgess, 1674-75. Commissioned Lieutenant, St. Mary's Co. Militia, 15 March, 1658; Lieutenant-Colonel, 31 Oct., 1660.
Parran, Mrs. James Bourne.
Howard, Mrs. Charles.

JEFFERSON, COLONEL PETER, 1708-1757. High Sheriff of Goochland Co., Va., 1739-40. Lieutenant-Colonel of Albemarle Co., 1745; Colonel, 1752. Member of the Virginia House of Burgesses, 1755.
Keyser, Mrs. R. Brent.
Buchanan, Miss Esther Sidney.
Randall, Mrs. Alexander Barton.
Cary, Mrs. Wilson Miles.
Cary, Miss Jane Margaret.

JEFFERSON, CAPTAIN THOMAS, 1679-1731. Justice of Henrico Co., Va., 1706-1718, and High Sheriff, 1718-19. Captain in the County Militia, 1708.
Keyser, Mrs. R. Brent.
Buchanan, Miss Esther Sidney.
Randall, Mrs. Alexander Barton.
Cary, Mrs. Wilson Miles.
Cary, Miss Jane Margaret.

JEFFERSON, PRESIDENT THOMAS, 1743-1826. Member of the Virginia House of Burgesses, 1769-73, and of Convention, 1774-76. Member of Congress. Governor of Virginia, 1779-81. President of the United States, 1800-1808. Author and Signer of Declaration of Independence.
Randall, Mrs. Alexander Barton.

JENNESS, CAPTAIN RICHARD, 1686-1769. Rye, New Hampshire. Representative, 1727-62. Captain, 1728.
Stewart, Mrs. David.
Hamilton, Mrs. W. T.

JENNESS, RICHARD, JR., 1717-1782. Member New Hampshire Assembly, 1765-73. Member of the New Hampshire Provincial Congress, 1775.
Hamilton, Mrs. W. T.
Stewart, Mrs. David.

JENNINGS, THOMAS, ——-1759. Chief Clerk of the Land Office. Justice, Anne Arundel Co., 1746-59.
Rogers, Mrs. Henry W.

JOHNS, KENSEY, 1722-1763. Justice, Anne Arundel Co., 1754. High Sheriff, 1760.
Earle, Miss Mary Isabel.
Milnor, Miss Mary Worthington.

JOHNSON, COLONEL BAKER, 1747-1811. Member of the Committee of Correspondence for Frederick Co., 1774. Member of Maryland Conventions, 1774, '75, '76. Colonel of the Fourth Maryland Regiment in the Revolution.
Mercein, Mrs. Thomas R.

JOHNSON, DOCTOR EDWARD, ——1797. Justice. Calvert

120

INDEX OF ANCESTORS AND DESCENDANTS.

Co., 1773. Member Committee of Calvert Co., 1775-76. Surveyor of Calvert Co., 1775. Judge of County Court, 1777.
Buchanan, Mrs. Roberdeau.

JOHNSON, CAPTAIN HENRY, ——1690. Justice, Baltimore Co., 1683-86; Burgess, 1683.
Hoffman, Mrs. R. Curzon.

JOHNSON, SIR NATHANIEL, Knight, ——1713. Governor of the Leeward Islands, 1686. Governor of South Carolina, 1701-09.
Morris, Miss Elizabeth M.

JOHNSON, GOVERNOR THOMAS, 1732-1819. Burgess, Anne Arundel Co., 1765. Delegate from Maryland to Continental Congress, 1774, and re-elected, 1777. Brigadier-General Maryland Forces, 6 January-4 July, 1776. Governor of Maryland, 1777. Justice of the Supreme Court of the United States, 1791.
Ward, Mrs. Frank X.
Rogers, Mrs. Henry W.

JOLIFFE, CAPTAIN JOHN, 1751-1777. Captain in 4th Regiment, Virginia Line. Died in service.
Manly, Mrs. L. Tyson.

JONES, PHILIP, ——1753. Surveyor of Baltimore Co., 1729. Justice of the County, 1731.
McIntire, Mrs. William Watson.
Goldsborough, Mrs. George Robins.

KENDALL, COLONEL WILLIAM. Collector of Revenue, Northampton Co., Va., 1660; Burgess, 1657, '62-63, '86; Speaker of the House, 1686.
Smith, Miss Virginia Hope Bryant.
Floyd, Miss Nannie Teackle.

KENDIG, HENRY. Member Committee of Safety, Lancaster Co., Penna., 1775.
McSherry, Mrs. H. Clinton.
Hoogewerff, Mrs. John A.

KENNON, RICHARD, ——1698. Justice of Henrico Co., Va., 1678. Member of the House of Burgesses, 1685-86.
Keyser, Mrs. R. Brent.
Randall, Mrs. Alexander Barton.
Cary, Miss Jane Margaret.

KEY, LIEUTENANT JOHN ROSS, 1754-1821. Second Lieutenant, Captain Price's Rifle Company, Frederick Co., Md., 20 June, 1775. In command of a Troop of Horse at Yorktown, 6 July, 1781.
Howard, Mrs. Charles.

KEY, PHILIP, 1696-1764. Burgess, St. Mary's Co., 1729, '36, 50-54. Member of Council, 1763-64.
Ramsay, Miss Martha Parker.
Howard, Mrs. Charles.

KING, COLONEL MILES, 1747-1814. Captain of Virginia Minute Men, July, 1775, to October, 1776. Represented Elizabeth City Co., Va., in the House of Delegates several times between 1784 and 1798.
Cottman, Mrs. J. Hough.
Cottman, Miss Elizabeth Stewart.

KIRKBRIDE, JOSEPH, 1662-1738. Member of Pennsylvania Assembly, 1698, 1716, '19.
Smith, Mrs Robert C.

121

Milnor, Miss Mary Worthington.

KIRKBRIDE, MAHLON. Member of the Pennsylvania Assembly, 1741.
Smith, Mrs Robert C.

KNAPP, LIEUTENANT JOHN, 1697-1763. Commissioned Lieutenant of Horse, in 9th Regiment, Connecticut Colony. October, 1741.
Dunn, Mrs. Herbert O.

KOLLOCK, COLONEL JACOB, 1692-1772. Justice of the Peace and of the Courts, Sussex Co., Del., 1726-27, 1764. Member of Assembly for the three lower counties, 1732-72; Speaker, 1759-65. Lieutenant, Captain John Shannon's Company, 25 June, 1746. Colonel of the Sussex Regiment in French and Indian War, 1756.
Poe, Mrs. Neilson, Jr.
Poultney, Mrs. Eugene.

KOLLOCK, SIMON, Justice of the Peace and of the Courts, Sussex Co., Del., 1725-27. High Sheriff of the County, 1730-33.
Beasten, Mrs. Charles.

LATIMER, JAMES. Justice of the Peace and Court of Common Pleas for New Castle, Del., 1769; Member Delaware Assembly, 1774. Member of Council of Safety, 1776. Justice Court of Common Pleas and Orphans' Court, 1777.
Cromwell, Mrs. Kennedy.

LAWRENCE, JOHN, 1743-1782. Member Committee of Observation, Frederick Co., 1775. Justice, 1777.
Hunt, Miss Anita Dunbar.
Hunt, Mrs. Dunbar.
Brent, Miss Ida S.
Keyser, Mrs. William.

LAWRENCE, CAPTAIN WILLIAM, 1623-1680. Captain, Queens Co. Militia, 1665-80. Commanded the "Flushing Foote Companie" at the surrender of New York to the Dutch, 1673. One of the patentees of Flushing, L. I., 1645.
Hoffman, Mrs. R. Curzon.

LAWSON, COLONEL ANTHONY. Colonel of Militia; active in the suppression of Bacon's Rebellion, 1676. Laid out City of Norfolk, Va., 1682. Justice, Lower Norfolk Co., 1678-9, '82, '98-99.
Smith, Miss Virginia Hope Bryant.

LAWTON, GEORGE, ——1693, Portsmouth, R. I. Deputy six years, 1665, '72, '75-76, '79-80. Assistant, 1680-86, '89-90.
Blackford, Mrs. Eugene.
Poultney, Mrs. Arthur E.

LEE, HANCOCK, 1653-1729. Burgess, Northumberland Co., Va., 1688.
Clarke, Mrs. Henry F.

LEE, COLONEL RICHARD I., ——1665. Secretary of the Colony of Virginia, and Member of Council, 1663.
Smith, Miss Virginia Hope Bryant.
Lyster, Mrs. Henry F. LeH.
Clarke, Mrs. Henry F.
Calvert, Mrs. Charles Baltimore.

LEE, COLONEL RICHARD II., 1647-1714. Member of the Virginia House of Burgesses, 1677; Colonel of Horse, 1680; Naval Officer for Potomac River, 1699.
Calvert, Mrs. Charles Baltimore.
Lyster, Mrs. Henry F. LeH.

INDEX OF ANCESTORS AND DESCENDANTS.

LEE, GOVERNOR THOMAS, 1690-1751. Member of Council of Virginia, 1732. President of the Council and Acting Governor, 1749.
Lyster, Mrs. Henry F. LeH.

LEE, THOMAS LUDWELL, 1730-1778. Member of the Virginia Committee of Safety, 1775. Judge of the General Court.
Lyster, Mrs. Henry F. LeH.

LEVERETT, SIR JOHN, 1616-1679. Captain in Parliamentary Army, 1644-45. Agent of the Bay Colony to the English Court. Major-General of the Massachusetts Forces, 1663-73. Deputy Governor. Governor of Massachusetts, 1673-79. Knighted by King Charles II., August, 1676, for important services as Governor of the Colony during King Philip's War. Died in office.
Johnson, Mrs. William Woolsey.

LEWIS, COLONEL CHARLES, 1729——. Captain in the French and Indian War, 1755. Colonel of Virginia Minute Men, 1775.
Reynolds, Mrs. William.
Tarleton, Mrs. Robert.
Colvin, Mrs. Alexander B.

LEWIS, COLONEL FIELDING, 1725-1781. Member of the Virginia House of Burgesses, 1773. Chairman of the Spottsylvania Co. Committee of Safety, 1775-76. Chairman of District Committee for the Counties of Caroline, Stafford, King George and Spottsylvania, 1776.
Lewis, Miss Virginia Tayloe.
Buell, Mrs. Daniel H.

LEWIS, JOHN, 1669-1725. Member of the Council of Virginia, 1715.
Reynolds, Mrs. William.
Tarleton, Mrs. Robert.
Lewis, Miss Virginia Tayloe.
Buell, Mrs. Daniel H.
McCandlish, Miss Evelyn Byrd.
Colvin, Mrs. Alexander B.

LEWIS, COLONEL JOHN, 1678-1762. Settled Augusta Co., Va., and located the town of Staunton, 1732. Justice, 1745. High Sheriff, 1748. Surveyor, 1751. Commissioned Colonel of Militia, 1752.
Dammann, Mrs. J. Francis.

LEWIS, ZACHARY, 1731-1803. Captain of Spotsylvania Foot Company, 1758. Served in French and Indian War.
Latané, Miss Lucy Temple.

LIGHTFOOT, HONORABLE PHILIP, 1689-1748. Member of the Council of Virginia, 1733-47. Judge of the General Court. Visitor of William and Mary College, where he founded two scholarships, 1720-28.
Reynolds, Mrs. William.
Tarleton, Mrs. Robert.
Colvin, Mrs. Alexander B.

LIGHTFOOT, LIEUTENANT PHILIP, 1751-1786. Lieutenant in Harrison's Artillery, Continental Line.
Reynolds, Mrs. William.
Tarleton, Mrs. Robert.
Colvin, Mrs. Alexander B.

LINGAN, GEORGE. —— 1708. Justice, Calvert Co., 1679-85; of Quorum, 1694. Burgess, 1695-96.
Dorsey, Miss Ella Loraine.

INDEX OF ANCESTORS AND DESCENDANTS.

LITTLETON, COLONEL NATHANIEL, ——1654. Chief Justice, Accomac Co., Va., 1640. Member of the Council of Virginia, 1652.
Rogers, Mrs. Henry W.
Floyd, Miss Nannie Teackle.

LITTLETON, COLONEL SOUTHEY, 1645-1679. Colonel, Virginia Forces, 1676. Served during Bacon's Rebellion.
Rogers, Mrs. Henry W.

LIVINGSTON, PETER VAN BRUGH, 1710-1793. President of the Provincial Congress, New York, 1775-76. Member of the Committee of One Hundred, 1775.
Livingston, Miss Elizabeth.

LIVINGSTON, COLONEL PHILIP, 1686-1749. Lord of Livingston Manor. Member of Assembly, 1709. Participated in the capture of Port Royal, 1710, and later Colonel of the Provincial Forces. Member of Council, 1725-49. Secretary for Indian Affairs, Province of New York, 1721-49.
Poultney, Mrs. Eugene.
Poe, Mrs. Neilson.
Livingston, Miss Elizabeth.

LIVINGSTON, ROBERT, I., 1654-1728. First Lord of the Manor of Livingston. Member of the Council, Province of New York, 1698, 1701. Member of Assembly, 1709-11.
Armstrong, Miss Mary Hughes.
Rowley, Mrs. C. W.
Poultney, Mrs. Eugene.
Poe, Mrs. Neilson
Livingston, Miss Elizabeth.

LIVINGSTON, ROBERT, II., ——

1790. Lord of Livingston Manor from 1749.
Poultney, Mrs. Eugene.
Poe, Mrs. Neilson.

LLOYD, EDWARD, I., ——1695. Burgess from Lower Norfolk Co., Va., 1644-45. Commander of Anne Arundel Co., Md., 30 July, 1650. Commissioner to make treaty with the Susquehannah Indians. 1652. Burgess, 1654. Member of the Council, 1658-66. A party to treaty with the Susquehannah Indians, 1661. Orders scouting parties against Indians, 20 June, 1662. Commissioner to confer with Virginia, 9 May, 1663.
Tilton, Miss Elizabeth.
Mackubin, Miss Florence.
Coolidge, Mrs. Charles Austin.
Bateman, Mrs. James M. H.
Stokes, Miss Eliza Hughes.
Magruder, Mrs. John Read.
Lürman, Mrs. Gustav W.
Beall, Mrs. Edward Sinclair.
Beall, Miss Louisa Ogle.
Winn, Miss Mary.
Shippen, Mrs. Edward.
Pennington, Miss Elizabeth Lloyd.
Roman, Miss Louisa Lowndes.
Allen, Mrs. Ethan.
Lough, Mrs. Ernest St. George.
Lürman, Mrs. Theodor G.
Tilghman, Miss Mary.
Lowndes, Mrs. Lloyd.
Paca, Miss Juliana Tilghman.
Turnbull, Mrs. John O.
Washburn, Mrs. Charles W.
Preston, Mrs. J. Alexander.
Carroll, Miss Sally Wethered.
Marshall, Mrs. Charles.
Merritt, Mrs. J. Alfred.
Presstman, Mrs. Benjamin.
Earle, Miss Mary Isabel.
Calvert, Mrs. Charles Baltimore.
Emory, Mrs. Campbell D.
Screven, Mrs. George P.
Trimble, Mrs. David C.

Sullivan, Mrs. Felix R.
Pitts, Mrs. Sullivan.
Howard, Mrs. Charles.
Norris, Mrs. Owen.
Dandridge, Miss Anne Spottswood.
Semple, Mrs. Percy.

LLOYD, EDWARD, II., 1670-1718. Burgess, Talbot Co., 1699-1702. President of the Council and Acting Governor of Maryland, 1709-14.
Roman, Miss Louisa Lowndes.
Lough, Mrs. Ernest St. George.
Lowndes, Mrs. Lloyd.
Marshall, Mrs. Charles.
Emory, Mrs. Campbell D.
Screven, Mrs. George P.
Trimble, Mrs. David C.
Sullivan, Mrs. Felix R.
Pitts, Mrs. Sullivan.
Magruder, Mrs. John Read.
Shippen, Mrs. Edward.
Pennington, Miss Elizabeth Lloyd.
Howard, Mrs. Charles.
Tilton, Miss Elizabeth.

LLOYD, EDWARD, III., 1711-1770. Burgess, Talbot Co., 1739. Member of Council.
Roman, Miss Louisa Lowndes.
Lough, Mrs. Ernest St. George.
Lowndes, Mrs. Lloyd.
Emory, Mrs. Campbell D.
Screven, Mrs. George P.
Trimble, Mrs. David C.
Sullivan, Mrs. Felix R.
Pitts, Mrs. Sullivan.
Magruder, Mrs. John Read.
Shippen, Mrs. Edward.
Pennington, Miss Elizabeth Lloyd.
Howard, Mrs. Charles.
Tilton, Miss Elizabeth.

LLOYD, EDWARD, IV., 1744-1796. Burgess, Talbot Co., 1771-73. Member Council of Safety, 1775. Member of Legislature until 1791.

Roman, Miss Louisa Lowndes.
Lough, Mrs. Ernest St. George.
Lowndes, Mrs. Lloyd.
Emory, Mrs. Campbell D.
Screven, Mrs. George P.
Trimble, Mrs. David C.
Sullivan, Mrs. Felix R.
Pitts, Mrs. Sullivan.
Magruder, Mrs. John Read.
Shippen, Mrs. Edward.
Pennington, Miss Elizabeth Lloyd.
Howard, Mrs. Charles.
Tilton, Miss Elizabeth.

LLOYD, JAMES, ——1723. Burgess, Talbot Co., 1712-20.
Lürman, Mrs. Theodor G.
Tilghman, Miss Mary.
Earle, Miss Mary Isabel.
Pitts, Mrs. Sullivan.
Norris, Mrs. Owen.
Dandridge, Miss Anne Spottswood.
Merritt, Mrs. J. Alfred.

LLOYD, COLONEL PHILEMON, 1646-1685. Captain of Horse on Chester and Wye Rivers, 1667; and served against the Indians. Colonel of Horse of Talbot, Kent and Cecil Counties, 1681. Burgess for Talbot County, 1671. Speaker of House of Burgesses, 1678, '81, '83, '84. Commissioner to negotiate treaty with Northern Indians (Five Nations) at Albany, 1682.
Mackubin, Miss Florence.
Coolidge, Mrs. Charles Austin.
Bateman, Mrs. James M. H.
Roman, Miss Louisa Lowndes.
Allen, Mrs. Ethan.
Lough, Mrs. Ernest St. George.
Lürman, Mrs. Theodor G.
Tilghman, Miss Mary.
Lowndes, Mrs. Lloyd.
Paca, Miss Juliana Tilghman.
Turnbull, Mrs. John O.
Washburn, Mrs. Charles W.
Preston, Mrs. J. Alexander.
Carroll, Miss Sally Wethered.

INDEX OF ANCESTORS AND DESCENDANTS.

Lürman, Mrs. Gustav W.
Marshall, Mrs. Charles.
Merritt, Mrs. J. Alfred.
Presstman, Mrs. Benjamin.
Earle, Miss Mary Isabel.
Calvert, Mrs. Charles Baltimore.
Emory, Mrs. Campbell D.
Screven, Mrs. George P.
Trimble, Mrs. David C.
Sullivan, Mrs. Felix R.
Pitts, Mrs. Sullivan.
Stokes, Miss Eliza Hughes.
Magruder, Mrs. John Read.
Beall, Mrs. Edward Sinclair.
Beall, Miss Louisa Ogle.
Winn, Miss Mary.
Shippen, Mrs. Edward.
Pennington, Miss Elizabeth Lloyd.
Howard, Mrs. Charles.
Norris, Mrs. Owen.
Dandridge, Miss Anne Spottswood.
Semple, Mrs. Percy.
Tilton, Miss Elizabeth.

LOGAN, JAMES, 1674-1751. Member of the Provincial Council of Pennsylvania, 1702-47. President of the Council and Acting Governor, 1736-38. Mayor of Philadelphia, 1723. Chief Justice of the Supreme Court of Pennsylvania, 1731-39.
Proudfit, Miss Mary Couper.

LOWE, COLONEL HENRY, ——1717. Commander of St. Mary's Co. Militia, 1696. Judge of the Provincial Court of Maryland, 1697. Deputy Commissary, 1695-1697.
Woods, Mrs. Daniel C.

LOWE, MAJOR JOHN, ——1701. Justice, St. Mary's Co., 1694-97; Burgess, 1697-1701.
Jenkins, Mrs. E. Austin.

LOWE, CAPTAIN MICHAEL, 1743-1820. Captain, Prince George's Co. Militia, 1776.
Jenkins, Mrs. E. Austin.

LOWNDES, CHRISTOPHER. Justice, Prince George's Co., 1753-75, and of the Quorum from 1769.
Lowndes, Mrs. Lloyd.

LUCAS, ROBERT. Member of Pennsylvania Assembly, 1683.
Smith, Mrs Robert C.

LUCKETT, WILLIAM. Captain of Militia, Frederick Co., 1758, in French and Indian War; Justice and County Commissioner, 1765.
Luckett, Miss Mary Stacker.

LUDLOW, GABRIEL, 1704——. Member of Assembly for Orange Co., N. Y., 1739-1745.
Carroll, Miss Sally Wethered.

LUDWELL, PHILIP, I. Member of the Council of Virginia, 1674-78, '81-87. Governor of Carolina, 1689-94.
Lyster, Mrs. Henry F. LeH.
Minor, Miss Mary Willis.

LUDWELL, PHILIP, II., 1672-1727. Member of the Council of Virginia, 1702.
Minor, Miss Mary Willis.
Lyster, Mrs. Henry F. LeH.

LUX, DARBY, 1698-1750. Commissioner to lay out Baltimore Town, 1730. Member of Maryland Assembly, 1748.
Keyser, Mrs. Samuel.
Jackson, Mrs. John J.
Comegys, Mrs. Joseph Parsons.
Black, Mrs. Charles H.
Thompson, Miss Charlotte de Macklot.
Wilson, Miss Mary Bowly.
Wilson, Miss Ella Chapman.
Rogers, Mrs. Henry W.
Wilson, Miss Emma.

Lux, Colonel Darby, ——
1795. Member Committee of Observation, 1775-76. Member Maryland Convention, 1775.
Black, Mrs. Charles H.

Lyman, John, 1623-1690. Ensign, Lieutenant, and Captain of Northampton (Mass.) Troops. In command at "Fall's Fight," near Deerfield, Mass., 18 May, 1676.
Fowler, Miss Amélie de Pau.

Lynde, Joseph, 1636-1727. Member of General Court. Colonel of Middlesex Regiment, Mass. One of the Committee of Safety, 1689. Representative, 1674, '79, '80.
Hamilton, Mrs. Levin Mayer.

Lynn, David. Justice, Frederick Co., 1748.
Boyd, Mrs. Allen Richards.

Lytle, Captain William, 1728-1779. Commissioned Captain, Pennsylvania Forces, 12 April, 1750.
Blackwell, Mrs. Josiah Low.

Maccubbin, Joseph, 1739-1800. Commissioned 2d Lieutenant, 22 February, 1776; 1st Lieutenant, 11 April, 1776, Maryland Militia.
Jenkins, Mrs. E. Austin.

Maccubbin, Nicholas, 1710-——. High Sheriff, Anne Arundel Co., 1732-34.
Mackubin, Miss Florence.
Calvert, Mrs. Charles Baltimore.

Maccubbin, Zachariah, ——
1756. High Sheriff of Anne Arundel Co., 1729-32.
Allen, Mrs. Ethan.
Beall, Mrs. Edward Sinclair.
Beall, Miss Louisa Ogle.
Mackubin, Miss Florence.
Turnbull, Mrs. John O.
Washburn, Mrs. Charles W.
Preston, Mrs. J. Alexander.
Carroll, Miss Sally Wethered.
Ligon, Miss Elizabeth Worthington Dorsey.
Calvert, Mrs. Charles Baltimore.
Winn, Miss Mary.

Macgill, Reverend James, 1701-1779. Rector of Queen Caroline Parish, Anne Arundel Co., 1730-76.
James, Mrs. Norman.
Macgill, Miss Louisa.
Carrington, Miss Henrietta Penniman.
Gibson, Mrs. George T. M.
Gary, Mrs. E. Stanley.
Harrison, Mrs. Edmund Pitts.
Penniman, Miss Rebecca.
Parsons, Mrs. Joel Burton.

Mackall, James John, 1717-1772. Burgess, Calvert Co., 1745-65.
Simpson, Mrs. Edward.

Mackall, Honorable James, 1677-1716. Burgess, 1712-1716.
Mackenzie, Miss Mary G. M.

Mackall, Colonel John, 1669-1739. Burgess from Calvert Co., 1704-39. Speaker of the House, 1725-34, '39.
Simpson, Mrs. Edward.
Mackall, Miss Sally Somervell.

Magruder, Samuel, ——1711. Burgess, Prince George's Co., 1705-1707.
Jenkins, Mrs. E. Austin.

Manigault, Gabriel, ——
1781. Member of South Carolina Assembly, 1748, '61, '72, etc. Treasurer of the Province, 1740.
Morris, Miss Elizabeth M.

INDEX OF ANCESTORS AND DESCENDANTS.

MARSHALL, CAPTAIN SAMUEL, ——1675. Killed in the "Swamp Fight," King Philip's War, 19 December, 1675.
Franklin, Mrs. Fabian.

MARSHALL, COLONEL THOS., 1730-1802. Lieutenant of Volunteers, Virginia Forces, in French and Indian War, 1755; Colonel of 2d Virginia Regiment in the Revolution.
Carroll, Mrs. Mary Randolph.
Page, Mrs. William C.

MARSHAM, RICHARD, ——1713. Justice, Calvert Co., 1679-81.
Parran, Mrs. James Bourne.

MARSTON, THOMAS, 1615-1690. Representative to the General Court of Massachusetts, 1677, and to the General Court of New Hampshire, 1680-84.
Stewart, Mrs. David.
Hamilton, Mrs. W. T.

MARTIAN, NICHOLAS, 1591-1657. Member of the Virginia House of Burgesses, 1632.
Buell, Mrs. Daniel H.
Minor, Miss Mary Willis.

MARTIN, COLONEL JAMES, ——1748. High Sheriff, Worcester Co., 1742-45. School Commissioner. Colonel, Worcester Co. Militia.
Campbell, Mrs. Duncan.
Campbell, Miss Ella Calvert.

MARTIN, COLONEL JAMES, 1742——. Colonel of Militia, Guilford, N. C., 1775.
Mercer, Mrs. Carroll.

MASON, COLONEL GEORGE, I., ——1686. Justice, Stafford Co., Va.; Sheriff, 1670; Clerk of the County Court, 1673. County Lieutenant, 1675. Burgess, 1676.
Rowland, Miss Elizabeth Mason.
Calvert, Mrs. Charles Baltimore.

MASON, COLONEL GEORGE, II., 1670-1716. Captain of Potomac Rangers. Justice, Stafford Co., Va., 1689-92. Sheriff of Stafford Co. County Lieutenant, 1699-1700.
Rowland, Miss Elizabeth Mason.
Calvert, Mrs. Charles Baltimore.

MASON, COLONEL GEORGE, III., 1692-1735. Justice, Stafford Co., Va., 1713; Burgess, 1718, '23, '26. County Lieutenant, 1719. Removed to Charles Co., Md., 1730.
Rowland, Miss Elizabeth Mason.

MASON, HUGH, 1606-1678. Member of General Court of Massachusetts. Magistrate. Captain of Watertown Company, 1652.
Hamilton, Mrs. Levin Mayer.

MASON, THOMSON, 1733-1785. Trustee of Leesburg, 1758. Member Virginia House of Burgesses, 1758-59, '61, '67-71, '74. Member of Assembly, 1777-79, '83. Judge of the General Court, 1778.
Rowland, Miss Elizabeth Mason.

MAYNADIER, REVEREND DANIEL, I., ——1745. Rector of St. Margaret's Parish, Anne Arundel Co., 1712. Rector of St. Peter's Parish, Talbot Co., 1714-15.

INDEX OF ANCESTORS AND DESCENDANTS.

Screven, Mrs. George P.
Trimble, Mrs. David C.
Sullivan, Mrs. Felix R.
Pitts, Mrs. Sullivan.

MAYNADIER, REVEREND DANIEL, II., 1724-1772. Rector of Great Choptank Parish, Dorchester Co., 1764-72.
Screven, Mrs. George P.
Trimble, Mrs. David C.
Sullivan, Mrs. Felix R.
Pitts, Mrs. Sullivan.

MCALLISTER, COLONEL RICHARD, ——1795. Justice, York Co., Penna., 1771-74. Member Committee of Safety, 1775. Member Provincial Congress. 1775. Colonel, 3d Battalion, York Co., 1775-77. County Lieutenant, 1777-80.
Morris, Mrs. Charles Manigault.
Morris, Miss Elizabeth M.

MCCLINTOCK, REVEREND SAMUEL, 1732-1804. Chaplain, 2d New Hampshire Regiment, June-July, 1775.
Stewart, Mrs. David.
Hamilton, Mrs. W. T.

MCKEAN, THOMAS, 1723-1817. Signer of the Declaration of Independence. President of Congress. Three times Governor of Pennsylvania. Chief Justice of Pennsylvania for twenty-two years.
Redwood, Mrs. Frank T.
Screven, Mrs. George P.
Sullivan, Mrs. Felix R.

MCKIM, LIEUTENANT THOS. 1710-1784. Commissioned by the Governor of Delaware, Lieutenant of Militia in the Upper Regiment from Brandywine Hundred, 1756. Justice of the Peace and Judge of the Court of Common Pleas, New Castle, Del., 1774.
von Kapff, Mrs. Frederick, Jr.
Wilson, Miss Mary Bowly.
Wetmore, Mrs. Russell.
Wilson, Miss Ella Chapman.
Hayes, Mrs. John S.
Heyward, Mrs. Wilson P.
Wilson, Miss Emma.
Wilson, Miss Ella C.

MCKINNIE, BARNABY. Justice, Bertie Co., N. C., 1724-28; Edgecombe Co., 1739. Member North Carolina Assembly, 1735.
Smith, Mrs. Frederick Henry.

MCPHERSON, COLONEL ROBERT, 1730-1789. Captain, 3d Pennsylvania Battalion, 1758, and in Forbes' expedition against Fort Duquesne. Sheriff of York Co., Penna., 1762-65; Justice, 1764-75. Member of Assembly, 1765-67; '81-85. County Treasurer, 1755, '68. Colonel of Pennsylvania Militia in the Revolution.
McCrackin, Mrs. Alexander.
Rogers, Mrs. Henry W.

MERRYMAN, JOHN, 1737-1814. Member Committee of Observation, Baltimore Co., 1774-76. Judge of Orphans' Court, Baltimore Co., 1784.
Black, Mrs. Charles H.

MIDDLETON, CAPTAIN THOS. 1674-1744. Prince George's Co., Md. Captain of Rangers in Indian disturbances, 1698.
Leakin, Miss Margaret Dobbin.
Sioussat, Mrs. Albert Willis.

MILLER, MICHAEL, ——1700. Burgess, Kent Co., 1685.
Chatard, Mrs. Thomas M.

MINOR, GARRETT. Member

of Committee of Safety, Louisa Co., Va., 1775.
Polk, Mrs. William Stewart.

MINOR, JOHN, 1735-1800. Member of Committee of Safety, Caroline Co., Va., 1774-75.
Poultney, Mrs. Arthur E.
Minor, Miss Mary Willis.

MITCHELL, WILLIAM, ——— 1685. Member of Council of Maryland, 1649.
Spencer, Mrs. Jervis.
Mullan, Mrs. John.
Boone, Mrs. Daniel A.

MOALE, JOHN, I., 1697-1740. Burgess, Baltimore Co., 1729.
Early, Mrs. Alexander R.
Slingluff, Mrs. Fielder C.
Nicholas, Mrs. Wilson Cary.

MOALE, JOHN, II., 1731-1798. Burgess from Baltimore Co., 1767. Member of Convention, 1774-75, and of Committee of Observation, 1775. Lieutenant-Colonel, Baltimore Town Battalion, 1776.
Early, Mrs. Alexander R.
Nicholas, Mrs. Wilson Cary.

MONROE, PRESIDENT JAMES, 1758-1831. Lieutenant Virginia Forces, 28 September, 1775. Aide de Camp to Lord Stirling, with rank of Major, 1777-78. Member of Virginia Assembly. United States Senator. President of the United States, 1817-25.
McIntire, Mrs. William Watson.

MOORE, BERNARD. Member of the Virginia House of Burgesses, 1748.
Clark, Mrs. Frank P.

MOORE, JOHN. Collector of the Port of Philadelphia, 1703.
Pitts, Mrs. Sullivan.
Dandridge, Miss Anne Spottswood.

MOORE, WILLIAM, 1699-1783. Colonel, First Associated Regiment, Chester Co., Penna., 1747-48, and re-commissioned in 1755. Member of Assembly. President of the County Court.
Pitts, Mrs. Sullivan.
Dandridge, Miss Anne Spottswood.

MORGAN, HENRY, ———1663. High Sheriff and Commander of the Militia of Kent Co., 1648. Justice, 1650-59. Burgess, 1659.
Emory, Mrs. Campbell D.
Pitts, Mrs. Sullivan.
Magruder, Mrs. John Read.
Shippen, Mrs. Edward.
Pennington, Miss Elizabeth Lloyd.
Lowndes, Mrs. Lloyd.
Sullivan, Mrs. Felix R.
Screven, Mrs. George P.
Howard, Mrs. Charles.

MORGAN, CAPTAIN JACOB, 1716-1792. Captain, 1st Battalion, Pennsylvania Troops, 1755. Captain in 2d Battalion, 1757. Adjutant, 1760.
O'Ferrall, Mrs. Frank F.

MORRIS, ANTHONY, 1654-1707. Judge of the Court of Common Pleas, 1692. Judge of Supreme Court of Pennsylvania, 1694. Member of Provincial Council, 1695. Mayor of Philadelphia, 1704.
Murray, Mrs. Francis Key.

MORRIS, HONORABLE LEWIS, I., 1671-1746. Chief Justice of New York, 1720-38. First Governor of the

Province of New Jersey, 1738-46.
Morris, Miss Elizabeth M.

MORRIS, HONORABLE LEWIS, II., 1698-1762. Judge of the High Court of Admiralty, Province of New York.
Morris, Miss Elizabeth M.

MORRIS, HONORABLE LEWIS, III., 1726-1798. Member of Congress, 1775. Signer the Declaration of Independence. Brigadier-General, New York State Militia.
Morris, Miss Elizabeth M.

MORRIS, HONORABLE ROBERT, 1734-1806. Signer of the Declaration of Independence.
Slingluff, Mrs. Fielder C.

MORTON, CAPTAIN JOHN, 1730-1779. Member of Committee of Safety, 1775. Captain in the Fourth Regiment Virginia Continental Line, 19 February, 1776.
Ridgely, Mrs. John.

MOSELEY, COLONEL EDWARD, 1661-1736. Colonel and Justice of Princess Anne Co., Va.; High Sheriff, 1707-8. Member of the House of Burgesses. Knight of the Golden Horseshoe, 1710-22.
Smith, Miss Virginia Hope Bryant.

MOSELEY, EDWARD HACK, ——1783. Burgess, Princess Anne Co., Va., 1761-69; Colonel and Sheriff of the County.
Smith, Miss Virginia Hope Bryant.

MOSELY, SAMUEL, 1641-1680. Commissioner to treat with Narragansett Indians. Commander of Troop in King Philip's War.
Hamilton, Mrs. Levin Mayer.

MOTTE, ISAAC, 1700-1770. For thirty years Treasurer of South Carolina.
Taylor, Mrs. Winfield J.

MUHLENBERG, MAJOR - GENERAL JOHN PETER GABRIEL, 1746-1807. Colonel of the Eighth Virginia Regiment, December, 1775. Brigadier-General, Continental Army, 21 February, 1777. Member of Congress, 1789-95, 1799-1801. United States Senator, 1801.
McSherry, Mrs. H. Clinton.
Hoogewerff, Mrs. John A.

MUMFORD, THOMAS. Went to Virginia with the First Supply, 1607. One of the Incorporators named in the second charter of Virginia, 28 May, 1609.
Mason, Mrs. John Thomson.

MURDOCK, REVEREND GEORGE, ——1761. Rector of Rock Creek Parish, Prince George's and Frederick Counties, 1726-61.
Mercein, Mrs. Thomas R.
Stokes, Miss Eliza Hughes.

MURDOCK, WILLIAM, ——1769. Burgess, Prince George's Co., 1749-69. Member of Committee to represent Maryland in the Stamp Act Congress, held in New York, October, 1765.
Kerfoot, Mrs. Samuel Humes.
Beckwith, Mrs. Franklin H.
Woods, Mrs. Daniel C.

MURRAY, DOCTOR WILLIAM (Cambridge), 1696-1763. Justice, Dorchester Co., 1734-57.
Pitts, Mrs. Sullivan.

MURRAY, DOCTOR WILLIAM (Chestertown), 1708-1769. Justice, Kent Co., 1750.
Pitts, Mrs. Sullivan.

NASH, COLONEL JOHN. Member of the Virginia House of Burgesses, 1755-65. Captain of a company in the Indian Wars. High Sheriff, Prince Edward Co., 1758.
Ligon, Miss Elizabeth Worthington Dorsey.

NEALE, CAPTAIN JAMES, 1615-1684. Member Provincial Council of Maryland, 1643-44, and 1660-61. Burgess, 1666. Commissioner of the Treasury, 1643. Attorney of Lord Baltimore at Amsterdam to protest against the seating of the Dutch and Swedes on the Delaware River and Bay. Commissioned Captain by Lord Baltimore (1661) to raise troops against the Dutch on Delaware Bay.
Keyser, Mrs. William.
Mackubin, Miss Florence.
Coolidge, Mrs. Charles Austin.
Bateman, Mrs. James M. H.
Tilton, Miss Elizabeth.
Hunt, Mrs. Dunbar.
Hunt, Miss Anita Dunbar.
Brent, Miss Nanine Maria.
Brent, Miss Ida S.
Sullivan, Mrs. Felix R.
Roman, Miss Louisa Lowndes.
Lough, Mrs. Ernest St. George.
Lürman, Mrs. Theodor G.
Tilghman, Miss Mary.
Lowndes, Mrs. Lloyd.
Paca, Miss Juliana Tilghman.
Turnbull, Mrs. John O.
Woods, Mrs. Daniel C.
Washburn, Mrs. Charles W.
Preston, Mrs. J. Alexander.
Trimble, Mrs. David C.
Pitts, Mrs. Sullivan.
Stokes, Miss Eliza Hughes.
Milnor, Miss Mary Worthington.

Magruder, Mrs. John Read.
Lürman, Mrs. Gustav W.
Beall, Mrs. Edward Sinclair.
Beall, Miss Louisa Ogle.
Winn, Miss Mary.
Shippen, Mrs. Edward.
Pennington, Miss Elizabeth Lloyd.
Williams, Mrs. Charles Phelps.
Manly, Mrs. L. Tyson.
Carroll, Miss Sally Wethered.
Marshall, Mrs. Charles.
Merritt, Mrs. J. Alfred.
Presstman, Mrs. Benjamin.
Denman, Mrs. H. B.
Redwood, Mrs. Frank T.
Earle, Miss Mary Isabel.
Calvert, Mrs. Charles Baltimore.
Emory, Mrs. Campbell D.
Screven, Mrs. George P.
Penniman, Mrs. George Dobbin.
Howard, Mrs. Charles.
Norris, Mrs. Owen.
Dandridge, Miss Anne Spottswood.
Mackenzie, Miss Mary G. M.
Semple, Mrs. Percy.
Baughman, Mrs. Mary Jane.
Jones, Mrs. George Alphonzo.

NELSON, MAJOR JOHN, 1750-1827. Captain, 7th Virginia, 28 October, 1776; retired, 4 September, 1778. Served subsequently as Major in a Virginia State Regiment.
Ober, Mrs. Robert.

NELSON, ROGER, 1735-1815. Second Lieutenant, 5th Maryland, 1779, and 1st Lieutenant, 1780. Wounded and taken prisoner at Camden, 1780. Transferred to Baylor's Dragoons, 1782, and served to the end of the war. Member of Congress, 1804-10.
Steele, Miss Rosa.
Beckwith, Mrs. Franklin H.

NELSON, SECRETARY THOMAS,

INDEX OF ANCESTORS AND DESCENDANTS.

NICHOLAS, 1716-1782. Member of the Council of Virginia, 1764. President of the Council. Secretary of State. One of the Governors of William and Mary College.
Ober, Mrs. Robert.

NICHOLAS, DOCTOR GEORGE, 1680-1734. Represented William and Mary College in the Virginia House of Burgesses, 1730.
Randall, Mrs. Alexander Barton.

NICHOLAS, ROBERT CARTER, 1728-1780. Member of the Virginia House of Burgesses, 1758, '66-74. Speaker, 1764-70. Treasurer of Virginia. Member of the various revolutionary conventions, and President, *pro tem.*, of that of 1775.
Carter, Miss Mary Coles.
Nicholas, Miss Cary Ann.
Nicholas, Miss Elizabeth Cary.
Randall, Mrs. Alexander Barton.

NICHOLSON, COLONEL JOSEPH, 1709-1787. High Sheriff of Kent Co., 1763-68; Colonel of the County Militia; Deputy Commissary for many years.
Shippen, Mrs. Edward.
Magruder, Mrs. John Read.

NICHOLSON, JOSEPH, JR., 1734-1786. Justice, Kent Co., 1760. Member of Maryland Convention, 1775.
Magruder, Mrs. John Read.

NICOLL, MATTHIAS, 1621-1687. Captain in the British Army, 1664. Secretary of the Province of New York, 1664-80. Member of the King's Council, 1667-80. Speaker of Provincial Assembly, 1683. Judge of the Court of Admiralty, 1686. Mayor of New York, 1672.
Mason, Mrs. John Thomson.

NICOLL, HONORABLE WILLIAM, 1657-1723. Member of Council, New York, 1691-98. Speaker of Provincial Assembly, 1702-18. Attorney-General, 1687-90.
Mason, Mrs. John Thomson.

NICOLS, REVEREND HENRY, 1678-1748. Rector of St. Michael's Church, Talbot Co., 1708-48.
Marshall, Mrs. Charles.
Merritt, Mrs. J. Alfred.

NOTLEY, HONORABLE THOS. ——1679. Burgess, St. Mary's Co., 1665-71, and for St. Mary's City, 1671-74. Member of Council, 1676-79. Deputy Governor, 1678.
Denman, Mrs. H. B.
Williams, Mrs. Charles Phelps.
Jones, Mrs. George Alphonzo.

OGDEN, JOHN, 1610-1681 (Elizabeth Towne). Magistrate, 1656. Of Upper House, General Court, 1660-61, Colony of Connecticut. Patentee, 1662. Member of King's Council, Province of New Jersey, 1665. Schout and Acting Governor of the English Colony in East Jersey, 1673, during the Dutch occupation.
Camak, Miss M. Annie.

OGLE, GOVERNOR SAMUEL, 1694-1752. Governor of Maryland, 1732, 1735-42, 1747-52.
Lewis, Miss Virginia Tayloe.
Beall, Miss Louisa Ogle.
Shawhan, Mrs. Charles S.

OWEN, ROBERT, ——1697. Jus-

133

tice, Merion, Pa., 1695-97. Member of Pennsylvania Assembly, 1695-97.
Blackford, Mrs. Eugene.
Poultney, Mrs. Arthur E.

PACA, AQUILA, ——1721. High Sheriff, Baltimore Co., 1702-03; Burgess, 1708.
Paca, Miss Juliana Tilghman.

PACA, WILLIAM, 1740-1799. Signer of the Declaration of Independence, 1776. Governor of Maryland, 1782-85.
Paca, Miss Juliana Tilghman.

PAGE, COLONEL JOHN, 1627-1692. Member of the Council of Virginia, 1683-92. Colonel of York Co.
Ober, Mrs. Robert.
Minor, Miss Mary Willis.
Keyser, Mrs. R. Brent.
Randall, Mrs. Alexander Barton.
Cary, Miss Jane Margaret.

PAGE, GOVERNOR JOHN, 1744-1808. Member of the Virginia House of Burgesses, 1771. Member of Council, 1773. Member of Congress, 1789-97. Governor of Virginia, 1802-03.
Minor, Miss Mary Willis.

PAGE, HONORABLE MANN I., 1691-1730. Member of the Council of Virginia, 1714-31.
Ober, Mrs. Robert.
Minor, Miss Mary Willis.
Keyser, Mrs. R. Brent.
Randall, Mrs. Alexander Barton.
Cary, Miss Jane Margaret.

PAGE, HONORABLE MANN II., 1718——. Member of the Virginia House of Burgesses, 1762-65. Visitor of William and Mary College, 1750.
Minor, Miss Mary Willis.

PAGE, HONORABLE MATTHEW, 1660-1704. One of the original Board of Trustees for William and Mary College, 1693. Member of the Council of Virginia, 1699.
Ober, Mrs. Robert.
Minor, Miss Mary Willis.
Keyser, Mrs. R. Brent.
Randall, Mrs. Alexander Barton.
Cary, Miss Jane Margaret.

PARKE, HONORABLE DANIEL. Member of the Council of Virginia, 1692. Captain-General and Governor of the Leeward Islands.
Goldsborough, Mrs. George Robins.

PARKE, WILLIAM, 1595-1685. Member of the Ancient and Honorable Artillery Company, 1638. Represented Roxbury, Mass., in the General Court, 1635-67, the longest known term of service under the old charter.
Williams, Miss Sue Campbell.
Mackenzie, Miss Mary G. M.

PARSONS, MAJOR-GENERAL SAMUEL HOLDEN, 1737-1789. Member of Connecticut Assembly eighteen consecutive sessions. King's Attorney, 1773. Major, 1770, Connecticut Forces. Major-General, 1780.
Winchester, Mrs. H. Carroll.

PARTRIDGE, REVEREND RALF, ——1658. Pastor of the Church at Duxbury, Mass., 1636-1658.
Powell, Mrs. William S.

PARTRIDGE, SAMUEL, 1645-1740. Quartermaster, Major John Pynchon's Troop, 1688. Deputy, 1683, '85,

'86. Assistant. Associate Judge, Hampshire County Court, 1685. Judge of the Court of Common Pleas, 1692-1740, Colony of Massachusetts Bay.
Jacobs, Mrs. Jesse Elliott.
Wood, Mrs. Joseph C.

PEABODY, LIEUTENANT FRANCIS, 1614-1697. Lieutenant in the Militia, Topsfield, Mass., 1668.
Powell, Mrs. William S.

PEALE, CHARLES WILLSON, 1741 - 1827. Captain of Pennsylvania Volunteers, 1776, and served in the battles of Trenton and Germantown. Member of Pennsylvania Legislature, 1779.
Atkinson, Mrs. Robert.
Gamble, Mrs. Robert Howard.
Iglehart, Mrs. C. Iredell.
Robinson, Miss Louisa Hall.

PEARCE, CAPTAIN DANIEL. Burgess, Kent Co., 1709-13.
Merritt, Mrs. J. Alfred.

PEARCE, WILLIAM, ——1720. Burgess, Cecil Co., 1694, 1706-07. Chief Judge, Kent Co., 1714-15.
Turnbull, Mrs. John O
Preston, Mrs. J. Alexander.
Carroll, Miss Sally Wethered.

PEARSON, ROBERT. Burgess of Trenton, N. J., 1746.
Thom, Mrs. J. Pembroke.
Duke, Mrs. Basil.

PEMBERTON, DOCTOR THOS., 1653-1693. As Surgeon, accompanied expedition to Canada, 1690.
Hall, Miss Elizabeth Ward.
Hall, Miss Mary Stickney.

PENGILLY, LIEUTENANT JOHN, ——1709. Ensign, Massachusetts Militia, 1692; Lieutenant, 1700.
Fisher, Mrs. William A.
Woodruff, Mrs. George C.

PENHALLOW, SAMUEL, 1665-1726. Deputy to the General Court, 1698. Speaker of the House, 1699. Treasurer, 1699-1726. Assistant, 1702. Secretary, 1704. Judge of Superior Court, 1714-17. Chief Justice, 1717 - 26. Commissary-General, 1712. Colony of New Hampshire.
Hall, Miss Elizabeth Ward.
Hall, Miss Mary Stickney.

PENNOCK, JOSEPH, 1677-1771. Member of Pennsylvania Assembly, 1716-28.
Martin, Mrs. Frank.

PEPPERRELL, LIEUTENANT-COLONEL WILLIAM, 1654-1754, Kittery, Me. Captain of the company of Provincial Militia (1714) Commandant of His Majesty's Fort at Kittery Point, 1714. Subsequently Lieutenant-Colonel of the Provincial Militia of York Co., Me. Justice of the Court of Common Pleas, 1715-30. Deputy to the General Court of Massachusetts, 1696 ——.
Belknap, Mrs. Charles.
Browne, Mrs. Samuel Tracy.
Asshcton, Mrs. William Herbert.

PERRY, WILLIAM, 1746-1799. Justice, Caroline Co., 1774. Receiver of Alienation Fees for the Proprietary of Maryland.
Markoe, Mrs. Frank.
Sibley, Mrs. Clarence.
Dugan, Mrs. Hammond.

PETERS, WILLIAM, ——circ, 1790. Came to Pennsylvania, 1736-7. Justice of

County Court, of Court of Common Pleas, and of Orphans' Court. Deputy Secretary of Province of Pennsylvania, and Clerk of the Provincial Court, 1757. Member of Pennsylvania Assembly, 1752-56.
Buchanan, Mrs. Roberdeau.

PEYTON, FRANCIS, ——1808. Member of the Virginia House of Burgesses, 1769-1774; Member of Convention, 1775.
Luckett, Miss Mary Stacker.

PEYTON, VALENTINE, 1686-1751. Justice, Prince William Co., Va., 1743. Sheriff, 1749; Burgess. 1736.
James, Mrs. Norman.
Luckett, Miss Mary Stacker.
Macgill, Miss Louisa.
Gibson, Mrs. George T. M.
Gary, Mrs. E. Stanley.
Gibson, Mrs. Charles H.
Cottman, Mrs. Clarence.
Powell, Miss Sarah Harrison.

PHELPS, WILLIAM, 1599-1672. One of the eight Commissioners appointed by the Bay Colony, 3 March, 1636, "to govern the people of Connecticut." Member of Court, in 1637, at Hartford, that declared war against the Pequots. Assistant, 1638-43.
Franklin, Mrs. Fabian.

PHILPOT, BRIAN, 1695——. Justice, Baltimore Co., 1750.
Ridgely, Mrs. John.
Philpot, Miss Mary Dennison.

PHILPOT, ENSIGN BRIAN, 1748-1812. Ensign, Smallwood's Regiment, 14 January, 1776.
Philpot, Miss Mary Dennison.

PILE, HONORABLE JOHN. Member of the Council of Maryland, 1649-50.
Brent, Miss Ida S.
Keyser, Mrs. William.
Hunt, Mrs. Dunbar.
Hunt, Miss Anita Dunbar.

PLAISTEAD, JOHN, 1660——. Judge of the Superior Court of New Hampshire, 1699. Chief Justice, 1716. Speaker of Assembly, 1695, 1718, '27.
Franklin, Mrs. Fabian.

PLAISTED, LIEUTENANT ROGER, ——1675. Deputy, 1663-64, '73. Lieutenant, Captain Charles Frost's Company, 1670. Killed (1675) in a fight with the Indians.
Franklin, Mrs. Fabian.

PLATER, ATTORNEY-GENERAL GEORGE, ——1707. Attorney-General of Maryland, 1691, '95-96.
Pitts, Mrs. Sullivan.
Magruder, Mrs. John Read.
Shippen, Mrs. Edward.
Pennington, Miss Elizabeth Lloyd.
Lowndes, Mrs. Lloyd.
Howard, Mrs. Charles.

PLATER, HONORABLE GEORGE, 1695-1755. Member of Council, 1732-55. Deputy Secretary of Maryland, 1755.
Roman, Miss Louisa Lowndes.
Lough, Mrs. Ernest St. George.
Pennington, Miss Elizabeth Lloyd.
Lowndes, Mrs. Lloyd.
Emory, Mrs. Campbell D.
Screven, Mrs. George P.
Trimble, Mrs. David C.
Sullivan, Mrs. Felix R.
Pitts, Mrs. Sullivan.
Magruder, Mrs. John Read.
Shippen, Mrs. Edward.

INDEX OF ANCESTORS AND DESCENDANTS.

Howard, Mrs. Charles.
Shawhan, Mrs. Charles S.
Tilton, Miss Elizabeth.

PLOWDEN, SIR EDMUND, 1590-1659. Founder, Governor, Captain-General, and Earl Palatine of New Albion (now New Jersey). Charter granted by Charles I.
Jenkins, Mrs. Michael.
Jenkins, Mrs. Edmund Plowden.
Hinckley, Mrs. Robert.
O'Donnell, Mrs. Columbus.

POLK, DAVID, 1705-1778. Justice, Somerset Co., 1763.
Polk, Miss Anna Maria.
Gorter, Mrs. Gosse Onno.
Jenkins, Mrs. E. Austin.

POLK, THOMAS, 1735-1793. Member of Provincial Assembly of North Carolina and signer of the Mecklenberg Declaration of Independence.
Brown, Miss Lizinka Campbell.

POPE, NATHANIEL, ——1660. Member of Maryland Assembly, 1642. Lieutenant-Colonel of Militia, Westmoreland Co., Va.
Minor, Miss Mary Willis.

POWELL, COLONEL LEVIN, 1738-1810. Member Committee of Observation, 1774. Major of Militia, 1775. Lieutenant-Colonel Grayson's Additional Continental Regiment, 1777-1778; Presidential Elector; member Virginia Convention, 1788.
Gibson, Mrs. Charles H.
Cottman, Mrs. Clarence.
Powell, Miss Sarah Harrison.
Semple, Mrs. Percy.

PRICE, COLONEL THOMAS,—— 1795. Justice, Frederick Co., 1762-1776. Captain of Riflemen, 1775. Major, 1776. Colonel, 2d Regiment, Maryland Line, 1777.
King, Miss Virginia.
Pearre, Miss Mary Smith Worthington.
Phenix, Miss Florence.
Blackiston, Mrs. A. Hooton.
Smith, Miss Clementine.
Smith, Miss Sallie Cox.

PRINCE, GOVERNOR THOMAS, 1600-1673. Assistant, Plymouth Colony, from 1635. Governor, 1634-38, and 1657-72. Member of the Council of War, and "went forth against the Pequot Indians," 1637. Commissioner for the United Colonies, 1645, '50, '61.
Green, Mrs. William.

PROVOST, DAVID, I., 1608-1656. Commander at Fort Good Hope, 1642-47. First of the "nine men," 1652. Sergeant, Blue Flag Company, Burgher Corps, New Amsterdam, 1653. First separate Schout at Breuckelen, 1655. Schout and Secretary of Breuckelen, Amersfoort and Midwont until his death.
Lürman, Mrs. Gustav W.

PROVOST, DAVID, II., 1670-1724. Captain in Colonel Abraham de Peyster's Regiment, New York City, 1700. Major, 1710. Lieutenant-Colonel, 1716. Member of General Assembly, 1702-11. Member of Council, 1708-10.
Lürman, Mrs. Gustav W.

QUINCY, LIEUTENANT-COLONEL EDMUND, 1627-1698, Braintree. Deputy to the General Court. Major. Lieutenant-Colonel in

INDEX OF ANCESTORS AND DESCENDANTS.

command of the Suffolk Regiment, 1698, Colony of Massachusetts Bay.
Woods, Mrs. Daniel C.

QUINCY, COLONEL JOHN, 1689-1767, Boston, Mass. Member of the House of Representatives, 1717, 1719-41; Speaker, 1729-41; Member of His Majesty's Council, 1742, 1747-53; Colonel of the Suffolk Regiment.
Woods, Mrs. Daniel C.

RAMSAY, DAVID, 1749-1815. Surgeon of the Charleston Artillery Company at siege of Savannah, 1781. Member of South Carolina Legislature, 1776-1781. Member of Council of South Carolina. Member of Congress, 1782, '85.
Ramsay, Miss Martha Parker.

RANDOLPH, ISHAM, 1687-1742. Member of Virginia House of Burgesses, 1738-40. Colonel of Militia, 1740. Adjutant-General of Virginia, 1738-42.
McLean, Mrs. Thomas Chalmers.
Gordon, Miss Margaret
Keyser, Mrs. R. Brent.
Buchanan, Miss Esther Sidney.
Randall, Mrs. Alexander Barton.
Cary, Mrs. Wilson Miles.
Cary, Miss Jane Margaret.

RANDOLPH, COLONEL RICHARD (of Curles), 1691-1748. Member of Virginia House of Burgesses, 1728, 1736-40. Treasurer of Virginia, 1736-42. Colonel of Henrico Co.
McLean, Mrs. Thomas Chalmers.
Gordon, Miss Margaret.
Keyser, Mrs. R. Brent.

Randall, Mrs. Alexander Barton.
Cary, Miss Jane Margaret.

RANDOLPH, COLONEL THOMAS, 1689-1730. Justice of Henrico Co., Va., from 1714, and Presiding Justice of Goochland Co., 1728. Colonel of Militia and County Lieutenant.
Keyser, Mrs. R. Brent.
Randall, Mrs. Alexander Barton.
Cary, Miss Jane Margaret.

RANDOLPH, COLONEL THOMAS MANN, 1741-1793. Member of the Virginia House of Burgesses, 1772-73, and of Convention, 1775-76. Colonel of Militia. Member of the Virginia Senate, 1776, and of the House of Delegates, 1784-88.
Keyser, Mrs. R. Brent.
Randall, Mrs. Alexander Barton.
Cary, Miss Jane Margaret.

RANDOLPH, WILLIAM, 1650-1711. Clerk of Henrico Co., Va., 1673-83. Captain, 1680. Attorney-General of Virginia, 1696. Speaker of the House of Burgesses, 1698. Colonel of his county.
McLean, Mrs. Thomas Chalmers.
Gordon, Miss Margaret.
Carroll, Mrs. Mary Randolph.
Page, Mrs. William C.
Randall, Mrs. Alexander Barton.
Keyser, Mrs. R. Brent.
Buchanan, Miss Esther Sidney.
Cary, Mrs. Wilson Miles.
Cary, Miss Jane Margaret.

RANDOLPH, COLONEL WILLIAM (of Tuckahoe), 1713-1745. Justice for Goochland Co., Va., 1735-44.

Member of the House of Burgesses, 1744. First Clerk of Albemarle Co. Colonel of Militia.
Keyser, Mrs. R. Brent.
Randall, Mrs. Alexander Barton.
Cary, Miss Jane Margaret.

RAPER, THOMAS. Member of New Jersey Assembly, 1708.
Smith, Mrs Robert C.

READE, GEORGE, ——1670. Member of the Virginia House of Burgesses, 1644. Member of Council, 1657-60.
Reynolds, Mrs. William.
Tarleton, Mrs. Robert.
Buell, Mrs. Daniel H.
Minor, Miss Mary Willis.
Colvin, Mrs. Alexander B.

REVELL, RANDALL, 1611——. Member of the Maryland Assembly, 1638. Burgess, Accomac Co., Va., 1660.
Whitridge, Mrs. William H.
Rogers, Mrs. Henry W.
Floyd, Miss Nannie Teackle.

RHOADS, SAMUEL. 1711-1784. Member of Philadelphia City Council, 1741; Mayor of Philadelphia, 1774. Member of Assembly of Pennsylvania, 1761, '62-64, '71-74. Delegate to Continental Congress, 1774.
Cromwell, Mrs. Kennedy.

RICHMOND, CAPTAIN EDWARD, 1632-1696. Lieutenant, 1676, in King Philip's War. Captain, 1684. Deputy to the Rhode Island Assembly, 1678-79, '86.
Mason, Mrs. John Thomson.

RIDGELY, CHARLES. ——1772. Justice, Baltimore Co., 1741-53. Burgess, 1751.
Moore, Mrs. Henry.

McBlair, Miss Emily.
Goodwin, Miss Elizabeth Taylor.
Smith, Mrs. Virginia McBlair.
Simpson, Mrs. Edward.
Turnbull, Mrs. John O.
Thompson, Miss Elizabeth Young.
Washburn, Mrs. Charles W.
Preston, Mrs. J. Alexander.
Gorter, Mrs. Albert L.
Carroll, Miss Sally Wethered.
Chatard, Mrs. Thomas M.
Beall, Mrs. Edward Sinclair.
Beall, Miss Louisa Ogle.
Winn, Miss Mary.
Smith, Mrs. Chandler Price.

RIDGELY, COLONEL HENRY, ——1710. Justice, Anne Arundel Co., 1686, '89, '92, '94. Burgess, 1692. Commissioned Captain of Foot, Maryland Militia, 4 September, 1689; Major, July, 1694; Lieutenant-Colonel, 9 October, 1694.
Fisher, Mrs. Charles D.
Carrington, Miss Henrietta Penniman.
Harrison, Mrs. Edmund Pitts.
Gill, Mrs. Martin Gillet.
Penniman, Miss Rebecca.
Nicholson, Mrs. Charles G.
Dorsey, Miss Ella Loraine.
Parsons, Mrs. Joel Burton.
Calvert, Mrs. Charles Baltimore.
Smith, Mrs. Chandler Price.
Mackubin, Miss Florence.

RIDGELY, HENRY, ——1750. Justice, Anne Arundel Co., 1730——; of Quorum, 1733-42.
Harrison, Mrs. Edmund Pitts.
Penniman, Miss Rebecca.
Parsons, Mrs. Joel Burton.
Smith, Mrs. Chandler Price.

RIDGELY, MAJOR HENRY, 1728-1791. Commanded Rangers in Indian War, 1755. Major of Anne Arundel Co. Militia, 1761-73; Colonel, 1773.
Marshall, Mrs. Charles.

RIDGELY, JOHN, 1723-1771.
Burgess, Baltimore Co.,
1767. Justice, 1750———;
of Quorum, 1752-53.
Simpson, Mrs. Edward.
Thompson, Miss Elizabeth Young.
Sloan, Mrs. Robert Neale.
Gorter, Mrs. Albert L.

RIDGELY, ROBERT, ———1681.
Commissioned Chief Clerk to the Secretary. Clerk of the Provincial Court, Register and Examiner of the High Court of Chancery, 19 January, 1670-71. Deputy Secretary of Maryland, 1671.
Moore, Mrs. Henry
McBlair, Miss Emily.
Goodwin, Miss Elizabeth Taylor.
Smith, Mrs. Virginia McBlair.
Simpson, Mrs. Edward.
Turnbull, Mrs. John O.
Thompson, Miss Elizabeth Young.
Washburn, Mrs. Charles W.
Preston, Mrs. J. Alexander.
Gorter, Mrs. Albert L.
Carroll, Miss Sally Wethered.
Ridgely, Mrs. Charles.
Beall, Mrs. Edward Sinclair.
Beall, Miss Louisa Ogle.
Winn, Miss Mary.
Smith, Mrs. Chandler Price.

RINGGOLD, MAJOR JAMES, ———1686. Major of Kent Co. Militia, 1678-83. Justice, Kent Co., 1661.
Merritt, Mrs. J. Alfred.

RINGGOLD, THOMAS, ———1711. Justice, Kent Co., 1695.
Earle, Miss Mary Isabel.

RINGGOLD, MAJOR WILLIAM. Member Committee of Observation, 1775. Captain, Queen Anne's Co. Militia, 16 March, 1776.
Earle, Miss Mary Isabel.

RISTEAU, JOHN. High Sheriff, Baltimore Co., 1742.
Semmes, Mrs. John E.

ROBERTS, HUGH, ———1708. Member of Council of Pennsylvania.
Presstman, Mrs. Benjamin.

ROBINS, GEORGE, 1697-1742. Burgess, Talbot Co., 1728-31.
Presstman, Mrs. Benjamin.
Stokes, Miss Eliza Hughes.
Semple, Mrs. Percy.

ROBINS, COLONEL OBEDIENCE, 1600-1662. Burgess for Accomac Co., Va., 1629-30, '44, '52. Commander of Accomac, 1632. Member of Council, 1656-59.
Floyd, Miss Nannie Teackle.

ROBINS, THOMAS, 1672-1721. Burgess, Talbot Co., 1709-17.
Presstman, Mrs. Benjamin.
Stokes, Miss Eliza Hughes.

ROBINSON, CHRISTOPHER, 1645-1693. Member of Council of Virginia, 1692; Secretary of State, 1692.
Page, Mrs. William C.

ROGERS, COLONEL NICHOLAS, 1753-1822. Aid to General Ducoudrais, 1777, and to General De Kalb, 1778. Member of Committee for the defense of Baltimore, 1780.
McIntire, Mrs. William Watson.
Goldsborough, Mrs. George Robins.

ROLFE, JOHN, 1585-1622. Member of Council of Virginia, 1619; Secretary of State and Recorder-General, 1617-19.
Tait, Mrs. John R.
Keyser, Mrs. R. Brent.

INDEX OF ANCESTORS AND DESCENDANTS.

Randall, Mrs. Alexander Barton.
Cary, Miss Jane Margaret.

ROLFE, LIEUTENANT THOMAS, 1616——. Permanent Commander of the Garrison of Chickahominy Fort, 1646.
Keyser, Mrs. R. Brent.
Randall, Mrs. Alexander Barton.
Cary, Miss Jane Margaret.

ROSCOE, WILLIAM, JR., 1699-1753. Burgess for Warwick Co., Va., 1736.
Jenkins, Mrs. T. Meredith.
Brooks, Mrs. Walter B., Jr.
White, Mrs. Miles, Jr.

ROSS, JOHN, 1696-1766. Mayor of Annapolis, 1748, 1764-65. Clerk to the Council of Maryland, 1729-64. Naval Officer of Patuxent, 1761-65.
Howard, Mrs. Charles.

ROUSBY, JOHN, I., ——1685. Clerk of the Upper House, 1671. Burgess for Calvert Co., 1681-83.
Pennington, Miss Elizabeth Lloyd.
Tilton, Miss Elizabeth.
Emory, Mrs. Campbell D.
Screven, Mrs. George P.
Trimble, Mrs. David C.
Sullivan, Mrs. Felix R.
Pitts, Mrs. Sullivan.
Magruder, Mrs. John Read.
Shippen, Mrs. Edward.
Lowndes, Mrs. Lloyd.
Howard, Mrs. Charles.

ROUSBY, JOHN, II., ——1744. Member of the Maryland House of Burgesses, 1714-21. Member of Council, 1721-36.
Emory, Mrs. Campbell D.
Screven, Mrs. George P.
Trimble, Mrs. David C.
Sullivan, Mrs. Felix R.
Pitts, Mrs. Sullivan.

Magruder, Mrs. John Read.
Shippen, Mrs. Edward.
Pennington, Miss Elizabeth Lloyd.
Lowndes, Mrs. Lloyd.
Howard, Mrs. Charles.
Tilton, Miss Elizabeth.

ROZER, COLONEL BENJAMIN, ——1680. High Sheriff of Charles Co., 1667 - 68. Member of Council, 1677-80.
Denman, Mrs. H. B.
Williams, Mrs. Charles Phelps.
Jones, Mrs. George Alphonzo.

ST. LEGER, SIR WARHAM. Incorporator named in Royal Charter of Virginia, 12 March, 1612.
Randall, Mrs. Alexander Barton.

SAMBORNE, LIEUTENANT JOHN, 1620-1692, Hampton, N. H. Ensign in the Hampton Company; promoted to Lieutenant, 15 October, 1679.
Stewart, Mrs. David.
Hamilton, Mrs. W. T.

SAMBORNE, CAPTAIN JONATHAN, 1672-1741. Captain of a Troop of Horse, in active service against Indians, 1724-26.
Stewart, Mrs. David.
Hamilton, Mrs. W. T.

SAMBORNE, PETER, 1713-1810. Member of New Hampshire Provincial Congress, 1775.
Stewart, Mrs. David.
Hamilton, Mrs. W. T.

SAMBORNE, TRISTRAM, 1691-1771. Representative for Kingston, N. H., 1734, '36-37.
Stewart, Mrs. David.
Hamilton, Mrs. W. T.

INDEX OF ANCESTORS AND DESCENDANTS.

SANDERLAIN, JAMES, ——1692. Justice, Chester Co., Penna., 1681. Member of Assembly for Chester, 1688-89.
Iglehart, Mrs. C. Iredell.
Robinson, Miss Louisa Hall.
Whitridge, Mrs. Horatio L.
Taylor, Mrs. Winfield J.
Turnbull, Mrs. Alexander Nisbet.
Garrett, Mrs. T. Harrison.

SANDS, COMFORT, 1748-1834. Member of Committee of Sixty to carry out non-importation resolutions of Congress, 1774. Member of New York Committee of One Hundred, 1775. Member of Provincial Congress, 1775. Auditor-General of New York, 1776-82. Member of New York Legislature, 1778.
Strother, Mrs. Nelson.

SAUGHIER, GEORGE. Member of Maryland Assembly, 1647-8.
McIntire, Mrs. William Watson.
Goldsborough, Mrs. George Robins.

SAUNDERS, HONORABLE JAMES, ——1707. Justice, Anne Arundel Co., 1692, '96. Burgess, 1692-1701. One of the Commissioners to lay out Annapolis, 1694-96. Member of Council of Maryland, 1701-1707.
Keyser, Mrs. Samuel.
Jackson, Mrs. John J.
Comegys, Mrs. Joseph Parsons.
Black, Mrs. Charles H.
Thompson, Miss Charlotte de Macklot.
Wilson, Miss Mary Bowly.
Wilson, Miss Ella Chapman.
Rogers, Mrs. Henry W.
Wilson, Miss Emma.

SCARBURGH, CAPTAIN EDMUND, ——1634. Member of the Virginia House of Burgesses, 1629-32. Justice, Northampton Co., 1632-33.
Bayard, Miss Ellen Howard.
Howard, Miss Marian Gilmor.
Bayard, Mrs. Richard Bassett.
King, Mrs. Joseph.
Marshall, Mrs. Edward Athelstan.
Whitridge, Mrs. William H.
Floyd, Miss Nannie Teackle.
Shippen, Mrs. Edward.

SCARBURGH, COLONEL EDMUND, ——1671. Member Virginia House of Burgesses, 1642-71. Speaker of the House, 1645. In command of the expedition against the Assateague Indians, 1659. Surveyor-General of Virginia.
Shippen, Mrs. Edward.
von Kapff, Mrs. Frederick.
Custis, Miss Lena Wise.
Custis, Miss Sarah Horsey.
Custis, Miss Clara Douglas.
Cator, Mrs. James H.
Bayard, Miss Ellen Howard.
Wilson, Mrs. James W.
Howard, Miss Marian Gilmor.
Bayard, Mrs. Richard Bassett.
King, Mrs. Joseph.
Marshall, Mrs. Edward Athelstan.
Whitridge, Mrs. William H.
Floyd, Miss Nannie Teackle.
Tiffany, Mrs. L. McLane.

SCHLEY, JOHN THOMAS, 1712-——. Member of Committees of Correspondence and Observation, Frederick Co., 1774-75.
Mercein, Mrs. Thomas R.

SCHUYLER, COLONEL PETER, 1657-1724. Lieutenant of Horse, 1685. Commanded a company at Schenectady, and in 1689 was in command of the fort at Albany. For many years Delegate to the Councils of the Five Nations. Mem-

INDEX OF ANCESTORS AND DESCENDANTS.

ber of the King's Council, 1692-1720, and, as President, Acting Governor of the Province.
Armstrong, Miss Mary Hughes.
Rowley, Mrs. C. W.

SCHUYLER, CAPTAIN PHILIP PIETERSE, 1600-1684. Captain of Foot at Schenectady, New York Provincial Forces, 1669.
Armstrong, Miss Mary Hughes.
Rowley, Mrs. C. W.
Lürman, Mrs. Gustav W.
Morris, Miss Elizabeth Manigault.

SCULL, NICHOLAS, 1687-1762. Sheriff of Philadelphia, 1744-46. Surveyor - General, 1748.
Blackwell, Mrs. Josiah Low.

SEWALL, HONORABLE HENRY, ——1665. Secretary of Maryland, 1661-65.
Keyser, Mrs. William.
Hunt, Mrs. Dunbar.
Hunt, Miss Anita Dunbar.
Brent, Miss Nanine Maria.
Brent, Miss Ida S.
Leakin, Miss Margaret Dobbin.
Steuart, Miss Mary Elizabeth.
Steuart, Miss Henrietta.
Sioussat, Mrs. Albert Willis.
Philpot, Miss Mary Dennison.
Williams, Mrs. Charles Phelps.
Thompson, Miss Elizabeth Young.
Fuller, Mrs. Oliver Clyde.
Gorter, Mrs. Albert L.
Denman, Mrs. H. B.
Redwood, Mrs. Frank T.
Screven, Mrs. George P.
Sullivan, Mrs. Felix R.
Milnor, Miss Mary Worthington.
Lürman, Mrs. Gustav W.
Beall, Miss Louisa Ogle.
Pennington, Miss Elizabeth Lloyd.
Blackiston, Mrs. A. Hooton.
Pearre, Miss Mary Smith Worthington.
Williams, Miss Elizabeth Chew.
McCrackin, Mrs. Alexander.
Jones, Mrs. George Alphonzo.
Baughman, Mrs. Mary Jane.

SEWALL, MAJOR NICHOLAS, 1655 - 1737. Member of Council, Deputy Governor, and Secretary of State, 1682-89.
Lürman, Mrs. Gustav W.
Leakin, Miss Margaret Dobbin.
Sioussat, Mrs. Albert Willis.
Thompson, Miss Elizabeth Young.
Fuller, Mrs. Oliver Clyde.
Gorter, Mrs. Albert L.
Philpot, Miss Mary Dennison.
Redwood, Mrs. Frank T.
Screven, Mrs. George P.
Sullivan, Mrs. Felix R.
Beall, Miss Louisa Ogle.
Pennington, Miss Elizabeth Lloyd.
Blackiston, Mrs. A. Hooton.
Pearre, Miss Mary Smith Worthington.
Williams, Miss Elizabeth Chew.
McCrackin, Mrs. Alexander.

SEYMOUR, HONORABLE FLORENTIUS, ——1681. Governor-General of Bermuda, 1663-68, '81.
Keyser, Mrs. William.
Hunt, Mrs. Dunbar.
Hunt, Miss Anita Dunbar.
Brent, Miss Nanine Maria.
Brent, Miss Ida S.

SHEPARD, REVEREND THOMAS, 1605-1649. Pastor of the Church at Cambridge. Mass., 1635-49. Took an active part in founding Harvard College.
Woods, Mrs. Daniel C.

SHEPARD, REVEREND THOMAS, JR., 1635-1677. Fellow of

143

INDEX OF ANCESTORS AND DESCENDANTS.

Harvard College, 1654-73, 1675-77.
Woods, Mrs. Daniel C.

SHEPPEARD, HERCULES, ——— 1705. Justice of the Peace and of the Courts, Sussex Co., Del., 1683-85. Member of Pennsylvania Assembly for Sussex Co., 1683-84.
Poe, Mrs. Neilson, Jr.
Poultney, Mrs. Eugene.
Beasten, Mrs. Charles.

SHEPPEARD, LIEUTENANT JOHN, ———1707. Burgess for Charles City Co., Va., 1654.
Floyd, Miss Nannie Teackle.

SHERBURNE, HENRY, ———1680, Portsmouth, N. H. Representative, 1660; Associate, 1652, '56-57.
Stewart, Mrs. David.
Hamilton, Mrs. W. T.

SHERBURNE, CAPTAIN SAMUEL, 1638-1691, Hampton, N. H. Captain of Militia, 1689; killed by Indians in King William's War.
Stewart, Mrs. David.
Hamilton, Mrs. W. T.

SHIPPEN, EDWARD, 1639-1712. Member of the Ancient and Honorable Artillery Company of Boston, 1669. Speaker of Pennsylvania Assembly, 1695. Member of Council, 1696-1712. Judge of the Supreme Court and Presiding Judge of the Court of Common Pleas, 1697. First Mayor of Philadelphia, 1701. Acting Deputy Governor, 1703. President of the Provincial Council, 1702-04.
Murray, Mrs. Francis Key.
McCandlish, Miss Evelyn Byrd.
Lürman, Mrs. Gustav W.
Randall, Mrs. Alexander Barton.

SHOEMAKER, LIEUTENANT THOMAS. Lieutenant, New York Provincial Forces, 1733.
Christopher, Mrs. John G.

SHRIVER, DAVID, 1735-1826. Member of Committee of Observation, 1774-75. Member of Maryland Convention, 1776. For many years Member of the House of Delegates, and of the State Senate.
Tomkins, Mrs. John Almy.
Mercein, Mrs. Thomas R.

SHUBRICK, HONORABLE THOMAS, ———1779. Member of the Legislative Council of South Carolina. Speaker of Assembly, 1776.
Taylor, Mrs. Winfield J.

SHUBRICK, COLONEL THOMAS, 1755-1809. Commissioned Captain 5th South Carolina Regiment, 15 January, 1778. Received thanks of Congress and a medal for gallantry at Eutaw Springs.
Taylor, Mrs. Winfield J.

SIM, COLONEL JOSEPH, ——— 1793. Member of Maryland Convention, 1775. Member of Privy Council of Maryland, 1777. Colonel of Prince George's Co. Militia, 1776.
Kerfoot, Mrs. Samuel Humes.
Steele, Miss Rosa.
Beckwith, Mrs. Franklin H.

SIMMS, COLONEL CHARLES, 1730-1819. Lieutenant and Colonel, 6th Virginia Line.
Cottman, Mrs. Clarence.
Powell, Miss Sarah Harrison.

SIMONDS, CAPTAIN JONAS, 1745-1808. Commissioned 2d Lieutenant, Pennsyl-

INDEX OF ANCESTORS AND DESCENDANTS.

vania Artillery, 1 May, 1775; 1st Lieutenant, 10 January, 1776; Captain-Lieutenant, 1 January, 1777; Captain, 13 September, 1778.
Cromwell, Mrs. Kennedy.

SINCLAIR, ROBERT, ———1704. Judge of the Court of Admiralty, 1690, Province of New York.
Mason, Mrs. John Thomson.

SKINNER, ANDREW. Clerk of Assembly, 1657. Clerk of Anne Arundel Co., 1661. Commissioned Ensign, 9 December, 1661.
Heyward, Mrs. Wilson P.

SLYE, CAPTAIN GERARD, 1662-1733. Commander of Fort Susquehannock. High Sheriff of St. Mary's Co., 1678.
Jenkins, Mrs. Michael.
Jenkins, Mrs. Edmund Plowden.
Hinckley, Mrs. Robert.
O'Donnell, Mrs. Columbus.

SLYE, CAPTAIN ROBERT, 1615-1670. One of the Commissioners of the Province and Member of Council of State in Maryland, 1655. Burgess from St. Mary's Co., 1658. Captain of Militia.
Jenkins, Mrs. Michael.
Jenkins, Mrs. Edmund Plowden.
Hinckley, Mrs. Robert.
O'Donnell, Mrs. Columbus.

SMITH, BENJAMIN, 1631-1713. Deputy, 1680-85; Assistant, 1686-1704; Colony of Rhode Island.
Wright, Mrs. D. Giraud.
Taylor, Mrs. B. Jones.

SMITH, DOCTOR CLEMENT, ———1792. Deputy Commissary, Calvert Co., 1752-77; High Sheriff, 1772-75.

Pearre, Miss Mary Smith Worthington.
Phenix, Miss Florence.
Blackiston, Mrs. A. Hooton.
Smith, Miss Clementine.
Smith, Miss Sallie Cox.

SMITH, DANIEL, 1665-1742. Member of New Jersey Assembly, 1716.
Smith, Mrs Robert C.

SMITH, DANIEL, JR. Surveyor-General of West Jersey, 1768.
Smith, Mrs Robert C.

SMITH, EDWARD, ———1675. Assistant at various times between 1654 and 1666. Deputy, 1665-69. Commissioner, 1655-59. Colony of Rhode Island.
Taylor, Mrs. B. Jones.
Wright, Mrs. D. Giraud.

SMITH, ISAAC, 1734-1813. Member of Committee of Safety, Accomac Co., Va., 1774. Delegate to Virginia Conventions, 1774, 1775, 1776.
Floyd, Miss Nannie Teackle.

SMITH, CAPTAIN JAMES, ———1760. Justice, Kent Co., 1697; Burgess, 1719-21, 1728. Clerk of Kent Co. for many years.
Shippen, Mrs. Edward.

SMITH, JOHN (of Baltimore, Md.) 1722-1794. Member of Pennsylvania Assembly, 1754-59. Removed to Baltimore, Md., 1759. Justice, 1774. Member Committee of Observation, 1775. On committee to superintend trade and import arms, 1775. Elected to Maryland Constitutional Convention, 1776. State Senator, 1781-91.
von Kapff, Mrs. Frederick.

INDEX OF ANCESTORS AND DESCENDANTS.

Wilson, Mrs. James W.
Keyser, Mrs. R. Brent.
Buchanan, Miss Esther Sidney.
Randall, Mrs. Alexander Barton.
Cary, Mrs. Wilson Miles.
Cary, Miss Jane Margaret.

SMITH, HONORABLE JOHN (of Pennsylvania). Member of Council of New Jersey, 1703-04.
Smith, Mrs Robert C.

SMITH, RICHARD. Attorney-General of Maryland, 1655-60. Burgess, Calvert Co., 1660-1667.
Kerfoot, Mrs. Samuel Humes.
Pearre, Miss Mary Smith Worthington.
Phenix, Miss Florence.
Blackiston, Mrs. A. Hooton.
Smith, Miss Clementine.
Smith, Miss Sallie Cox.
Steele, Miss Rosa.
Penniman, Mrs. George Dobbin.
Thompson, Miss Elizabeth Young.
Mackall, Miss Sally Somervell.
Gorter, Mrs. Albert L.
Batre, Mrs. Alfred.
Chatard, Mrs. Thomas M.
Lemmon, Mrs. J. Southgate.
Redwood, Mrs. Frank T.
Williams, Miss Elizabeth Chew.
Calvert, Mrs. Charles Baltimore.
Screven, Mrs. George P.
Sullivan, Mrs. Felix R.
Beall, Mrs. Edward Sinclair.
Beall, Miss Louisa Ogle.
Winn, Miss Mary.
Beckwith, Mrs. Franklin H.
Woods, Mrs. Daniel C.

SMITH, RICHARD, JR., ———1714. Captain Calvert Co. Militia, 1689. Surveyor-General, 1693.
Penniman, Mrs. George Dobbin.

SMITH, ROBERT, 1698-1791. Judge of the Court of Common Pleas, Burlington, N. J., 1755.
Smith, Mrs. Robert C.

SMITH, SAMUEL, 1693-1784. High Sheriff, Lancaster Co., Penna., 1735-37. Member Pennsylvania Assembly, 1737-38. Justice, 1741, '49-50, and, in 1751, Presiding Justice of the Orphans' Court.
Keyser, Mrs. R. Brent.
Buchanan, Miss Esther Sidney.
Randall, Mrs. Alexander Barton.
Cary, Mrs. Wilson Miles.
Cary, Miss Jane Margaret.

SMITH, LIEUTENANT SAMUEL, 1602-1680. An "antient Serjeant" at Wethersfield, Conn., and Deputy there, 1640-61. Lieutenant of Hadley Troop, 1663-78, and Deputy to the General Court, Colony of Massachusetts Bay, 1661-73. Commissioner to negotiate with the Mohawks, 1667.
Stockbridge, Mrs. Henry, Jr

SMITH, SIMON, ———1712. Warwick, Rhode Island. Deputy, 1705. Captain, 1704. Attorney-General, 1706-09. Speaker of the House of Deputies, 1711.
Wright, Mrs. D. Giraud.
Taylor, Mrs. B. Jones.

SMITH, COLONEL WALTER, ———1711. Captain of Foot, Calvert Co. Militia, 4 September, 1689; Major, 1695; Justice, 1694, and of Quorum, 1696. Burgess, 1696-1704, 1708-11. Chief Judge Calvert Co. Court, 10 May, 1699.
Pearre, Miss Mary Smith Worthington.

146

INDEX OF ANCESTORS AND DESCENDANTS.

Phenix, Miss Florence.
Blackiston, Mrs. A. Hooton.
Smith, Miss Clementine.
Smith, Miss Sallie Cox.
Steele, Miss Rosa.
Thompson, Miss Elizabeth Young.
Beckwith, Mrs. Franklin H.
Gorter, Mrs. Albert L.
Batre, Mrs. Alfred.
Lemmon, Mrs. J. Southgate.
Philpot, Miss Mary Dennison.
Redwood, Mrs. Frank T.
Williams, Miss Elizabeth Chew.
Calvert, Mrs. Charles Baltimore.
Screven, Mrs. George P.
Sullivan, Mrs. Felix R.
Beall, Mrs. Edward Sinclair
Beall, Miss Louisa Ogle.
Winn, Miss Mary.
Woods, Mrs. Daniel C.

SMITH, WALTER, JR., ——1734. Deputy Commissary, Calvert Co., 1722-30; Burgess, 1719-22; High Sheriff, 1725; Justice, 1726, and of Quorum, 1727-34.
Pearre, Miss Mary Smith Worthington.
Phenix, Miss Florence.
Blackiston, Mrs. A. Hooton.
Smith, Miss Clementine.
Smith, Miss Sallie Cox.
Thompson, Miss Elizabeth Young.
Gorter, Mrs. Albert L.
Redwood, Mrs. Frank T.
Williams, Miss Elizabeth Chew.
Screven, Mrs. George P.
Sullivan, Mrs. Felix R.

SMITH, HONORABLE WILLIAM, 1728-1814. Sheriff of Lancaster Co., Penna., 1756, '60. Removed to Baltimore, Md., 1760. Member Committee of Correspondence, 1774. Committee of Observation, 1775. Member of Congress, 1777, '89, '91. Auditor of the Treasury of the United States, 1791. Presidential Elector, 1792.
von Kapff, Mrs. Frederick.
Wilson, Mrs. James W.
Iglehart, Mrs. C. Iredell.
Robinson, Miss Louisa Hall.
Whitridge, Mrs. Horatio L.
Turnbull, Mrs. Alexander Nisbet.
Garrett, Mrs. T. Harrison.

SNOWDEN, MAJOR THOMAS, 1751-1803. Member of Committee of Observation, 1774. Commissioned Major, Prince George's Co. Militia, 18 March, 1776.
Marshall, Mrs. Charles.

SNOWDEN, RICHARD, ——1711. Captain Provincial Forces, 1700-1703.
Hough, Miss Ethel.

SOANE, HENRY, ——1662. Member of the Virginia House of Burgesses, 1652-62, and Speaker of the House, 1661-62.
Keyser, Mrs. R. Brent.
Buchanan, Miss Esther Sidney.
Randall, Mrs. Alexander Barton.
Cary, Mrs. Wilson Miles.
Cary, Miss Jane Margaret.

SOMERVELL, COLONEL ALEXANDER, 1734-1783. High Sheriff, Calvert Co., 1769-72, '74. Justice, 1773. Member of Assembly, 1774. Colonel of Calvert Co. Militia.
Penniman, Mrs. George Dobbin.

SOMERVELL, JAMES, 1694-1750. Justice, Calvert Co., 1741-44, '47-50. High Sheriff, 1744-47.
Penniman, Mrs. George Dobbin.

INDEX OF ANCESTORS AND DESCENDANTS.

SOMERVELL, JAMES, II. Member Maryland Conventions, 1774-76.
Mackall, Miss Sally Somervell.

SOUTHWORTH, CONSTANT, 1615-1679. Deputy to General Court, 1647-59. Treasurer of Duxbury, Mass., 1659-78. Commissary-General, 1675.
Powell, Mrs. William S.

SPENCER, ENSIGN JARED (Haddam, Conn.). Commissioned, 1656. Served in King Philip's War. Representative, 1674, '78-80, '83, '95.
Hodges, Mrs. J. S. B.

SPRING, JOHN, 1630-1717. Lieutenant of Militia. Member General Court of Massachusetts.
Hamilton, Mrs. Levin Mayer.

SPOTSWOOD, GOVERNOR ALEXANDER, 1676-1740. Governor of Virginia, 1710-22. Appointed, 1740. Major-General to command the forces raised in America to coöperate with Admiral Vernon in the West Indies, but died before taking command.
Clark, Mrs. Frank P.
Dandridge, Miss Anne Spottswood.

SPRAGUE, FRANCIS, ——1666. Original purchaser of Dartmouth, 1652. Proprietor of Bridgewater, 1645.
Huse, Mrs. Harry P.

STAATS, MAJOR ABRAHAM, M. D., ——1694. Captain, 1669, and Major of Foot at Albany. Surgeon at Rensselaerwyck. Member of the Council at Beverwyck, and its President in 1644.
Morris, Miss Elizabeth M.

STACY, MAHLON, ——1704. Member of New Jersey Assembly, 1681-82, '88, '97, 1701. Member of Council, 1703.
Smith, Mrs Robert C.

STANDISH, CAPTAIN MILES, 1584-1656. February 27, 1621, he received the first military commission given in this country. Captain and commander of the military forces of Plymouth Colony, 1620-56. Magistrate and Assistant, 1627-56, of the town of Duxbury, Mass., which he founded in 1627.
Thomsen, Mrs. John J.
Ridgely, Mrs. John.

STANLEY, CAPTAIN JOHN, 1624-1706. Sergeant, 1669; Ensign, 1674; Lieutenant, 1675; Captain, 1676, Hartford Co. Militia. Served in King Philip's War "up the river," Colony of Connecticut.
Goddard, Mrs. Henry P.

STANTON, THOMAS, 1615-1677. Interpreter-General for New England Colonies. Member General Court. Magistrate. Indian Commissioner.
Hamilton, Mrs. Levin Mayer.

STEELE, CAPTAIN WILLIAM, 1707-1780. Captain of one of the Associated Companies of Lancaster Co., Penna., in 1756.
Mills, Mrs. Abraham Gilbert.

STEGGE, CAPTAIN THOMAS, ——1651. Speaker of the Virginia House of Burgesses, 1642. Parliamentary Com-

missioner for the reduction of Virginia, 1651.
Poultney, Mrs. Arthur E.
Minor, Miss Mary Willis.
Randall, Mrs. Alexander Barton.

STEPHAN, GENERAL ADAM, ——1791. Major, Indian War, 1754. Colonel, 1765. Brigadier-General, 1776.
Dandridge, Miss Anne Spottswood.

STERETT, JAMES, ——1796. Member of Committee of Observation. Baltimore Town, 1775.
Simpson, Mrs. Edward.

STERETT, CAPTAIN JOHN, 1750-1787. Member Committee of Observation, Baltimore Co., 1776. Captain, Baltimore Co. Militia, 1776.
Simpson, Mrs. Edward.
Sloan, Mrs. Robert Neale.

STEUART, DOCTOR GEORGE, ——1780. Commissioner of the Land Office, 1753-57. Mayor of Annapolis, 1759-63. Member of Council.
Steuart, Miss Mary Elizabeth.
Steuart, Miss Henrietta.

STEVENS, COLONEL WILLIAM, ——1687. Burgess, Somerset Co., 1658, '69. Member of Council.
Zunts, Miss Sue Howard.

STEVENSON, GEORGE, Carlisle, Pa. Justice of the Peace and Courts, 1749-50, 1777, etc.
Lyster, Mrs. Henry F. LeH.

STICKNEY, LIEUTENANT WILLIAM, 1592-1665. A founder of Rowley, Mass., 1639. Lieutenant, 1661.
Hall, Miss Elizabeth Ward.
Hall, Miss Mary Stickney.

STITH, DRURY, ——1770. Burgess for Brunswick Co., Va., 1748, '52.
Johnston, Miss Maria Stith.
Robbins, Mrs. Henry S.

STITH, GRIFFIN, 1720-1784. Clerk of Northampton Co. (Va.) Court, 1743-83. Member of Committee of Observation, 1774.
Johnston, Miss Maria Stith.
Robbins, Mrs. Henry S.

STITH, MAJOR JOHN. Major of Militia and Justice of Henrico Co., Va., 1680. High Sheriff Charles City Co. 1691. Burgess, 1685, 1692-93.
Johnston, Miss Maria Stith.
Robbins, Mrs. Henry S.

STOCKLEY, ALEXANDER, ——1787. Member of the Committee of Safety, Accomac Co., Va., 1774.
Floyd, Miss Nannie Teackle.

STOCKTON, HONORABLE JOHN, 1701-1757. Presiding Judge of the Court of Common Pleas, New Jersey.
Williams, Mrs. John Witherspoon.

STOCKTON, LIEUTENANT RICHARD, 1606-1707. First Lieutenant, 1665, Flushing (L. I.) Troop of Horse, and of the Foot Company, 1667.
O'Ferrall, Mrs. Frank F.
Huse, Mrs. Harry P.

STONE, JOHN, ——1698. Justice, Charles Co., 1670-1687; High Sheriff of the county, 1694; Justice of the Provincial Court of Maryland, 1695-96.
Parran, Mrs. James Bourne.

STONE, CAPTAIN THOMAS, 1677-1727. Burgess for

Charles Co., 1715; Justice, 1717-1727.
Parran, Mrs. James Bourne.

STONE, GOVERNOR WILLIAM, 1604-1660. Governor of Maryland, 1648-55.
Parran, Mrs. James Bourne.

STROTHER, CAPTAIN WILLIAM DABNEY. Captain in 2d Georgia Regiment; on roll for August, 1778.
Clarke, Mrs. Henry F.

SWIFT, JOHN, I., Bucks County and Philadelphia, Pa. Justice of the Peace, 1685, 1715, '17-19, '22, '25-27; Member of Assembly, 1689, '92-93, '95, 1699-1701, 1704-07, '12-16, '18, '21-28.
Poe, Mrs. Neilson, Jr.
Poultney, Mrs. Eugene.

SWIFT, JOHN, II., 1720-1802. Member of the Common Council of Philadelphia, 1757-76; Collector of the Port, 1762-72. Justice of the Peace and of the Courts, Bucks Co., Pa., 1774-1802.
Poe, Mrs. Neilson, Jr.
Poultney, Mrs. Eugene.

SYLVESTER, CAPTAIN JOSEPH, 1638-1690, Scituate, Mass. Captain, under Colonel Church, in the Maine Expedition, 1689. Died, 1690, in Sir William Phipps' Quebec Expedition.
Mason, Mrs. John Thomson.

TALIAFERRO, JOHN, ——1720. Member of the Virginia House of Burgesses. Lieutenant, commanding Rangers, 1692. Sheriff of Essex Co., 1699.
Reynolds, Mrs. William.
Tarleton, Mrs. Robert.
Colvin, Mrs. Alexander B.

TANEY, MICHAEL, ——1692. High Sheriff of Calvert Co., Md., 1685-89.
Brent, Miss Ida S.
Keyser, Mrs. William.
Hunt, Mrs. Dunbar.
Hunt, Miss Anita Dunbar.

TASKER, HONORABLE BENJAMIN, 1690-1768. President of Council of Maryland. Acting Governor, 1752. Commissioner to Pennsylvania, 1752. Delegate to Colonial Congress at Albany, 1754.
Brown, Miss Lizinka Campbell.
Roman, Miss Louisa Lowndes.
Lough, Mrs. Ernest St. George.
Lowndes, Mrs. Lloyd.
Lewis, Miss Virginia Tayloe.
Lemmon, Mrs. J. Southgate.
Beall, Mrs. Edward Sinclair.
Beall, Miss Louisa Ogle.
Winn, Miss Mary.
Shawham, Mrs. Charles S.

TASKER, CAPTAIN THOMAS, ——1700. Justice, Calvert Co., 1685, '90-92. Burgess, 1692-97. Member of Council, 1698-1700. Justice, Provincial Court, 1694. Treasurer of Maryland, 1695.
Roman, Miss Louisa Lowndes.
Lough, Mrs. Ernest St. George.
Pennington, Miss Elizabeth Lloyd.
Lowndes, Mrs. Lloyd.
Chatard, Mrs. Thomas M.
Lemmon, Mrs. J. Southgate.
Beall, Mrs. Edward Sinclair.
Beall, Miss Louisa Ogle.
Winn, Miss Mary.
Shippen, Mrs. Edward.
Sullivan, Mrs. Felix R.
Screven, Mrs. George P.
Howard, Mrs. Charles.

TAYLOE, COLONEL JOHN, I., 1687-1747. Sheriff of Rich-

mond Co., Va., 1713.
Member of the Council of
Virginia, 1732.
*Lewis, Miss Virginia Tayloe.
Emory, Mrs. Campbell D.
Screven, Mrs. George P.
Trimble, Mrs. David C.
Sullivan, Mrs. Felix R.
Pitts, Mrs. Sullivan.
Magruder, Mrs. John Read.
Shippen, Mrs. Edward.
Pennington, M i s s Elizabeth
Lloyd.
Lowndes, Mrs. Lloyd.
Howard, Mrs. Charles.
Shawhan, Mrs. Charles S.
Tilton, Miss Elizabeth.*

TAYLOE, COLONEL JOHN II.,
———1779. Member of the
Council of Virginia, 1772.
Councillor of State, 1776.
*Emory, Mrs. Campbell D.
Screven, Mrs. George P.
Trimble, Mrs. David C.
Sullivan, Mrs. Felix R.
Pitts, Mrs. Sullivan.
Magruder, Mrs. John Read.
Shippen, Mrs. Edward.
Pennington, M i s s Elizabeth
Lloyd.
Lowndes, Mrs. Lloyd.
Howard, Mrs. Charles.
Shawhan, Mrs. Charles S.
Tilton, Miss Elizabeth.*

TAYLOE, COLONEL WILLIAM,
———1710. Justice, Rappahannock Co., Va., 1686.
High Sheriff, 1688 - 89,
1705-07. County Lieutenant of Richmond Co.,
1705. Burgess, 1705-10.
*Shippen, Mrs. Edward.
Tilton, Miss Elizabeth.
Emory, Mrs. Campbell D.
Screven, Mrs. George P.
Trimble, Mrs. David C.
Sullivan, Mrs. Felix R.
Pitts, Mrs. Sullivan.
Magruder, Mrs. John Read.
Pennington, M i s s Elizabeth
Lloyd.
Lowndes, Mrs. Lloyd.
Howard, Mrs. Charles.*

TAYLOR, COLONEL JAMES,
1674-1729. Burgess, King
and Queen Co., Va., 1702.
Clarke, Mrs. Henry F.

TAYLOR, CAPTAIN THOMAS,
———1657. Member of the
Virginia House of Burgesses, 1646.
*Nicholas, Miss Cary Ann.
Nicholas, Miss Elizabeth Cary.
Keyser, Mrs. R. Brent.
Randall, Mrs. Alexander Barton.
Cary, Miss Jane Margaret.*

TEACKLE, JOHN, 1693-1721.
Member Virginia House
of Burgesses, 1721.
*von Kapff, Mrs. Frederick.
Cox, Mrs. James W., Jr.
Giffen, Miss Lilian.
Giffen, Mrs. James Fortescue.
Giffen, Miss Louise.
Bayard, Miss Ellen Howard.
Wilson, Mrs. James W.
Howard, Miss Marian Gilmor.
Bayard, Mrs. Richard Bassett.
King, Mrs. Joseph.
Marshall, Mrs. Edward Athelstan.
Whitridge, Mrs. William H.
Floyd, Miss Nannie Teackle.*

TEACKLE, THOMAS, 1736-1784.
Member of the Committee
of Safety, Accomac Co.,
Va., 1774.
Floyd, Miss Nannie Teackle.

THACHER, REVEREND THOS.,
1620-1678. First pastor of
Old South Church, Boston, 16 February, 1670.
Powell, Mrs. William S.

THOMAS, COLONEL EDWARD.
Commissioned Lieutenant-Colonel, Heard's Battalion of Minute Men, 12
February, 1776. Colonel
1st Regiment, Essex Co.
(N. J.) Militia, 23 February, 1776. Colonel Detached Militia, 18 July,

1776. Detailed to join General Washington at Trenton, to form the Flying Camp, 16 July, 1776.
Smith, Mrs. Robert C.

THOMAS, EVAN, 1738-1826. Member Committee of Observation for Frederick Co., 1774-75.
Fisher, Mrs. Charles D.
Roberts, Mrs. John B.

THOMAS, LIEUTENANT PHILIP, 1600-1675. Member of the High Commission governing Maryland, 1656, and one of those who, in 1659, surrendered the Government to Lord Baltimore. Lieutenant Provincial Forces of Maryland before 1656.
Roberts, Mrs. John B.
Fisher, Mrs. Charles D.
Marshall, Mrs. Charles.
Hough, Miss Ethel.

THOMAS, DOCTOR PHILIP, 1747-1815. Delegate to Congress held at Annapolis, 1774; member of the Committee of Observation, Frederick Co., 1775; member of House of Delegates, 1777; Presidential Elector at first election of Washington.
Carroll, Mrs. Mary Randolph.

THOMAS, TRISTRAM, 1701-1769. Justice, Talbot Co., 1745-46, '51-54.
Markoe, Mrs. Frank.
Sibley, Mrs. Clarence.
Dugan, Mrs. Hammond.

THOMAS, MAJOR WILLIAM, 1714-1795. Burgess, St. Mary's Co., 1761, 1769-71; member of Committee of Safety, 1775; Delegate to Assembly from St. Mary's Co., 1777, '79, '81; Major in the Provincial Militia.
Parran, Mrs. James Bourne.

THOMPSON, COLONEL JOHN. Burgess, Cecil Co., 1694.
Bayard, Miss Ellen Howard.

THOMSON, STEVENS, 1670-1714. Attorney-General of Virginia, 1703-14.
Rowland, Miss Elizabeth Mason.

THORNBURGH, LIEUTENANT-COLONEL JOSEPH, ——— 1820. Wagonmaster-General. Commissioned Lieutenant - Colonel, 18 June, 1777.
Birckhead, Mrs. James, Jr.

THOROWGOOD, CAPTAIN ADAM, 1602-1640. Member Virginia House of Burgesses, 1629-30, '32. Member of Council, 1637.
Rowland, Miss Elizabeth Mason.
Milnor, Miss Mary Worthington.
Shippen, Mrs. Edward.
Smith, Miss Virginia Hope Bryant.
Floyd, Miss Nannie Teackle.

THURSTON, EDWARD, 1617-1707. Deputy to Rhode Island Assembly, 1667-88.
Mason, Mrs. John Thomson.

TILGHMAN, JAMES, 1743-1809. Burgess, Queen Anne's Co., 1762. Member of Maryland Convention, 1775-76. Member of the Council of Safety, 1776.
Earle, Miss Mary Isabel.

TILGHMAN, HONORABLE MATTHEW, 1718-1790. Justice, Talbot Co., 1741; Burgess, 1751-1774; Speaker, 1773-74; President of Maryland Assembly, 1774-76, and of Constitutional Convention, 1776. Delegate to Continental Congress, 1774-76. Member of Senate of Maryland till 1783.
Coolidge, Mrs. Charles Austin.

INDEX OF ANCESTORS AND DESCENDANTS.

Bateman, Mrs. James M. H.
Paca, Miss Juliana Tilghman.

TILGHMAN, DOCTOR RICHARD, 1626-1675. High Sheriff of Talbot Co., 1670-71.
Beall, Miss Louisa Ogle.
Coolidge, Mrs. Charles Austin.
Bateman, Mrs. James M. H.
Lürman, Mrs. Theodor G.
Tilghman, Miss Mary.
Paca, Miss Juliana Tilghman.
Presstman, Mrs. Benjamin.
Earle, Miss Mary Isabel.
Stokes, Miss Eliza Hughes.
Lürman, Mrs. Gustav W.
Norris, Mrs. Owen.
Merritt, Mrs. Alfred.
Semple, Mrs. Percy.

TILGHMAN, COLONEL RICHARD, 1672-1738. Burgess, Talbot Co., 1698-1702. Member of Council from 1711; Chancellor, 1725
Coolidge, Mrs. Charles Austin.
Bateman, Mrs. James M. H.
Lürman, Mrs. Theodor G.
Tilghman, Miss Mary.
Paca, Miss Juliana Tilghman.
Presstman, Mrs. Benjamin.
Earle, Miss Mary Isabel.
Pitts, Mrs. Sullivan.
Stokes, Miss Eliza Hughes.
Lürman, Mrs. Gustav W.
Beall, Miss Louisa Ogle.
Norris, Mrs. Owen.
Semple, Mrs. Percy.
Dandridge, Miss Anne Spottswood.

TILGHMAN, RICHARD, III., 1705-1768. Justice of the Provincial Court, 1746-54.
Earle, Miss Mary Isabel.
Lürman, Mrs. Gustav W.
Beall, Miss Louisa Ogle.

TILGHMAN, LIEUTENANT-COLONEL TENCH, 1744-1786. Captain, Maryland Flying Camp, 1776. Aid to General Washington, with rank of Lieutenant-Colonel; served through the war. Selected to convey to Congress the news of the surrender of Cornwallis, 1781.
Bateman, Mrs. James M. H.

TILGHMAN, WILLIAM, 1711-1782. Burgess, Queen Anne's Co., 1734-38.
Lürman, Mrs. Theodor G.
Tilghman, Miss Mary.
Norris, Mrs. Owen.
Dandridge, Miss Anne Spottswood.

TIMOTHY, LOUIS. One of the founders of the Philadelphia Library, 1731, and its Librarian, 1732-33.
Wright, Mrs. D. Giraud.
Taylor, Mrs. B. Jones.

TODD, CAPTAIN THOMAS, 1622-1676. Burgess for Baltimore Co., Md., 1674-1675.
Waller, Mrs. Robert Alexander.
Hoffman, Mrs. R. Curzon.
Price, Mrs. Sterling W.
Semmes, Mrs. John E.

TOLLEY, THOMAS, ——1732. Burgess for Baltimore Co., 1721-31; Justice, 1726, '30. Commissioner to lay out Joppa, 1724. Commissioner to lay out Baltimore, 1729.
Conrad, Mrs. Lawrence Lewis.
Ligon, Miss Elizabeth Worthington Dorsey.
Milnor, Miss Mary Worthington.
Smith, Mrs. Chandler Price.

TOLLEY, COLONEL WALTER, ——1782. Burgess for Baltimore Co., 1754; Justice, 1754-64. Member Maryland Conventions, 1774-76. Colonel of Gunpowder Battalion, 1776.
Conrad, Mrs. Lawrence Lewis.
Ligon, Miss Elizabeth Worthington Dorsey.

153

Milnor, Miss Mary Worthington.
Smith, Mrs. Chandler Price.

TOWNSEND, HENRY, ——1695. Member of Rhode Island Assembly, 1650, '53. One of the original patentees of Flushing, 1656.
Milnor, Miss Mary Worthington.
Hodges, Mrs. J. S. B.

TOWNSEND, JOHN, ——1668. Member of Rhode Island Assembly, 1650, and successive years. One of the original patentees of Flushing, 1656.
Milnor, Miss Mary Worthington.

TOWNSHEND, CAPTAIN RICHARD, 1595-1648. Member Virginia House of Burgesses, 1629, '42. Member of Council, 1642.
Story, Mrs. B. T.

TRAILL, ROBERT, ——1781. Collector of Customs, Port of Portsmouth, 1764.
Washburn, Mrs. Charles W.

TRAVERS, COLONEL WILLIAM, ——1685. Speaker of the Virginia House of Burgesses, 1677.
Carroll, Mrs. Mary Randolph.
Page, Mrs. William C.

TREAT, HONORABLE RICHARD, 1584 - 1669, Wethersfield, Conn. Deputy, 1644-58; Assistant, 1658-65; named, in the Royal Charter, one of the Patentees for Connecticut, 1662.
Woods, Mrs. Daniel C.
Chatard, Mrs. Thomas M.
Williams, Miss Rebecca Dalrymple.
Mackenzie, Miss Mary G. M.

TREAT, GOVERNOR ROBERT, 1622-1710. Commander at Great Swamp Fight. Major commanding Connecticut troops at the battles of Hadley and Springfield. Deputy Governor, 1676-86. Governor, 1686-1701. In the encounter with the Indians at Bloody Brook, 18 September, 1675, his arrival with the Connecticut Forces turned the tide.
Woods, Mrs. Daniel C.

TREZEVANT, THEODORE, 1722-1797. Member of South Carolina Provincial Congress, 1775.
Wright, Mrs. D. Giraud.
Taylor, Mrs. B. Jones.

TRIPPE, LIEUTENANT - COLONEL HENRY, 1632-1697. Justice, Dorchester Co., 1671; Burgess, 1671-81. Lieutenant-Colonel Maryland Militia.
Cox, Mrs. James W., Jr.

TROWBRIDGE, LIEUTENANT JAMES, 1636-1717, Newton. Deputy to the General Court from Cambridge, 1700 and 1703. Served in King Philip's War. Colony of Massachusetts Bay.
Hall, Miss Elizabeth Ward.
Hall, Miss Mary Stickney.

TURBUTT, FOSTER, 1679-1720. Clerk of Talbot Co. Burgess, 1715-16.
Markoe, Mrs. Frank.
Sibley, Mrs. Clarence.
Dugan, Mrs. Hammond.

TURBUTT, MICHAEL, ——1696. Justice, Talbot Co., 1687-80.
Markoe, Mrs. Frank.
Sibley, Mrs. Clarence.
Dugan, Mrs. Hammond.

TYBOUT, JAMES, Kent Co., Del. Lieutenant, French and Indian War.
Beasten, Mrs. Charles.

INDEX OF ANCESTORS AND DESCENDANTS.

TYLER, ROBERT, ——1674. Justice, Calvert Co., 1670.
Mercein, Mrs. Thomas R.
Stokes, Miss Eliza Hughes.

TYNG, WILLIAM, of Boston, later of Braintree, Mass. Representative, 1639-44, '47, '49-51; Treasurer of the Colony, 1640-44; Captain of the Braintree Militia.
Woods, Mrs. Daniel C.

VAN CORTLANDT, HONORABLE OLAFF STEVENS, 1600-1684. Colonel of the Burgher Corps, 1649. One of the "eight men," 1645, and one of the "nine men," 1663. Burgomaster of New York, 1655-64, the last before the English conquest. Lord of Cortlandt Manor.
Morris, Miss Elizabeth M.
Lürman, Mrs. Gustav W.
Mason, Mrs. John Thomson.

VAN CORTLANDT, HONORABLE STEPHANUS, 1643-1700. Colonel of the King's County Regiment, 1671-93. Mayor of New York, 1677. Member of the Council of New York, 1680-1700.
Morris, Miss Elizabeth M.
Lürman, Mrs. Gustav W.

VAN COWENHOVEN, WOLFORT GERRITTSE. Schepen (Alderman) of New Amsterdam, 1654. Secretary of Town Council, 1658. Commissioner to Holland, 1653.
Hoffman, Mrs. R. Curzon.

VAN RENSSELAER, COLONEL JEREMIAS, ——1674. Second Patroon of Rensselaerwyck. Member of the Colonial Assembly, and Speaker, 1664. Colonel of Militia at Albany.
Mason, Mrs. John Thomson.

VAN RENSSELAER, KILIAEN, ——1646. First Patroon of Rensselaerwyck.
Mason, Mrs. John Thomson.

VAN SLICHTENHORST, BRANT ARENTSE. First resident Director of the Colony of Rensselaerwyck, 1646-48, and commander of the fort at Rensselaerwyck.
Armstrong, Miss Mary Hughes.
Rowley, Mrs. C. W.
Morris, Miss Elizabeth Manigault.

VAN SWEARINGEN, GARRETT, ——1698. High Sheriff, St. Mary's Co., 1687-88.
Lürman, Mrs. Theodor G.
Tilghman, Miss Mary.
Norris, Mrs. Owen.
Spencer, Mrs. Jervis.
Tait, Mrs. John R.
Rogers, Mrs. Charles Lyon.
Mullan, Mrs. John.
Whitney, Mrs. George E.
Holladay, Mrs. Samuel W.

VAUGHAN, CAPTAIN ROBERT. Member of Assembly, 1637-47, '62. Lieutenant, 1642. Captain, 1647. Commander of the Isle of Kent, 1647-53.
Merritt, Mrs. J. Alfred.

VENABLE, CAPTAIN ABRAHAM, 1701-1768. Member of the Virginia House of Burgesses, 1748. Captain of Virginia Forces in the Indian Wars.
Ligon, Miss Elizabeth Worthington Dorsey.

VERNON, RANDAL, 1640-1725. Member of Provincial Assembly of Pennsylvania, 1687.
Griswold, Miss Ellen Howell.

VER PLANCK, ABRAHAM ISAACSEN, 1616-1690. One of the "twelve men," the

first representative Assembly of the Dutch in New Netherland.
Lürman, Mrs. Gustav W.

VER PLANCK, ENSIGN GELEYN, 1637-1684. Ensign, 1673. In garrison at the fort in New York City. Schepen of Nieuw Amsterdam, and Alderman of New York.
Lürman, Mrs. Gustav W.

VER PLANCK, ENSIGN PHILIP, 1695-1771. Ensign in Colonel Vetch's Regiment, Massachusetts Colonial Forces, 1711. Commissioner to the Six Nations, 1746. Commissioner for fortifications, 1755. Member of New York Provincial Assembly, 1734-68. One of the Governors of King's College, 1754-71.
Lürman, Mrs. Gustav W.

WADE, CAPTAIN JONATHAN, ——1689. Ipswich, Mass. Captain of the Three County Troop of Horse, King Philip's War, 1676.
Hall, Miss Elizabeth Ward.
Hall, Miss Mary Stickney.

WAINWRIGHT, COLONEL JOHN, ——1708. Colonel of Massachusetts Militia, 1707.
Bond, Mrs. Hugh Lennox, Jr.

WALKE, ANTHONY, 1692-1768. Member of Virginia House of Burgesses, and Judge of Princess Anne County Court.
Smith, Miss Virginia Hope Bryant.

WALKE, ANTHONY, JR., 1726-1782. Member of Virginia House of Burgesses.
Smith, Miss Virginia Hope Bryant.

WALLER, BENJAMIN, 1716-1786. Member of the Virginia House of Burgesses, 1748.
Atkinson, Mrs. Matthew S.

WALLINGFORD, THOMAS, 1695-1771, of Stafford Co., N. H. Colonel of the County Militia. Associate Justice, Supreme Court of New Hampshire, 1748-71.
Turnbull, Mrs. Alexander Nisbet.
Garrett, Mrs. T. Harrison.

WARD, SETH. Member of the Virginia House of Burgesses, 1766-68.
McIntosh, Mrs. David Gregg.

WARD, WILLIAM, 1597-1687. Deputy from Sudbury, Colony of Massachusetts Bay, 1644; Marlborough, 1666. One of the founders of the town of Marlborough, 1660. In garrison at Sudbury in King Philip's War.
Hall, Miss Elizabeth Ward.
Hall, Miss Mary Stickney.

WARDLAW, CAPTAIN HUGH, ——1802. Captain of South Carolina Militia, 1775.
Miles, Mrs Francis T.

WARFIELD, DOCTOR CHARLES ALEXANDER, 1751-1813. Member of Committee of Observation, 1774. Major of Anne Arundel Co. Militia.
Marshall, Mrs. Charles.

WARING FRANCIS, 1717-1771. Member of the Virginia House of Burgesses, 1758, '64. Signer of the Westmoreland Protest, 1765.
Latané, Miss Lucy Temple.

WARING, THOMAS, ——1754. Member of the Virginia House of Burgesses, 1736.

Justice, Essex Co., 1720-1740.
Latané, Miss Lucy Temple.

WARNER, COLONEL AUGUSTINE, SR., 1611-1674. Member of the Virginia House of Burgesses, 1652-55. Member of Council, 1659-74.
Lewis, Miss Virginia Tayloe.
Buell, Mrs. Daniel H.

WARNER, COLONEL AUGUSTINE, JR., 1642-1681. Speaker of the Virginia House of Burgesses, 1675-1677.
Reynolds, Mrs. William.
Tarleton, Mrs. Robert.
Lewis, Miss Virginia Tayloe.
Buell, Mrs. Daniel H.
McCandlish, Miss Evelyn Byrd.
Colvin, Mrs. Alexander B.

WARNER, WILLIAM, ——1706. Member of Governor Markham's Council, 1681. Member of Pennsylvania Assembly, 1682-83. Justice at Upland Court, 1681. Justice of Swede's Court.
Huse, Mrs. Harry P.

WARREN, COLONEL HUMPHREY, ——1694. Colonel of Charles Co. Militia, 1694.
Parran, Mrs. James Bourne.

WASHINGTON, COLONEL JOHN, 1629-1677. Member of the Virginia House of Burgesses, 1666-76. Commanded expedition against the Seneca Indians, 1675.
Buell, Mrs. Daniel H.

WATERMAN, RICHARD, 1590-1673. One of the thirteen original proprietors of Providence Plantations, 1636.
Wright, Mrs. D. Giraud.
Taylor, Mrs. B. Jones.

WATSON, THOMAS, ——1737. Justice of Bucks Co., Penna., 1715, '17, 26-27. Member of Assembly, 1717-25.
Smith, Mrs. Thomas Marsh.

WEBSTER, GOVERNOR JOHN, 1590-1661. An original settler of Hartford and a founder of the Colony of Connecticut. Deputy, 1637. Assistant, Hartford, 1639-55. Deputy-Governor, 1655. Governor, 1656. First Magistrate, 1657-59. Judge of the Court, Hadley, Mass., 1660.
Stockbridge, Mrs. Henry, Jr.

WEIRE, MAJOR JOHN, ——1675. Burgess for Rappahannock Co., Va., 1663.
Howard, Mrs. Charles.

WEISER, COLONEL CONRAD, 1696-1760. Commissioned Colonel of Pennsylvania Forces, 31 October, 1755.
McSherry, Mrs. H. Clinton.
Hoogewerff, Mrs. John A.

WEST, GOVERNOR JOHN, 1590-1659. Burgess, 1629. Justice, York Co., Va., 1634. Councillor, 1631-59. Governor of Virginia, 1635-37. Quartermaster-General, 1641.
Clark, Mrs. Frank P.
Dandridge, Miss Anne Spottswood.

WEST, COLONEL JOHN, ——1689. Major, Virginia Forces, 1678. Senior Justice and Colonel of Militia, New Kent Co., Va., 1680.
Clark, Mrs. Frank P.
Dandridge, Miss Anne Spottswood.

WEST, LIEUTENANT-COLONEL JOHN, 1639-1703. High Sheriff of Accomac Co.,

Va., 1664, 1667. Justice, 1663-1703. Captain of Militia, 1665. Major, 1675. Lieutenant-Colonel, 1679.
von Kapff, Mrs. Frederick.
Bayard, Miss Ellen Howard.
Wilson, Mrs. James W.
Howard, Miss Marian Gilmor.
Bayard, Mrs. Richard Bassett.
King, Mrs. Joseph.
Marshall, Mrs. Edward Athelstan.
Whitridge, Mrs. William H.
Floyd, Miss Nannie Teackle.
Shippen, Mrs. Edward.

WEST, COLONEL NATHANIEL. Member of the Virginia House of Burgesses, 1702.
Clark, Mrs. Frank P.
Dandridge, Miss Anne Spottswood.

WETHERILL, CHRISTOPHER, ——1711. One of the original proprietors, and member of the Proprietary Council of West Jersey, 1688-1707.
O'Ferrall, Mrs. Frank F.

WHARTON, COLONEL JESSE, ——1676. President of Council of Maryland, 1672-76. Deputy Governor, 1676.
Keyser, Mrs. William.
Hunt, Mrs. Dunbar.
Hunt, Miss Anita Dunbar.
Brent, Miss Nanine Maria.
Brent, Miss Ida S.

WHEELWRIGHT, LIEUTENANT JEREMIAH, 1678-1770. Lieutenant in Louisburg expedition, 1745.
Belknap, Mrs. Charles.
Browne, Mrs. Samuel Tracy.
Assheton, Mrs. William Herbert.

WHEELWRIGHT, REVEREND JOHN, 1599-1679. Minister at Boston, Exeter, Wells, Hampton and Salisbury. Founder of Exeter, N. H.
Belknap, Mrs. Charles.
Browne, Mrs. Samuel Tracy.
Assheton, Mrs. William Herbert.

WHEELWRIGHT, COLONEL JOHN, 1664-1745. Representative, 1692, 1699. Assistant, 1708-1732. Judge of Inferior Court, 1702-29; of Probate Court, 1715. Colonel of Massachusetts Bay Colony Militia, 1731.
Belknap, Mrs. Charles.
Browne, Mrs. Samuel Tracy.
Assheton, Mrs. William Herbert.

WHEELWRIGHT, COLONEL SAMUEL, 1635-1700. Deputy, 1671, '77, 81. Commissary, 1691. Assistant, 1695-99. Judge of Inferior Court, 1692-1700; of Probate Court, 1694.
Belknap, Mrs. Charles.
Browne, Mrs. Samuel Tracy.
Assheton, Mrs. William Herbert.

WHIPPLE, ELDER JOHN, 1605-1669. Deputy to the General Court, 1640, '42, '46, '50, '53. Ruling Elder of the First Church, Ipswich, Mass.
Washburn, Mrs. Charles W.

WHIPPLE, CAPTAIN JOHN, 1626-1683 (Ipswich, Mass.). Representative, 1674, '76, '79, 83. Captain of a Troop of Horse, serving under Major Savage in King Philip's War, 1676.
Washburn, Mrs. Charles W.

WHIPPLE, MATTHEW, 1658-1738 (Ipswich, Mass.). Justice of the Sessions Court. Representative, 1718, '19, '29.
Washburn, Mrs. Charles W.

INDEX OF ANCESTORS AND DESCENDANTS.

WHITE, NATHANIEL, 1629-1711. Deputy, General Court, Connecticut, 1678-82. Lieutenant of Militia at Middletown, Conn., 1679.
Currie, Mrs. C. George.

WHITE, COLONEL THOMAS, 1704-1779. Deputy Surveyor of Baltimore Co. Major of the County Militia in 1736, and subsequently Colonel.
Ringgold, Mrs. James T.

WHITELOCK, ISAAC, 1712-1781. Member of Pennsylvania Assembly, 1772.
Huse, Mrs. Harry P.

WHITTEMORE, LIEUTENANT PELATIAH (of Charlestown, Mass.), 1680———. In command at Kittery, Me., 1704-5.
Belknap, Mrs. Charles.
Browne, Mrs. Samuel Tracy.
Assheton, Mrs. William Herbert.

WHITING, COLONEL HENRY, 1655-1729. Member of Council of Virginia, 1691. Treasurer, 1692-93.
Ramsay, Mrs. Henry Ashton.
Ramsay, Miss Martha Parker.

WICKES, MAJOR JOSEPH, ——1694. Burgess, Kent Co., 1654, '57-59, '69, '78, '82. Major of Kent Co. Militia, 1683.
Merritt, Mrs. J. Alfred.

WILKINS, JOHN, JR., Bedford, Pa. Captain in Colonel Spencer's Regiment, 1776-78; Member of Convention, 1776.
Lyster, Mrs. Henry F. LeH.

WILLITT, CAPTAIN THOMAS, 1610-1674. Captain, Plymouth Co. Militia, 1648.
Member of Council of War, 1653. Member General Council, 1672. First English Mayor of New York, 1665. Served on expedition which captured New York from the Dutch, 1664.
Goddard, Mrs. Henry P.

WILLIAMS, COLONEL JOSEPH, 1708-1798. Colonel of Massachusetts Militia, 1755-58. Representative, 1765. Chairman of Roxbury Committee, "Boston Massacre," 1770.
McCoy, Mrs. Harry.
Williams, Miss Rebecca Dalrymple.
Chatard, Mrs. Thomas M.
Williams, Miss Sue Campbell.
Mackenzie, Miss Mary G. M.

WILLIAMS, CAPTAIN STEPHEN, 1640-1720, Roxbury, Mass. Captain of a Troop of Horse in active service on the frontier, 1707-12.
Williams, Miss Rebecca Dalrymple.
Chatard, Mrs. Thomas M.
Mackenzie, Miss Mary G. M.

WILLIAMSON, LIEUTENANT-COLONEL MICAJAH, 1740-1796. Commanded at siege of Augusta, 1781.
Campbell, Miss Ella Calvert.
Williams, Miss Sue Campbell.

WILLING, CHARLES, 1710-1754. Mayor of Philadelphia, 1748, '54.
Murray, Mrs. Francis Key.
McCandlish, Miss Evelyn Byrd.
Lürman, Mrs. Gustav W.
Randall, Mrs. Alexander Barton.

WILLOUGHBY, CAPTAIN THOMAS, 1601-1658. Member of the Virginia House

INDEX OF ANCESTORS AND DESCENDANTS.

of Burgesses, 1629-32; member of Council, 1644-46, 1650.
Clarke, Mrs. Henry F.
Page, Mrs. William C.

WILMER, SIMON. Burgess, Kent Co., 1698.
Merritt, Mrs. J. Alfred.
Earle, Miss Mary Isabel.

WILSON, EPHRAIM, 1664-1732. High Sheriff, Somerset Co., 1693.
Goldsborough, Mrs. Worthington.

WILSON, COLONEL WILLIAM, 1646-1713. Major, Elizabeth City Co., Va., 1692, and Colonel, 1698. For many years Presiding Justice of the County Court. Member of the Virginia House of Burgesses, 1685, '92, 1702. Naval Officer for the Lower James, 1699-1710.
Keyser, Mrs. R. Brent.
Nicholas, Miss Cary Ann.
Nicholas, Miss Elizabeth Cary.
Randall, Mrs. Alexander Barton.
Cary, Miss Jane Margaret.

WINDER, COLONEL JOHN, ——1698. Justice, Somerset Co., 1666-80; Captain in the County Militia, 1687; Lieutenant-Colonel, 1697.
Pennington, Miss Elizabeth Lloyd.

WINDER, GOVERNOR LEVIN, 1757-1819. Lieutenant of Smallwood's Maryland Regiment, 14 January, 1776; Captain, 1st Maryland, 10 December, 1776; Major, 17 April, 1777; Lieutenant-Colonel, 5th Maryland, 27 April, 1781. Governor of Maryland, 1812-15.
Pennington, Miss Elizabeth Lloyd.

WINDER, WILLIAM, 1714-1792. Justice, Somerset Co., 1757-70; of Quorum, 1763-1770.
Pennington, Miss Elizabeth Lloyd.

WINGATE, COLONEL JOSHUA, 1679-1769. Deputy to the General Court, Province of New Hampshire, from Hampton, 1715, '27-31. Captain, 1716. Major, 1730. In 1745, being then Colonel, dispatched two companies of his regiment for service at Louisburg, Cape Breton.
Hall, Miss Elizabeth Ward.
Hall, Miss Mary Stickney.

WINN, JOSEPH, ——1714. Ensign in the Phips Expedition to Quebec, 1690.
Beall, Mrs. Edward Sinclair.
Beall, Miss Louisa Ogle.
Winn, Miss Mary.

WINN, TIMOTHY, 1740-1800. Ensign in Captain Ebenezer Cox's Company, French and Indian War, 1762.
Beall, Mrs. Edward Sinclair.
Beall, Miss Louisa Ogle.
Winn, Miss Mary.

WOOD, WILLIAM. Member of New Jersey Assembly, 1686-87, '97.
Huse, Mrs. Harry P.

WOOLMAN, RICHARD, ——1681. Justice, Anne Arundel Co., 1658. Chief Judge, Talbot Co., 1661-81. Burgess, Anne Arundel Co., 1659; Talbot Co., 1662-81. Commissioned Captain of Foot, Talbot Co., 6 December, 1662.
Tilghman, Miss Mary.
Lürman, Mrs. Theodor G.
Emory, Mrs. Campbell D.
Norris, Mrs. Owen.
Tilton, Miss Elizabeth.

INDEX OF ANCESTORS AND DESCENDANTS.

WOOLSTON, JOHN, I., ———
1698. Member of Assembly, West Jersey, 1696-97.
Canby, Miss Laura.
Huse, Mrs. Harry P.

WOOLSTON, JOHN, II., 1708-1791. Member of Pennsylvania Assembly, 1749-51.
Canby, Miss Laura.
Huse, Mrs. Harry P.

WORMLEY, COLONEL CHRISTOPHER, ———1701. Member of the Council of Virginia, 1686.
Page, Mrs. William C.

WORMLEY, RALPH, I., ———1651. Justice, York Co., Va., 1637-47. Member of the Virginia House of Burgesses, 1644-49. Member of Council, 1650-51.
Minor, Miss Mary Willis.
Keyser, Mrs. R. Brent.
Randall, Mrs. Alexander Barton.
Cary, Miss Jane Margaret.

WORMLEY, RALPH, II., 1650-1701. Member of the Council of Virginia, 1676. Secretary of State, 1693. President of the Council. President of the first Board of Trustees of William and Mary College, 1693.
Minor, Miss Mary Willis.
Keyser, Mrs. R. Brent.
Randall, Mrs. Alexander Barton.
Cary, Miss Jane Margaret.
Lyster, Mrs. Henry F. LeH.

WORTHINGTON, CAPTAIN JOHN, 1650-1701. Justice, Anne Arundel Co., 1692. Burgess, 1699. Captain of the County Militia.
Conrad, Mrs. Lawrence Lewis.
Pearre, Miss Mary Smith Worthington.
Blackiston, Mrs. A. Hooton.

Gill, Mrs. Martin Gillet.
Nicholson, Mrs. Charles G.
Ligon, Miss Elizabeth Worthington Dorsey.
Calvert, Mrs. Charles Baltimore.
Mercein, Mrs. Thomas R.
Milnor, Miss Mary Worthington.
Smith, Mrs. Chandler Price.
Dorsey, Miss Ella Lorraine.

WORTHINGTON, MAJOR NICHOLAS, 1733-1793. Justice, Anne Arundel Co., 1767. Judge of the Orphans' Court, 1778. Member Committee of Safety, 1775. Member of Assembly, 1777. Major, Severn Battalion, Anne Arundel Co.
Nicholson, Mrs. Charles G.
Calvert, Mrs. Charles Baltimore.

WORTHINGTON, SAMUEL, 1733-1815. Member Committee of Observation, Baltimore Co., 1774; Delegate to General Assembly, 1781.
Conrad, Mrs. Lawrence Lewis.
Milnor, Miss Mary Worthington.

WORTHINGTON, THOMAS, 1691-1753. Burgess, Anne Arundel Co., 1745.
Nicholson, Mrs. Charles G.

WRIGHT, SOLOMON, 1675-1729. Burgess, Queen Anne's Co., 1722-27.
Orrick, Mrs. Henry Abert.

WRIGHT, SOLOMON, JR., 1717-1792. Member of Annapolis Convention, 1774. Judge of Court of Appeals, 1778.
Orrick, Mrs. Henry Abert.

YARDLEY, THOMAS. Member of the Provincial Assembly of Pennsylvania, 1715, '22. Justice of the Peace, 1725-27.

INDEX OF ANCESTORS AND DESCENDANTS.

Canby, Miss Laura.
Manly, Mrs. L. Tyson.

YEARDLEY, COLONEL ARGALL,
——1656. Justice of Northampton Co., Va., 1640. Commander of the county, 1642-44. Member of Council, 1644, 1652.
Shippen, Mrs. Edward.
von Kapff, Mrs. Frederick.
Bayard, Miss Ellen Howard.
Wilson, Mrs. James W.
Howard, Miss Marian Gilmor.
Bayard, Mrs. Richard Bassett.
King, Mrs. Joseph.
Marshall, Mrs. Edward Athelstan.
Floyd, Miss Nannie Teackle.

YEARDLEY, SIR GEORGE, Knight, 1580-1627. Deputy Governor of Virginia, 1616. Governor, 1619-21, 1626-27.
Shippen, Mrs. Edward.
von Kapff, Mrs. Frederick.
Bayard, Miss Ellen Howard.
Wilson, Mrs. James W.
Howard, Miss Marian Gilmor.
Bayard, Mrs. Richard Bassett.
King, Mrs. Joseph.
Marshall, Mrs. Edward Athelstan.
Floyd, Miss Nannie Teackle.

YEATES, HONORABLE JASPER,
——1720. Justice, Chester Co., Penna., 1694. Member of Council, 1700-1704.
Iglehart, Mrs. C. Iredell.
Robinson, Miss Louisa Hall.
Whitridge, Mrs. Horatio L.
Taylor, Mrs. Winfield J.
Turnbull, Mrs. Alexander Nisbet.
Garrett, Mrs. T. Harrison.

YOUNG, COLONEL BENJAMIN,
——1754. Member of the Council of Maryland. Judge of the High Court of Admiralty, Chief Justice of the Provincial Court, and Judge of the Land Office.
Denman, Mrs. H. B.
Williams, Mrs. Charles Phelps.
Jones, Mrs. George Alphonzo.

YOUNG, COLONEL SAMUEL, 1667-1723. Justice, Anne Arundel Co., 1692; Burgess, 1692. Member of Council, 1716. Chief Justice of the Provincial Court.
Murdoch, Miss Sallie Howard.
Batre, Mrs. Alfred.

CORRIGENDA.

Page 10, line 3, *after* Atkinson, Mrs. Matthew S., *read* (Eliza Blow.)

Page 24, line 30, *for* Davies, Miss Jennie Haywood, *read* Daves, Miss Jennie Haywood.

Page 32, line 14, *for* Hamilton, Mrs. Levin Mayer, *read* Hamilton, Mrs. Lewis Mayer.

Page 90, first column, line 25, *for* Hamilton, Mrs. Levin Mayer, *read* Hamilton, Mrs. Lewis Mayer.

Page 104, first column, line 34, *for* Hamilton, Mrs. Levin Mayer, *read* Hamilton, Mrs. Lewis Mayer.

Page 127, first column, line 22, *for* Hamilton, Mrs. Levin Mayer, *read* Hamilton, Mrs. Lewis Mayer.

Page 128, second column, line 33, *for* Hamilton, Mrs. Levin Mayer, *read* Hamilton, Mrs. Lewis Mayer.

Page 131, second column, line 4, *for* Hamilton, Mrs. Levin Mayer, *read* Hamilton, Mrs. Lewis Mayer.

Page 148, first column, line 24, *for* Hamilton, Mrs. Levin Mayer, *read* Hamilton, Mrs. Lewis Mayer.

Page 148, second column, line 39, *for* Hamilton, Mrs. Levin Mayer, *read* Hamilton, Mrs. Lewis Mayer.

Page 32, line 22, *for* Harrison, Mrs. Edward Pitts, *read* Harrison, Mrs. Edmond Pitts.

Page 36, line 29, *for* Joseph Yeates, *read* Jasper Yeates.

Page 46, line 17, *for* Edward Neale I, *read* Edward Lloyd I.

Page 46, *after* Markoe, Mrs. Frank, *read* (Maria Thomas.)

Page 52, line 24, *for* Nicholas, Mrs. Wilson Cary (Augusta Neville), *read* Nicholas, Mrs. Wilson Cary (Augusta Moale.)

Page, 76 *after* Turnbull, Mrs. John O., *add* Fifth in descent from Gabriel Ludlow.

Page 102, first column, to descendants of Captain Edmund Craske, *add* Wilson, Miss Ella Chapman.

Page 102, first column, to descendants of Captain John Craske, *add* Wilson, Miss Ella Chapman.

Page 126, second column, to descendants of Gabriel Ludlow, *add* Turnbull, Mrs. John O., and Preston, Mrs. J. A.

The name of JONATHAN HAZARD should be cancelled on p. 116, l. 5. He is not eligible under the rules of the New York Society.

MEMBERS DECEASED.

MRS. CHARLES BLACK.
Died March 16th, 1894.

MRS. JAMES TRAPIER RINGGOLD.
Died April 2d, 1896.

MRS. CHANDLER P. SMITH.
Died April 7th, 1896.

MRS. CHARLES HOWARD.
Died September 9th, 1897.

MRS. J. J. THOMSEN.
Died February 4th, 1898.

MRS. RICHARD ODEN MULLIKIN.
Died February 11th, 1898.

MISS MARY D. PHILPOT.
Died February 26th, 1898.

MRS. H. B. DENMAN.
Died 1898.

MRS. JOHN MULLAN.
Died September 4th, 1898.

MRS. JOHN RITCHIE.
Died October 20th, 1898.

www.ingramcontent.com/pod-product-compliance
Lightning Source LLC
Chambersburg PA
CBHW030434190426
43202CB00036B/666